Alan Butler has had a lifelong fascination for ancient history and especially for the Megalithic period in Western Europe. He has studied carefully over the last couple of decades in order to acquire the best possible understanding of ancient astronomy and is also something of an expert on the evolution of calendars and measuring systems. On his own, and also together with Christopher Knight, he has written a number of books on these subjects. Alan is also a humorist and a radio and stage playwright. He lives in East Yorkshire but travels extensively these days, both throughout Britain and across the world, lecturing and taking part in documentaries.

Other books by Alan Butler
The Goddess the Grail and the Lodge
The Virgin and the Pentacle
Sheep

With Christopher Knight
Civilization One
Who Built the Moon?
Solomon's Powerbrokers (published in paperback
   as *The Hiram Key Revisited*)
Before the Pyramids

How to Read Prehistoric Monuments

Understanding Our Ancient Heritage

Alan Butler

WATKINS PUBLISHING
LONDON

This edition first published in the UK and USA 2011 by
Watkins Publishing, Sixth Floor, Castle House,
75–76 Wells Street, London W1T 3QH

1 3 5 7 9 10 8 6 4 2

Designed and typeset by Jerry Goldie Graphic Design
All photographs from author's collection
except pp.244 & 247 © Graeme Peacock
Line drawings by Stephen Dew

Printed and bound by Imago in China

British Library Cataloguing-in-Publication Data Available

Library of Congress Cataloging-in-Publication Data Available

ISBN: 978-1-907486-44-9

www.watkinspublishing.co.uk

Distributed in the USA and Canada by Sterling Publishing Co., Inc.
387 Park Avenue South, New York, NY 10016-8810

For information about custom editions, special sales, premium and
corporate purchases, please contact Sterling Special Sales
Department at 800-805-5489 or specialsales@sterlingpub.com

I would like to dedicate this book to the countless men and women from the past who toiled away, century after century, to leave us some of the most fascinating and enigmatic structures in the world.

Acknowledgements

My thanks go, as always, to my ever-patient wife Kate, who has trudged over hill and dale with me without complaint for over 16 years.

In addition I owe a debt of gratitude to my publishers, and especially to Michael Mann and Penny Stopa. And of course I cannot forget my ever patient editor, Shelagh Boyd, who proposes here, tweaks there and polishes everywhere to make the book readable.

Contents

LIST OF ILLUSTRATIONS

Introduction

The term 'prehistoric' was coined by the French researcher Paul Tournal to describe articles found in French caves that were made by man more than 10,000 years ago. What he meant by prehistoric was merely 'something created before written history began'. Generally speaking, in the British Isles this would refer to anything that came before the Roman invasion of these islands in AD 43 because prior to that time there was no literate culture living in Britain.

Bearing in mind that man first came to Britain about 500,000 years ago, it is fair to say that for our species in this particular location there have been about 2,000 years of recorded history and, according to the latest thinking, close to 498,000 years of prehistory! In terms of prehistoric monuments this isn't quite as daunting as it sounds because for a very long time our ancestors did not build any sort of structure that was durable enough to stand the test of time. Evidence of humanity in this extremely remote period comes from finds of 'edged tools' mostly made from flint, the earliest of which come from Norfolk and Suffolk. The people who made these tools were hunter-gatherers, who earned their living foraging for plants, seeds and roots, as well as harvesting shellfish and hunting larger species of prey. As the name hunter-gatherer implies, it is unlikely that such groups would have stayed in any particular place for very long. Communities were probably extremely small and they were tied to the availability of potential food sources in any given location.

This general pattern of existence for early humans in the British Isles was heavily affected by climatic conditions. Repeated cold snaps and major ice ages came and went, forcing early human communities south and back into the slightly warmer areas of continental Europe. The last ice age finally retreated about 10,000 years ago and, once it finished, humans flooded back into the British Isles again to take advantage of the natural resources that gradually became available once more. During this whole fantastically long period of time very little altered in terms of human advancement, probably because, as the saying goes, 'if it isn't broken don't fix it'. In other words, the hunter-gatherer's life worked well for the communities in question. Population levels probably remained more or less stable and there was not much reason for anything to change. We might take an example from the indigenous people of Australia who, until the arrival of Europeans in the late 18th century, lived a life that had probably changed very little in tens of thousands of years. Why should it? Australian Aborigines were the masters of their environment – skilled at all the tasks necessary to maintain the population and well able to earn a living from the land.

The situation in Britain was probably very similar, except for the interruptions caused by periodic ice ages, and there is no reason to believe that anything would have changed right up to the present time, had it not been for something that took place much further east. Around 10,000 years ago, in parts of what is now Syria and also along the Nile in Egypt, someone decided to break from the normal routines of hunter-gatherer life in a way that would have a profound bearing on our entire species. Instead of simply harvesting what nature was good enough to supply, they decided to lend a hand. There is strong evidence that people in these two locations began to deliberately plant cereal crops.

There were distinct advantages to the first attempts at agriculture. Crops deliberately planted could be kept safe from grazing by wild animals, ensuring that the bulk of the crop would be available for human use. Also, with a surplus of grain it became possible to store food against leaner times to a far greater degree than had been the case for the hunter-gatherers. But it did mean a dramatic change in lifestyle. Although hunting forays could still be undertaken – and were for thousands of years after farming began – communities had to remain in one place, in order to benefit from their hard work.

Another important change was the 'ownership' of land. It wouldn't have made any sense whatsoever to clear land and plant crops, only to allow the next roving band of people who happened to wander by to reap the benefit of one's ingenuity and toil. If necessary, violence might be the only recourse to prevent theft of crops, especially in times of famine.

Farming brought about a fundamental change in the way human communities thought and acted, and it arrived in the British Isles around 6,500 years ago, in the period we refer to as the Neolithic. Although Britain was still in the Stone Age at this time, people began to make clearings in the lush forests in order to plant the first crops of wheat and barley. At the same time a more settled existence allowed the domestication of animals such as sheep, goats, cattle and pigs. And perhaps not surprisingly it was soon after this period that people began to create structures that can still be found on the British landscape today.

Why should this be the case? There are probably a number of reasons and proclaiming ownership of a particular location surely had to be one of them. A really impressive structure, be it for practical or ritual purposes, might tell any would-be passing opportunist a great deal about a community. If it had been possible for a village or a collection of villages to cut and face wood, dig deep ditches and erect banks or even cut and drag stones across the landscape, the same people would probably represent a formidable foe and so it might be more prudent to leave them alone.

Such are the range and type of structures that have been left to us from pre-historic times it is impossible to generalize about either the motivation that caused them to be built or, in many cases, their true intended function. Some of these structures, even the very early ones, are massive in scope. As an example we might mention the first super-henges. As I will explain more fully in due course, a henge is usually circular and consists of one or a series of ditches and banks. The intended purpose of henges is somewhat contentious but of their scale there is little doubt. Sometime around 3500 BC, both in the south but especially in the north of England, a positive frenzy of henge building took place. An array of three such super-henges near Ripon in Yorkshire is so large that St Paul's Cathedral could easily be fitted inside any one of them. The ditches of these Class IIA henges (*see* Henges) were once very deep and the banks commensurately high. They must have represented a great effort on the part of the communities that created them and they were obviously not undertaken without a great deal of thought and planning.

One thing is more or less certain; people wanted to *belong* to a particular location and to respond positively to a specific landscape. They almost certainly also wanted to talk to their gods in a language they thought those selfsame gods would understand – 'Gods are self-evidently big, and so, in at least some cases, the structures built for them should also be large.'

Of course many of the enigmatic prehistoric structures dotted about the landscape of the British Isles had a very practical purpose. Hill forts were used to defend territory, and were probably a means of demonstrating potential power and fighting acumen. Barrows and burial chambers were the abode of the dead, and simple enclosure banjos or other banks and ditches were almost certainly created to protect animals and to keep them restricted to a specific area.

It may well be that some of the structures which are generally considered these days to be of purely 'ritual' or 'religious' importance may also have had very practical applications in the everyday lives of prehistoric communities. Together with my colleague Christopher Knight, I have demonstrated that this was certainly the case with the super-henges.

Developing research is now beginning to show that there was a great deal of continuity in terms of the population of the British Isles. A recent genetic study has shown that a man who died in Cheddar, Somerset, 9,000 years ago, and whose bones were discovered recently, has a direct descendant still living in the locality. Cheddar Man is related, through his mitochondrial DNA, to a history teacher who still resides in the same town!

Nevertheless, such an amazing and quite unexpected discovery should not blind us to the fact that new peoples were arriving in the British Isles regularly throughout the Stone Age, the Bronze Age and the Iron Age, supplementing the local population, bringing new innovations, changing religious patterns and instigating the creation of perpetually new and different structures.

Archaeology has come on in leaps and bounds across the last few decades. It has ever more techniques at its disposal that can be used in teasing out the truth of any prehistoric site. Reconstructive archaeology in particular has been an invaluable tool in terms of finding out what our ancestors were really thinking and doing, by thinking and doing it ourselves. We have to try and get ourselves into the mindset of people who in many ways were a great deal like us, but whose motivations, religious beliefs and practical necessities were sometimes dramatically different. If we can do that, we stand a chance of understanding exactly what many of the prehistoric structures were really about.

There is no doubt that when one talks about prehistoric monuments in the British Isles, many people's minds turn to the really impressive structures such as Stonehenge, Avebury or Silbury Hill, all in Wiltshire. However, and despite the impressive nature of these creations, the whole body of England, Wales, Scotland and Ireland are positively awash with pre-historic monuments, dating from the Stone Age, right up until the arrival of the Roman legions in the 1st century.

From the tiniest fairy ring, right up to the most complex and massive hill fort, all these 'scratchings in the soil' have something important to tell us about the way our direct ancestors thought, acted and lived their lives. To my mind nothing is better or more exciting than struggling across some muddy field or up a precipitous hill in order to look directly at something that may have been created in that spot as much as 6,000 years ago. I hope that what is contained in this book allows people who have these same fascinations to better understand what they are looking at when their goal is reached.

I have tried to bring together the most up-to-date explanations for all the types of prehistoric monument I mention, but there is nothing at all wrong with using the same intuition, imagination and logic that went into their creation. There is surely little in this world more thrilling than being able to answer a question that remains a puzzle, even to the experts.

Using *How to Read Prehistoric Monuments*, you will be able to find your way to a vast storehouse of history written large on the landscape. I hope that to do so brings you closer to the soul of our long-lost grandfathers and grand-mothers. Like us they lived their everyday lives. They had their joys and sorrows; they feasted and starved, loved and hated and, just like us, they sought to make sense of the vast starry skies and the caprices of nature. In terms of intelligence they were no different than we are today because our brains have changed very little during what seems to us to be a vast span of time; they could be ingenious and were able to come up with answers to problems that we might find difficult to address in our highly technological world.

Before you start looking at the many classifications and explanations that follow, take a peek at 'About the Book' so that you can get the most out of what is on offer. It is my intention that this book will bring you as much pleasure to read and to refer to as it has brought me to research and write. There is nothing more rewarding than the puzzle of the past and certainly nothing more enigmatic than the many thousands of often misunderstood prehistoric monuments that positively litter the landscape of the British Isles. Wherever you are, you will never be more than a few miles from one, so get on your boots, pack a few sandwiches and go on a journey in time.

About the Book

*H*ow to Read Prehistoric Monuments is divided into two basic parts. First there is an A–Z section. I have included this in order to cut through the jargon that inevitably attracts itself to a subject as potentially complex as prehistoric archaeology. All the major words associated with prehistoric structures located in the British Isles are mentioned in the A–Z and you will also find examples in each case of where such structures can be found.

This first section of the book is very important, not least because you will know what you are looking at when you find yourself at any prehistoric structure or site across our islands. Jargon is inevitable in any scientific study and some of the words used to describe collections of stones, tombs, enclosures or whatever can seem extremely confusing at first. If you are in Cornwall, England, you might happen upon a 'fougou'. You probably won't have the slightest idea what a fougou might be, and it probably won't help if you then learn that fougou is just a local name for a 'souterrain'. That's where the A–Z comes in, because there you will discover that fougou or souterrain are simply names for artificial caves. You will quickly learn, if you have not done so already, that experts such as archaeologists need to use long and confusing names for all manner of simple things. We can forgive them for doing so, because they are opening up the world of the past to us in a way that has never been possible before.

I have tried, where appropriate, to include examples of sites in all parts of the British Isles, but there are times when this will not be the case. A fougou can only be found in Cornwall, whereas a 'broch' is a peculiarly Scottish structure.

In the A–Z section you will also find words that do not describe 'sites' specifically but names or words associated with our prehistoric past that I think you may find useful.

Not all prehistoric sites across our islands are especially easy to find, in fact the majority are not. For this reason, whenever I have mentioned a particular site I have given a longitude and latitude position for it. Not only will this allow you to find the site in question on a detailed local map, but if you have such a device you could also feed these co-ordinates into a GPS satellite navigation system. These little hand-held gadgets (not to be confused with the ones that are generally meant for use in cars) are becoming more and more popular with walkers; they are now relatively inexpensive and are a real boon when pin-pointing a very small site – for example, an isolated rock containing prehistoric art. However, there is another reason for including longitude and latitude of the sites mentioned in the book and that relates to the use of Google Earth.

If there are any readers who are not already familiar with Google Earth, let me explain that it is a computer program, which at the time of publication of this book is free to download. It allows the user to look, in most cases in great detail, at aerial photographs of almost anywhere on the surface of the Earth. It is easy to use and, in addition to being able to find a location by its name, it is possible to look at a specific spot using its exact longitude and latitude, which are shown at the bottom of the screen.

Google Earth is a godsend to anyone who is trying to understand our ancient past. Part of the problem with many archaeological sites is that they have been badly eroded by the passing of so many centuries, and of course some of them have also been disturbed by people. Nevertheless, if any particular site is fairly large – or even in many cases if it isn't – no amount of disturbance will hide it from the prying eyes of the cameras in the sky. If you want to get an appreciation of what any particular monument or site actually looks like – which is often difficult on the ground, Google Earth will invariably show you, and it can be a mind-blowing experience. If you have Google Earth, next time you are at your computer, open the program and type 'Old Oswestry' into the 'Fly to' box. The program will now automatically take you to the part of the English–Welsh border where Old Oswestry hill fort is located. Now zoom in to the label for Old Oswestry and you will see an impressive Iron Age hill fort in all its staggering detail. Although nothing beats actually being there, Google Earth offers you the chance to see a full and extensive prehistoric site in a way that would be quite impossible from ground level.

Google Earth also shows up 'parch marks' or 'crop marks' (both of which you will find described in the A–Z section) which are basically the 'ghosts' of prehistoric and even more recent sites on the landscape that have disappeared altogether when viewed at ground level. All in all, Google Earth is a valuable tool and its presence has led to the discovery of many ancient sites that were previously unrecognized. And of course for our purposes it means you can always look at any particular site before you set off to see it at first hand. For long, dark, cold winter days, Google Earth can be a good friend, leading you to discover all sorts of fascinating places and to look at so many of the locations mentioned in this book.

The computer can also be of use to you in other ways. There are many good internet sites these days that deal specifically with our prehistoric past. Two of the best are 'The Modern Antiquarian' and 'The Megalithic Portal'. Not only will these offer you information about specific locations and prehistoric sites, but many contain comments placed there by other visitors to sites. It is always fascinating to learn what other people think and you could pick up hints and tips about accessing places or finding the most difficult ones amidst what can sometimes seem to be a confusing landscape. If you are visiting a particular area of the British Isles, these sites will offer you a county-by-county breakdown of the sites you can see there – far more than could ever be included in one book.

To make life a little easier I have included at the end of the book a list of sites cross-referenced for specific counties. It could be that you are planning a trip to a specific area of the British Isles and that you want to know what pre-historic sites are available there. If so, look at the list of counties and find the ones to which you will be travelling. There you will see page numbers connecting you to sites mentioned in the book.

A slight word of warning is necessary before you set off with your haversack and sandwiches. Many of the prehistoric structures and locations in the British

Isles – even quite a few mentioned in this book – are to be found in very remote locations. This is inevitable because the more isolated a site is, the better the chance that it has avoided development or too much interference from people. Scrambling up precipitous slopes or across wind-blown hills isn't appropriate for everyone, and to get to some of the most lonely examples of our prehistoric past you will need to be fairly fit.

The same rules apply as would be appropriate for anyone setting out into the countryside for a long walk. Be prepared, have foul-weather gear with you and let someone know where you are going before you set off. But if you are getting somewhat long in the tooth, or are not as fit as you would wish to be, don't panic, because there are also many fascinating places that can be approached by car and which are easier to negotiate. If you are in doubt, do a little surfing on the internet, because in almost every case you can learn from other people's experiences.

It is sometimes especially rewarding, particularly when one starts out on the road to becoming a 'prehistoric nut', to go and see some of the sites that have been reconstructed. After all, walking amongst the roundhouses of an Iron Age village will demonstrate not only what one actually looked like but also offer an insight into the way people lived back then. A good friend of mine, who will remain nameless, recently described some prehistoric sites as being little more than 'grassy hills' and of course that is what many of them look like these days. But with a picture of the reality 'as it was' in your mind, you will make more sense of what you are looking at and it will become all the more fascinating.

The second section of the book is dedicated to specific locations that I have found fascinating and which, I hope, are amongst the best and most interesting prehistoric sites available. In most cases, these are also amongst the most famous examples of our prehistoric past, but not always, because there are some amazing locations up and down these islands that are hardly known at all but which are extremely important. There are even some that should rank as 'world-class treasures' but which are not being protected in any way and I hope that once you have seen some of these you, like me, will try to bring gentle pressure to bear on the relevant authorities to give these sites the attention and TLC they rightfully deserve.

It goes without saying that we should not interfere in any way with prehistoric sites but rather enjoy them and then leave them for others to discover. Treasure hunters of the past did incalculable damage to our understanding of our ancient heritage, a trend which sadly continues into the present. Once the ground of any site has been disturbed by those who are not trained to understand context and stratification, the damage can never be repaired and a mountain of knowledge could be lost.

Countless numbers of people have trodden the fields and hills of the lovely British Isles before we came along. What they left behind is part of their legacy to us. There is a good chance that many of us carry the same genes as the people who erected Stonehenge or who carved the portal stones at Newgrange, so, in a sense, when we visit some of the remarkable prehistoric sites of the British Isles, we are simply going home.

Happy hunting.

British History Timeline

500000 BC	The first inhabitants of Britain arrive from the European continent.
6500 BC	Rising seas swamp the land bridge between Britain and France. Britain becomes an island.

4000 BC	The **Neolithic** period begins.
3500 BC	Sometime prior to this date hunter-gatherers in Britain became the first farmers. Cursus are laid down in Britain and the first henges and super-henges are created. Long barrows begin to appear.
3000 BC	More elaborate burial chambers are created and stone circles are created for the first time in Britain. Long barrows continue to be created.
2300 BC	The beaker people start to arrive in Britain. Some round barrows are created.

2100 BC	The start of the **Bronze Age** in Britain. More stone circles appear and more elaborate tombs are created. Bronze Age burials become the norm and individual 'chieftain' burials begin to replace earlier communal burials. Round barrows become common. Stone avenues and individual huge standing stones are erected. This is the golden age of the

Megalith builders and much of our prehistoric heritage is traceable to this period.

2000 BC Stonehenge is completed after many different stages. The age of great Megalithic structures eventually begins to draw to a close as cultures change and new immigrants to Britain alter old traditions.

1200 BC Instead of isolated communities, villages become more common, though the latest research shows that villages actually existed right back to the Old Stone Age.

---

750 BC Iron smelting is brought to Britain and the **Iron Age** begins. Souterrain building begins in Britain.

500 BC The peoples we know as the Celts started to arrive in Britain from Central Europe. The complexion of British society gradually changes, as no doubt did languages and cultural practices.

100 BC Broch building begins in Scotland.

55 BC The first invasion of Britain by the Romans under Julius Caesar.

AD 44 **Roman Britain.** The second invasion of Britain by the Romans under the leadership of the Emperor Claudius.

AD 75 Villa building begins in Britain and legionary fortresses are gradually constructed in England, Wales and parts of Scotland.

AD 410 The Roman legions are withdrawn from Britain and the incursion of the Anglo-Saxon people begins.

AD 624 King Raedwald buried with the Sutton Hoo treasure.

AD 889 The Anglo-Saxon Chronicle is commenced and monastic records are kept. True prehistory ends.

PART I

A–Z Section

Backsight (*see* Foresights and Backsights)

Barrow

Generally speaking the word 'barrow' is used in archaeology to describe a burial mound. Barrows come in a number of different forms and were used across a long period of time.

Figure 1: The various types of round barrow to be found in the British Isles

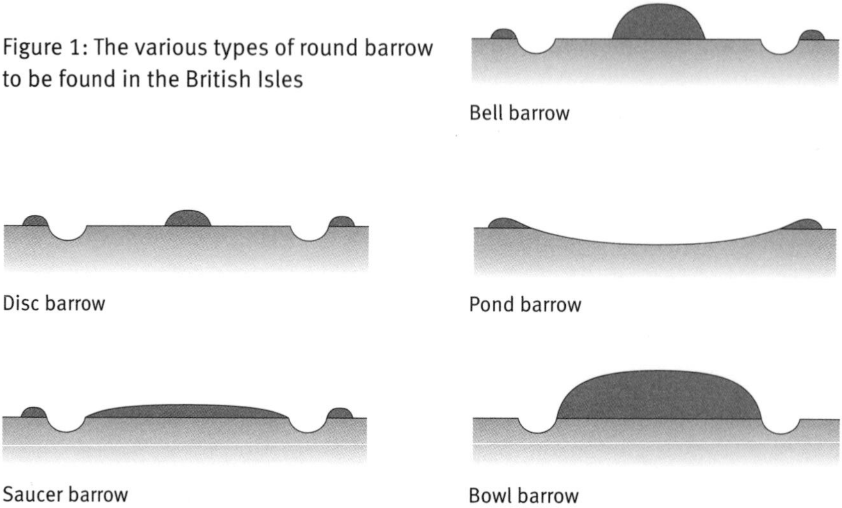

Bell barrow

Disc barrow

Pond barrow

Saucer barrow

Bowl barrow

Bell Barrow

A disc barrow is a type of round barrow and is distinguished by being a tumulus (*see* Tumulus) within a ditch, though in this case the mound is separated from the ditch by a berm (*see* Berm). The bell barrow is merely a variant form of round barrow and gained its name because when seen in profile in looks like a bell (*see* Round Barrows).

Disc Barrow

Disc barrows represent the most recent forms of bell barrow. They differ from the bell barrow because the berm (*see* Berm) is much wider than is the case with a bell barrow, an obviously intended strategy that made the barrow look

Examples of bell barrows:

Winterbourne Stoke, near Amesbury, Wiltshire, England

LATITUDE: 51° 10' 25.99" N   LONGITUDE: 1° 51' 24.98" W

This is part of a series of barrows. In addition to the bell barrow there are also disc barrows to be seen.

Amesbury Down Triple Bell Barrow, Wiltshire, England

LATITUDE: 51° 10' 12.93" N   LONGITUDE: 1° 50' 2.62" W

Amesbury stands within a very significant area for prehistoric monuments and there are three bell barrows at this site.

Aldbourne Four Barrows, Wiltshire, England

LATITUDE: 51° 29' 36.82" N   LONGITUDE: 1° 38' 28.65" W

This is part of a barrow cemetery and the barrows stand out particularly well in the autumn.

Examples of disc barrows:

Oakley Down Barrow Cemetery, Sixpenny Handley, Dorset, England

LATITUDE: 50° 57' 16.35" N   LONGITUDE: 1° 58' 27.73" W

I am as much taken by the name of the village at Sixpenny Handley as by the barrows, which are also impressive.

Flowerdown Disc Barrow, Littleton, Winchester, Hampshire, England

LATITUDE: 51° 5' 5.66" N   LONGITUDE: 1° 20' 40.59" W

A large and well preserved example, with other barrows close by.

Setley Plain, Brockenhurst, Hampshire, England

LATITUDE: 50° 47' 53.53" N   LONGITUDE: 1° 34' 47.8" W

These are the only disc barrows to be seen in the New Forest area of England and are well worth a visit.

more distinctive. For this reason the disc barrow is sometimes referred to as a 'fancy barrow' (*see* Round Barrows).

Long Barrows

Long barrows were created during the New Stone Age and are therefore often referred to as 'Neolithic'. Some long barrows were made entirely from earth (earthen long barrows), whilst others were much more complex and were lined with large stones.

The burial practices of our Neolithic ancestors remain something of a puzzle. Although long barrows have sometimes been found to contain bones from a large number of different individuals (occasionally dozens), not all the bones from any given person are present. What is more, it is certain that the bones ultimately placed in long barrows were de-fleshed first, either deliberately (by human intervention) or by leaving them exposed for the flesh to decompose naturally.

Some long barrows have recessed entries and it is thought (with good evidence) that these structures remained, possibly for long periods of time, as centres of religious rites in which the bones of dead ancestors played an important but little understood part.

Figure 2: Entrance to a long barrow

A really interesting fact about the Neolithic period in Britain is that we have little understanding of how the majority of people were buried. We find no cemeteries from the period and individual (whole) burials are rare. Bearing in mind that only certain bones found their way into long barrows, it could be that the Neolithic people performed a sort of 'sky burial', similar to techniques used in Tibet, in which the bodies of the deceased were placed in the open to decompose naturally; though this has to be conjecture.

Many long barrows have been destroyed by subsequent building and farming but they are very common and so there are still many to be seen, across England especially, some of which remain extremely impressive.

In structure, long barrows are rectangular or sometimes trapezoid earth mounds, and some have a long ancestry. Patient archaeological investigation across decades has shown that many long barrows began as relatively small enclosures containing earth mounds, on top of which was a timber structure (a palisade). It was within this fence that the burial chamber was created. Examples differed but some long barrows were quite grand, with ceremonial entrances or short avenues marked by sturdy posts.

Burial practices within the barrows differed from place to place. In some cases all the burials were put in the chamber at once. In other examples the store of bones was added to across a long period of time.

It may be that the bones chosen for placement in the long barrows were from individuals who enjoyed a high status within their society but if this is the case, the relative lack of grave goods is something of a puzzle.

Some time after this initial phase, large stone cairns were built over the original structures (*see* Cairn) and then the whole structure was covered with earth. A typical undisturbed long barrow might contain the skulls and long bones of many men, women and children, though no complete skeletons.

There are certainly in excess of 300 long barrows to be found in the British Isles, and there would have been many more that did not survive the ravages of time. The greatest concentration of long barrows is in the south and east of England, since different burial techniques predominated further north and in Ireland.

Examples of long barrows:

Street House, near Loftus in North Yorkshire, England

LATITUDE: 54° 33′ 57.71″ N   LONGITUDE: 0° 51′ 41.59″ W

Set amongst the ironstone mining areas of North Yorkshire, Street House is quite close to the sea and near to the charming Saltburn-by-the-Sea.

West Kennet Long Barrow, Salisbury Plain, Wiltshire, England
(*See* Impressive Sites section)

LATITUDE: 51° 24′ 30.78″ N   LONGITUDE: 1° 51′ 4″ W

Probably the best-known long barrow in England, and part of a ritual landscape that covers a huge area in southern England.

Belas Knap Long Barrow, near Cheltenham, Gloucestershire, England
(*See* Impressive Sites section)

LATITUDE: 51° 24′ 30.78″ N   LONGITUDE: 1° 51′ 4″ W

The remains of 31 different individuals were found within Belas Knap Long Barrow, demonstrating that long barrows formed community graves.

Uley Long Barrow, Dursley, Gloucestershire, England

LATITUDE: 51° 41′ 52.2″ N   LONGITUDE: 2° 18′ 19.2″ W

Uley Long Barrow was found to contain at least one Roman burial, proving that such sites were revered for a very long period.

Lambourn Seven Barrows, Lambourn, Berkshire, England
(*See* Impressive Sites section)

LATITUDE: 51° 32′ 33.41″ N   LONGITUDE: 1° 31′ 37.12″ W

Stand by for a shock. There are not 7 barrows at this site but actually 26, though you may not be able to spot them all.

Julliberrie's Grave, Chilham, Kent, England

LATITUDE: 51° 14′ 22.38″ N   LONGITUDE: 0° 58′ 33.22″ E

This is a lovely site but badly damaged in the distant past by the excavation of chalk, which may have destroyed the burials.

Pond Barrows

A pond barrow differs slightly from a round barrow in both structure and possibly in purpose. Pond barrows are hard to recognize since they were not necessarily huge or impressive to begin with. They consist of a mound surrounded by a depression and then a banked rim. Very few burials or grave goods have ever been found beneath pond barrows and it has been suggested that they may not have been intended for burials at all. Perhaps they were sites of ceremonial gatherings – social, ritual or religious – or they may even have marked wells or entrances into the 'underworld'. Pond barrows remain something of a mystery. Pond barrows are most likely to be found in the English counties of Dorset and Wiltshire. (*See* Round Barrows.)

Round Barrows

Although they are also burial mounds, round barrows differ significantly from the long barrow. Usually they are rather later in date, generally being attributed to the Bronze Age (though there are earlier, Neolithic examples too). As their name implies round barrows are circular in shape and they are one of the most common of prehistoric structures to be found across the British Isles.

The means of constructing round barrows varied markedly across the British landscape. Some were simple conical piles of earth, which contained at their centre either a full burial or the cremated remains of an individual. Other

---

Examples of pond barrows:

Culliford Tree, Came Wood, Dorset, England

LATITUDE: 50° 40' 0.75" N   LONGITUDE: 2° 25' 33.45" W

There are lots of trees on this site that obscure the barrows somewhat, but their presence may have preserved the barrows from ploughing.

Kingley Vale Barrow Cemetery, near Chichester, West Sussex, England

LATITUDE: 50° 53' 31.48" N   LONGITUDE: 0° 50' 7.44" W

These barrows are not too easy to find and are certainly not well signposted, however, for the determined they are a must.

round barrows were made from alternate layers of earth and stones. Some also contained timber and even basket-work or wattle-and-daub components.

Clearly our ancient ancestors (and perhaps our not so ancient ancestors too) held a reverence for round barrows. Quite frequently archaeologists have discovered new burials or cremations cut into the sides or the top of round barrows. Some of these were put in place many centuries after the barrow in question was first created.

There are many sub-classifications of round barrows. These include bell barrows, bowl barrows, disc barrows and saucer barrows. In most cases the difference is academic and due to regional preferences or the different forces of ageing that have affected the barrows during the intervening period.

Round barrows contained either a complete burial, in other words the entire skeleton of an individual, or else the cremated bones of a particular person. It is thought that round barrows were first created around 2500 BC and since they only contained one burial, it appears that society at the time was undergoing a significant change. The effort necessary to create such a structure for a single individual was considerable and this surely suggests a person of some rank within the community. Some experts have suggested that the rise of the use of round barrow burials indicates a greater stratification of society from the late Stone Age on, and the rise of tighter and more cohesive 'tribes' tied to specific locations.

Burials at the centre of round barrows may have been merely placed in a chamber dug from the earth or into chalk, or they might be contained in a stone-lined cist (coffin). Grave goods are frequently found in round barrows. These might include tools of various sorts, items of personal adornment (some made from copper, bronze or gold) and occasionally high-status items from far off, such as amber beads from the Baltic. It appears that there was little difference in status between men and women in cultures that flourished across Britain at the time, since significant barrows were quite frequently raised for female burials.

Many, if not most round barrows, have a ditch around them, probably a natural consequence of removing the earth necessary to raise the barrow, and on those occasions when round barrows have disappeared due to subsequent ploughing over thousands of years, the only distinguishable feature on the

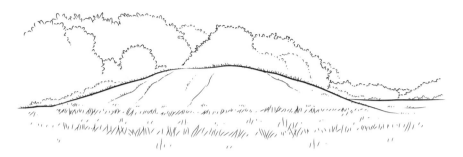

Figure 3: A typical round barrow

landscape may be the 'ghost' of this ditch, which can be seen as 'parch marks' on aerial photographs.

Although round barrows are the most common of prehistoric monuments and can be found distributed all over the landscape, there is a greater number in the area around Wessex and in Yorkshire. Whether this is because there was more prosperity in these areas is not known, but seems likely. Round barrows are also often found grouped together (barrow cemeteries), which could be another indication that families of a high status chose to bury and glorify their members in the same area.

Many round barrows across the British Isles remain in good condition, though where they are obvious they have often been dug out during the last few centuries. It is thought that the earliest round barrows were created by a culture that has become known as the 'beaker people' (*see* Beaker People), who gained the name due to the distinctive shape of the pottery goods they produced. However, round barrows of one sort or another are found across many parts of Europe and they cannot be attributed to a single culture.

The importance of round barrows and their contents cannot be underestimated. To find grave goods of stone, pottery or metal, alongside datable human remains is a godsend to archaeologists and the contents of round barrows have therefore heavily influenced our knowledge of the people who built them, as well as giving us a more complete chronological timeline for periods such as the start of the Bronze Age in Britain. Since many of the grave goods were self-evidently imported from far away, we can also gain a better

Examples of round barrows:

How Tallon, Barningham near Richmond, County Durham, England

LATITUDE: 54° 27' 55.09" N   LONGITUDE: 1° 55' 5.6" W

There is also a stone circle at How Tallon, though the round barrow is obviously from a considerably later period.

Hinderwell Beacon, Loftus, Redcar and Cleveland, England

LATITUDE: 54° 32' 59.56" N   LONGITUDE: 0° 46' 20.35" W

This part of Redcar and Cleveland contains a great many round barrows.

Duggleby Howe, Kirby Grindalythe, North Yorkshire, England

LATITUDE: 54° 5' 21.4" N   LONGITUDE: 0° 39' 10.53" W

This is one of the largest round barrows in Britain and is unusual in that it dates not from the Bronze Age but from the Neolithic era.

Lilla Howe Round Barrow, Grosmont, North Yorkshire, England

LATITUDE: 54° 22' 32.16" N   LONGITUDE: 0° 37' 51.95" W

This site is marked by the Lilla Cross, which defined the edge of a boundary of land once belonging to the beautiful Whitby Abbey.

Martin's Down Round Barrows, Littlebredy, near Dorchester, Dorset, England

LATITUDE: 50° 42' 59.24" N   LONGITUDE: 2° 36' 12.56" W

The barrows at Martin's Down are close to the A35 and so quite easy to find.

Bind Barrow, Burton Bradstock, near Bridport, Dorset, England

LATITUDE: 50° 41' 48.95" N   LONGITUDE: 2° 42' 59.49" W

The mound was damaged by military activity during the Second World War but is still worth a look. There is a good café garden close by at Hive Beach.

Rainbarrows Round Barrow, Dorset, England

LATITUDE: 50° 43' 35.05" N   LONGITUDE: 2° 22' 36.86" W

You will find Rainbarrows at the edge of the enchantingly named Puddletown Forest and on the equally intriguing Duddle Heath.

understanding of the level of long-distance trading that was taking place at the time the barrows were created.

There is some suggestion that the popularity of creating round barrows for single high-status burials somewhat 'took over' from the communal structures, such as the monumental stone circles, and it is possible that significant changes were taking place within society at this time. Personal wealth appears to have become more of an issue, as opposed to the effort that had been expounded by the whole of society on single, grandiose structures, such as the earlier henges and regional 'giant schemes' such as Stonehenge, Avebury and Silbury Hill.

Berm

Berm is an architectural term and is used in archaeology to describe the area of flat land between a ditch and a mound in the case of a barrow. The berm is present in bell barrows and disc barrows.

Broch

Brochs are only found in Scotland but even if you live in the south of the British Isles, it's worth the effort to go and visit some of these fascinating structures. Brochs, though certainly not as old as some of the prehistoric sites mentioned in this book, do deserve to be here because we now know that most of them were built just before, during, or just after the Roman invasion of Britain. Where dating for brochs does exist they seem to have been created in the period round about 100 BC.

Brochs are the most impressive of the type of 'roundhouse' that is peculiar to Scotland. Some brochs are large and still in relatively good condition. They have a dry stone construction and in their ruined state might easily be mistaken for the stumps of old stone windmills.

The word 'broch' derives from a Scottish word 'brough', which has many meanings but in this context is generally taken to mean 'fort', though whether this was originally the purpose of brochs remains a matter of hotly debated contention. Brochs are commonly located in the far northeast of Scotland, on Orkney and Shetland, though there are also some examples to be found to

Examples of brochs:

South Yarrows Broch, Wick, Caithness, Scotland

LATITUDE: 58° 22' 25.41" N   LONGITUDE: 3° 10' 59.59" W

The ground around the broch is quite rough and probably not ideally suited to anyone infirm or not well shod. The broch itself is fascinating.

Mousa Broch, Shetland, Scotland
(*See* Impressive Sites section)

LATITUDE: 59° 59' 45.37" N   LONGITUDE: 1° 10' 50.46" W

Undoubtedly the best preserved of all the brochs but it is in a very isolated position on Mousa Island and is something of an adventure to get to.

Clickimin Broch, Lerwick, Shetlands, Scotland

LATITUDE: 60° 8' 57.83" N   LONGITUDE: 1° 9' 51.33" W

The scenery around Clickimin Broch will take your breath away and the site is one of the 'must see' locations for broch pilgrims in particular.

Midhowe Broch, Orkney, Scotland

LATITUDE: 59° 9' 31.08" N   LONGITUDE: 3° 6' 0.09" W

One of the best brochs in Orkney and like all the prehistoric sites on this magical island it is set amidst stunning scenery.

Figure 4: A typical broch

the west and on the larger Western Isles. Brochs may have been simply a local peculiarity that spoke legions about the 'power' of local landowners and chieftains, though it does seem likely, mainly as a result of the position of many brochs, that they did serve some defensive purpose.

Bronze Age

Apart from copper, bronze was the first metal tamed by humanity and its introduction revolutionized many aspects of human life. For thousands of years people had used tools and weapons made from various forms of stone, bone and wood but nothing the Stone Age people of the world possessed came close to the usefulness and toughness of cast bronze.

Bronze is an alloy of copper and tin. It was first utilized in the Near East as early as 3300 to 3000 BC but it did not arrive in Britain until after around 2000 BC, which was quite late since the technology took that long to gravitate so far west. Britain was luckier than many regions of Europe or Asia in that significant deposits of tin were available in the southwest (Cornwall). Copper is more common but tin may have represented a significant opportunity to trade in southwest Britain and certainly found its way to the Continent. Its existence (together with gold in Wales) has been postulated as one of the reasons for the Roman invasion of Britain.

Burial Chamber

The term 'burial chamber' is often used to describe a range of different sorts of structures thought to have been originally designed to house the dead, though in a specific sense it relates to a particular type of tomb, mainly those created during the Megalithic period (*see* Megalithic Period). Such tombs are to be found across Britain. They are often, but not always, defined by having been created around a number of large flat stones, arranged in the form of a stone placed
on top of two uprights, thus creating a shelter within which the burial can take place.

This initial structure was then covered by an earth or stone bank.

Sometimes a long tunnel was created in order to connect the inner chamber with the outside world. It has been suggested that this passage (*see* Passage Grave) was meant to represent the birth canal (of the Earth), whilst the chamber itself symbolized the womb. Since it was common in ancient times for people to be buried in the foetal position it is entirely possible that prehistoric peoples equated death with birth – perhaps as a rebirth into a different sort of existence.

In many cases across the British landscape the contents of a burial chamber have long since disappeared, as has the earth bank that once covered it. This leaves the three or more large stones at the centre open to the elements. Under these circumstances the structure is known as a 'dolmen' (*see* Dolmen). There are so many different sorts of tombs left to us from prehistory that I have dealt with them under their own specific headings. (*See* Chambered Cairns, Chambered Long Barrows, Corbelled Tombs and Gallery Graves.)

Burial Mound

Burial mound is a term that refers to almost any sort of mound of earth, stones, timber and earth, wattle and earth etc. structure that was built over a site where burials had taken place. In general the terms 'barrow' for much of Britain and 'cairn' for Scotland are more appropriate. (*See* Barrow and Cairn)

Burnt Mound (*Fulacht fiadh* in Irish)

In many parts of the British Isles, piles of stones have been found, sometimes quite large ones, that have clearly been subjected to significant heat. This has caused them to fracture in a way that is consistent with being placed in cold water, with a resultant sudden shock. The mounds are often crescent-shaped and are associated with a trough, which must once have contained water and a hearth where the stones were first heated. It is interesting, though perhaps inevitable, that burnt mounds and the troughs that go with them are almost always found near water courses.

Various suggestions have been put forward to explain what the burnt mounds and troughs were used for. One of the most likely (at least at first sight) is that they represent places where meat, hunted locally, was cooked during hunting expeditions. This would be fine were it not for the fact that there is a total absence of bones in any of the sites, even those where the nature of the soil should have allowed for such organic material to have survived. It seems unlikely, if not impossible, that no trace of anyone's meal has been located at the burnt mounds and so experts have cast around for a more likely explanation. The most plausible seems to be 'sweat lodges'.

Although there is no historical evidence for the existence of sweat lodges in Britain this is not surprising, since the earliest of the burnt mounds date back to the Stone Age (though they vary greatly in date). It was noted by Europeans who first took the trouble to learn something of the lives of the indigenous peoples of North America that the men of some tribes often got together to create a sort of sauna. This may have been for simple relaxation but it is known that in many cases the American sweat lodges had a ceremonial and a religious purpose.

It is quite conceivable that our own ancient ancestors also happened upon a way of relaxing and of getting warm in a chilly climate and the mechanisms in place around burnt mounds, especially the presence of the trough and the hearth, offer evidence that this was indeed the case.

Many burnt mounds are now indistinct or practically impossible to see and I have avoided giving examples of locations because this, at best, is the worst sort of 'grassy lump' that could come at the end of a significant walk. If you do come upon a burnt mound it is worth imagining our ancient forebears relaxing after a hard day's hunting or, later in history, once the farming chores were out of the way. We can imagine that some primitive form of shelter or hut was used to collect the resulting steam. Such a structure would have disappeared soon after the practice ceased. It is thought that some burnt mounds were used across a considerable period of time.

Very few burnt mounds can be readily seen on the landscape and in cases where they have been excavated anything significant found has often been taken to local, regional or national museums. However, there are hundreds of examples, so they are certainly significant and can usually be located on high-scale, local Ordnance Survey maps.

Cairn

Cairn is a peculiarly Scottish word and refers to a pile of stones, deliberately and artificially placed on the landscape for any one of many different reasons. Cairns are often found at the top of hills, marking a particular water course on moorland or upland paths. Cairns have been built for countless centuries and there is no doubt that some of them have their origins back in the mists of prehistory, though they are still being created today.

It has, for example, been a habit of walkers in Scotland, and now across all of the British Isles, to pick up a small stone from the bottom of a hill or mountain and to place it on the cairn that is often to be found at the hill's summit. Long-lived cairns are marked on Ordnance Survey maps and herein lies part of the reason for their existence.

In prehistoric times the British Isles were sparsely populated and comprised a range of different sorts of countryside, much of which was boggy, tree-covered or exposed to the elements. Even in these remote times people had to get about, to trade, to hunt, or simply to visit other communities. Paths will not have been well marked but to stray from them could have meant danger or death, especially in the winter months. The existence of cairns represented a visual aid to travellers that they were on a well-used track and maintenance of such signposts was everyone's responsibility. For those who enjoy donning stout boots and trekking across the vast uplands that still exist in many places, cairns remain a good visible sign that 'someone has gone this way before' and that they are probably on a known and used track. In this sense, the cairn is just as important today as it ever was.

Keep your eyes open. There are far too many cairns in the British Isles to list in this or any book but you will see them almost everywhere. They are a friendly reminder that you are not alone and some of them have been made and remade since the Stone Age. This is living history on the landscape.

Cairn Tombs

In parts of Scotland, and especially around Inverness, there exists a type of burial similar to the barrow burials found further south in Britain. What sets

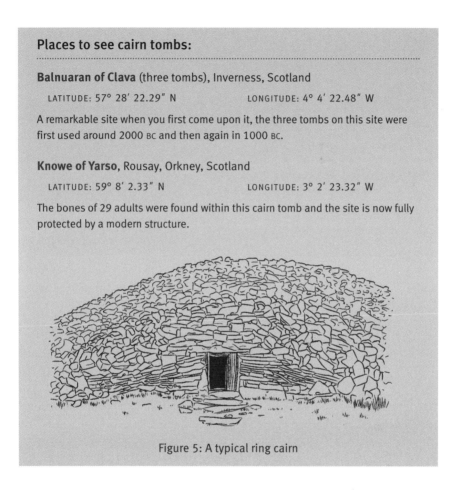

Places to see cairn tombs:

Balnuaran of Clava (three tombs), Inverness, Scotland

LATITUDE: 57° 28' 22.29" N   LONGITUDE: 4° 4' 22.48" W

A remarkable site when you first come upon it, the three tombs on this site were first used around 2000 BC and then again in 1000 BC.

Knowe of Yarso, Rousay, Orkney, Scotland

LATITUDE: 59° 8' 2.33" N   LONGITUDE: 3° 2' 23.32" W

The bones of 29 adults were found within this cairn tomb and the site is now fully protected by a modern structure.

Figure 5: A typical ring cairn

these Scottish examples apart is that rather than being covered by earth, they were carefully covered with both large and small stones. The effect is the same but the medium is different and cairn tombs often stand out more on the landscape than barrows do.

The Scottish examples, especially the ones around Inverness, are often called 'Clava Cairns', though in fact this name refers to three specific cairn burials at Balnuaran of Clava, Inverness.

There are two different types of cairn tombs in Scotland. One variety is a corbelled passage grave (*See* Corbelled Tomb and Passage Grave) with a single chamber and a short entrance passage. The passage usually faces southwest (towards midwinter sunset). The other type of cairn tomb had no apparent entrance and no specifically created roof to the chamber. It is, essentially a ring of stones.

Cairn tombs are invariably surrounded by a series of standing stones, and a kerb of stones often also surrounds the cairn.

Capstone

The word 'capstone' in relation to prehistoric monuments usually refers to the topmost stone of a dolmen (*see* Dolmen). Some of these are massive in scale but are only generally on view today because the mound that once covered the dolmen has been removed or has weathered away.

Carvings

Our prehistoric ancestors in Britain were certainly not reluctant to leave their mark on the landscape in ways other than creating monuments of one sort or another. As far as we are aware no culture in Britain before the coming of the Romans in the 1st century AD had what could be considered 'a written language' but they may well have had signs and signals that meant 'something' to others of their tribe or society.

Carvings in stone are to be found in many places across Britain and Ireland. The most famous and numerous of these are the cup and ring markings that appear almost everywhere, but these are far from being alone. Such carvings are generally known these days as 'rock art'.

Some of the finest rock art to be seen in the British Isles is to be found in the Boyne Valley in Ireland. There it is associated with a number of passage tombs. Large stones that once surrounded the mounds were carved into a series of abstract shapes, though it has been suggested by numerous researchers that the shapes found at Knowth, Newgrange and other sites were not abstract at all. We find spirals, lozenges, radiating lines, swirls and circles, all of which may have meant something quite significant to those who created them. It has even been suggested that there was an astronomical or cosmological meaning

Figure 6: A carved stone

Figure 7: Rock carvings

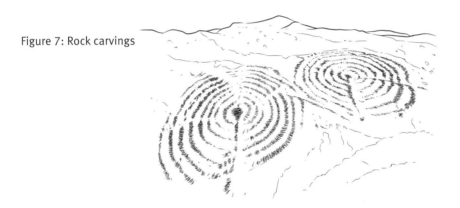

to these now long-forgotten forms of communication and that at least some of them may have made reference to the astronomical sightings that were possible in and from such sites.

Spirals are also common throughout the British Isles, and there are far more exotic stone carvings, such as the swastikas that were found on Ilkley Moor. Some modern experts suggest that this extraordinary stone (the one on the site is a replica and the original is in the museum in Ilkley) is medieval in date, but other people remain convinced it is prehistoric. As far as the spirals are concerned, the eminent researcher and tireless measurer of standing stones

Places to see good rock carvings:

Swastika Stone, Ilkley Moor, West Yorkshire, England

LATITUDE: 53° 55′ 4.29″ N   LONGITUDE: 1° 51′ 19.23″ W

This site is particularly close to my heart since it is close to where I was born. Ilkley Moor is beautiful, ancient and fascinating but a steep climb.

Hare Law Crags (Gled Law), Berwick upon Tweed, England

LATITUDE: 55° 34′ 8.17″ N   LONGITUDE: 1° 59′ 2.91″ W

This site is on private land so exercise a little caution and be considerate. The carvings are evocative and quite breathtaking.

Old Bewick Rock Carvings, near Alnwick, Northumberland, England

LATITUDE: 55° 29′ 16.8″ N   LONGITUDE: 1° 52′ 35.58″ W

This is a fairly tough adventure and certainly not for the faint-hearted. If you are fit, and you can find the rock art, you will be well rewarded.

Roughting Linn, Berwick upon Tweed, England

LATITUDE: 55° 37′ 25.5″ N   LONGITUDE: 2° 1′ 31.48″ W

This site can be found on a sandstone outcrop and, although a private site, is accessible on a footpath. There were probably more carvings originally.

Townhead, Dumfries and Galloway, Scotland

LATITUDE: 54° 48′ 5.79″ N   LONGITUDE: 4° 1′ 38.24″ W

All I can say about this site is 'wow'! Be prepared to spend a considerable time poking about and you might even find something new.

Achnabreck, Argyll, Scotland

LATITUDE: 56° 3′ 39.32″ N   LONGITUDE: 5° 26′ 39.14″ W

The Kilmartin area is a veritable wonderland of prehistoric structures and signs. There are many cup and ring markings to be seen.

and stone circles, Alexander Thom (*see* Thom, Alexander), has shown just how carefully these were sometimes created and carved. They may relate to the movement of the Sun throughout the year.

It is easy to understand how such rock carvings were made once bronze and then iron were introduced to the prehistoric tool box, but in earlier times even the most rudimentary carvings must have represented a long and laborious effort. Rather than being a simple 'we were here' they undoubtedly had great meaning for those who toiled away, hour after hour, in order to create them, but with no context these carvings, many of which probably still remain to be discovered, are enigmatic.

Causewayed Enclosures

Causewayed enclosures were once known as causewayed camps but since it has now been demonstrated that these structures were not necessarily domestic in nature, the new term has begun to predominate.

Causewayed enclosures are not a uniquely British structure. They are found in even greater numbers in France and have also been recognized in other European countries. The typical causewayed enclosure is defined by ditches and banks, interspersed with ways in and out of the structure, which is where the word 'causewayed' comes from. They may be roughly circular but are not always so and there can be from one to four sets of ditches and banks defining a causewayed enclosure.

Most of these structures date to the Neolithic period and it has been suggested that they relate to a time when totally settled farming communities had not fully developed. They could have been meeting places for diverse and widespread communities, or places where ritual or religious ceremonies took place. What is generally accepted these days is that nobody lived in the causewayed enclosures on a permanent basis. In reality causewayed enclosures may have served a number of purposes – for example they are frequently the site of burials, either contemporary with the structure or later. The archaeologist Aubrey Burl has suggested that causewayed enclosures fell out of fashion around 3000 BC, at which time, in Britain at least, they were superseded by other structures, such as henges.

Some of the examples of causewayed enclosures to be found in the British Isles are still very impressive. They usually occur in lowland areas and are not thought to have been used for defensive purposes.

Places to see causewayed enclosures:

Robin Hood's Ball, near Amesbury, Wiltshire, England

LATITUDE: 51° 12' 45.18" N   LONGITUDE: 1° 51' 9.09" W

Caution is necessary since this site is on a live firing range used by the British Army. Although you can get close to the site, watch for the red flags flying and stay on the path.

Coombe Hill, Jevington, East Sussex, England

LATITUDE: 50° 47' 50.49" N   LONGITUDE: 0° 14' 1.5" E

This site remained sacred for a very long period of time. It is Neolithic in origin but was used in Bronze Age times and also by the Romans.

Windmill Hill, Avebury, Wiltshire, England

LATITUDE: 51° 26' 27.55" N   LONGITUDE: 1° 52' 29.32" W

This is the largest causewayed enclosure in Britain and covers 92,957 square yards (85,000 square metres). It is set amidst the most active prehistoric landscape imaginable.

Hambledon Hill, near Blandford Forum, Dorset, England
(*See* Impressive Sites section)

LATITUDE: 50° 54' 40.21" N   LONGITUDE: 2° 13' 13.78" W

This is a very early site, first established even before most of the tree cover in the surrounding area had been removed. Indications of warfare have been unearthed here.

Hembury, Honiton, Devon, England

LATITUDE: 50° 49' 12.15" N   LONGITUDE: 3° 15' 33.68" W

On this site was found some of the earliest Neolithic pottery ever to be unearthed in the British Isles. The site was used much later by the Romans.

Caves

It is self-evident that our earliest ancestors took refuge in naturally created caves. Even to a culture refined enough to create substantial dwellings it is obviously preferable to utilize a form of shelter that nature has created free of charge. However, extensive evidence shows that caves have meant much more to human beings than just a place to keep dry and warm during inclement weather.

Britain does not have the wealth of rock paintings inside caves that are to be found elsewhere in the world, and especially in France, though there are some examples to be seen, such as a painting of a woolly mammoth recently found in a cave in the Cheddar Gorge in Somerset, which is estimated to be at least 30,000 years old. Others, this time of a horse and a lion, were found in a cave at Cresswell Crags, Sheffield. Paintings of birds and also an animal much like an ibex have also been recognized at Cresswell.

Despite the relative lack of rock paintings in Britain, archaeologists love to dig into the floors of caves because what they find there gives a great snapshot of humanity in Britain right back to 50,000 years ago, a time when Neanderthals were resident in Britain. Though what they find in such excavations cannot be considered prehistoric monuments, and so therefore don't rightfully belong in this book, it would be remiss of me not to mention them at all.

Layer upon layer, the debris and detritus that come to light during cave excavations show a timeline of life in the British Isles; nor does this record finish with the end of hunting and gathering in our islands. Many caves have been used up until recent times, either as places of habitation, storage or as workshops.

Some caves are completely man-made (*see* Mines and Quarries) and are the sites of countless hours of human labour to extract minerals or metal ores. Since it is inevitable that people will leave evidence wherever they happen to be, the man-made caves are also a favoured resort of archaeologists, who are constantly trying to fill in the many sketchy details concerning the lives of our ancient ancestors.

Of course, apart from being historically significant, caves are also great fun to explore, though many of them are also very dangerous and it is advisable for all but the expert to stick to caves that are known to be safe and secure and which are not prone to rapid flooding.

Places to see prehistoric caves:

Kents Cavern, Wellswood, Torquay, England

LATITUDE: 50° 27′ 59.01″ N   LONGITUDE: 3° 30′ 7.89″ W

The cavern is well signposted and quite fascinating – if you like caves.

Cresswell Crags, Sheffield, South Yorkshire, England

LATITUDE: 53° 15′ 45.38″ N   LONGITUDE: 1° 11′ 36.05″ W

This is a limestone crag positively honeycombed with caves, many of which were of significant interest to our really ancient ancestors.

Cheddar Gorge, Somerset, England

LATITUDE: 51° 17′ 5.4″ N   LONGITUDE: 2° 45′ 25.87″ W

Undoubtedly the most famous of the English caves. The site is now quite commercial and of special fascination to younger people.

Cemeteries

As opposed to individual burials, be they in chambers or barrows, we take the word cemetery to indicate a place set aside specifically for the interment of the dead en masse. Archaeologists love cemeteries, not only because of the reliable dating evidence that comes from human or in fact any bones, but for a whole series of reasons that are becoming more and more relevant.

Large samples of skeletons offer much evidence concerning rate and age of mortality at a particular period and in some cases they can also indicate how individuals died, such as, for example, cemeteries that came about as a result of battles or wars. In some cases it has been possible to extract DNA from even very ancient skeletons – a technique that is becoming more and more refined as time passes. This in turn helps to establish patterns of possible migration or it can show, as in the case of Cheddar Man and his still-living relative, that some human families stay in the same place for incredible periods of time.

Mass burials in cemeteries are also useful when the individual graves contain 'grave goods' in terms of pottery, tools or adornments.

Unfortunately, in the British Isles, there are no cemeteries until the arrival of the Bronze Age. Before this time burials were communal (*see* Long Barrows), and despite the fact that significant numbers of bones have been found in long barrows, full, articulated skeletons are never found in such settings.

Even the advent of round barrows (*see* Round Barrows) with their individual burials, offer a limited amount of useful evidence in the way that a large cemetery would. True, round barrows often exist in clusters, leading to the supposition that the people buried in them may be from the same 'dynastic' family but many of the round barrows were robbed during the last three or four hundred years, often without any scientific record being kept. Round barrows are also just as likely to contain cremated burials as inhumations, which again offer limited evidence compared to the sort that comes from whole, articulated skeletons.

Around the 12th century BC 'something' happened in the British Isles that started to change the nature of society in our islands. This is a period during which a great deal of disruption was taking place further afield and especially in the Mediterranean region. The British Isles may have been subjected to invasions by peoples from outside the islands or mass migration could have taken place. At any rate, we find that burial practices began to change around this time. Cremation became the norm and cemeteries began to appear.

With the advent of the Iron Age our ancestors once again became generally unhelpful to modern archaeology and its need for evidence. It appears that in most places the bodies of the dead were 'exposed' to the elements, as had taken place earlier in our history. Generally speaking only individual bones are found from this period, often buried in a post hole or under the former walls of buildings. There are some exceptions to this rule. In Yorkshire for example, around 400 BC, locals established long cemeteries in which individuals were buried side by side, and in the far southwest of Britain some burials took place in stone-lined graves.

All in all it might be suggested that the burial practices of the prehistoric peoples of the British Isles were such that although individual burials are found, some of which are of very high status, the possibility for amassing useful evidence of the sort that comes from Roman and later cemeteries is limited.

Chalk Figures (*See* Hill Figures)

Chambered Cairns

A chambered cairn is a particular form of burial site. It consists of a usually fairly large central chamber, often but not always made of stones, around which further stones are piled, forming the 'cairn' (*see* Cairn). Chambered cairns come from the Neolithic period (after 4000 BC) and are particularly numerous in Scotland.

Places to see chambered cairns:

Arthur's Stone Chambered Cairn, near Hay-on-Wye, Herefordshire, England
(*See* Impressive Sites section)

LATITUDE: 52° 4' 53.66" N   LONGITUDE: 2° 59' 43.28" W

This is one of hundreds of sites named for the famed King Arthur but it clearly had nothing to do with him. There isn't too much to see but it's interesting all the same.

Unstan Chambered Cairn, near Howe, Orkney Mainland, Scotland

LATITUDE: 58° 59' 11.89" N   LONGITUDE: 3° 14' 51.63" W

This is a great tomb to explore and a great deal of pottery was found at the site which has now given its name to a 'type' of pottery.

Maeshowe Chambered Cairn, Orkney Mainland, Scotland
(*See* Impressive Sites section)

LATITUDE: 58° 59' 46.28" N   LONGITUDE: 3° 11' 13.55" W

Superlatives fail when trying to describe Maeshowe. It is simply breathtaking and the absolute pinnacle of prehistoric knowledge and engineering.

Midhowe Chambered Cairn, Rousay, Orkney, Scotland

LATITUDE: 59° 9' 27.9" N   LONGITUDE: 3° 5' 53.69" W

This is a very impressive tomb and it wins out for all history buffs because it is also very close to one of Orkney's important brochs.

Some chambered cairns were fairly elaborate structures being also passage graves (*see* Passage Grave). There are definite regional differences between the way chambered cairns were created. Many were not simply random piles of stones but were arranged methodically and with great care. The cairn itself may or may not be covered with earth, though if it is the finished structure takes on the look of a round barrow when seen from a distance. Some of the chambered cairns, especially the ones in parts of northern Scotland and Orkney are extremely impressive, well preserved and well worth a visit.

Chambered Tomb

There are a number of different sorts of chambered tomb that can still be seen across the length and breadth of the British Isles. All consist of a central chamber, or sometimes more than one, in which individual burials or more commonly mass burials of disarticulated bones took place. The chambered cairn mentioned above is an example of a chambered tomb but so are dolmens (*see* Dolmen), chambered long barrows (*see* Long Barrow), corbelled tombs (*see* Corbelled Tomb) and chambered tumulus (*see* Tumulus).

Chambered tombs may or may not have a passage leading to the chamber but many do. In such cases it has been suggested that the passage together with the tomb represents a birth canal and a womb. This suggestion has to be conjecture because we know pitifully little about either the religious beliefs or the ultimate burial practices of people who lived so long ago and who have left nothing in terms of written evidence. Chambered tombs come from a wealth of different periods, according to their type. All are fascinating and well worth the effort necessary to seek them out and explore them.

Cist

Cist is the name given to a generally small, often stone-lined box in which burials, cremations and sometimes funereal goods were placed by our prehistoric ancestors. Cists are sometimes found at the centre of monuments such as a long barrow (*see* Long Barrow) and they were occasionally found cut into existing barrows or mounds and are therefore of a later date. The presence of grave goods in cists means they have always been of great interest to treasure seekers and to the early antiquarians of the 18th and 19th century. As a result, many were robbed, though without the meticulous care taken when such enlightening discoveries are made by modern archaeologists. The word 'cist' is originally Greek and is generally pronounced 'kist'.

Corbelled Tomb

Many prehistoric tombs were constructed by placing large stones upright, with one or more capstones on top, thus providing a chamber in which bones could be placed. The whole was then usually covered with earth, which may or may not have survived. However, there are examples of tombs in the British Isles in which the method of construction is much more sophisticated. In these examples, which are known as corbelled tombs, layers of carefully selected stones were used to cover the chamber. Each layer of stones overhangs the layer underneath until eventually the layers come together to form a conical roof over the chamber. There are some particularly good examples of corbelled tombs in both Ireland and Scotland, which represent some of the most magnificent structures left to us from our prehistoric past.

Places to see corbelled tombs:

Newgrange, Boyne Valley, near Drogheda, Ireland
(*See* Impressive Sites section)

LATITUDE: 53° 41' 40.69" N   LONGITUDE: 6° 28' 31.67" W

This may be the most famous tomb of its type in the British Isles, if not the world. It has been sympathetically reconstructed and is breathtaking.

Maeshowe Chambered Cairn, Orkney, Scotland
(*See* Impressive Sites section)

LATITUDE: 58° 59' 46.28" N   LONGITUDE: 3° 11' 13.55" W

Many people visiting Maeshowe find it difficult, if not impossible, to accept that this tremendous feat of engineering could possibly be so old.

The technique of creating tombs was not a 'development' of the dolmen because some examples of corbelled tombs are extremely ancient. Newgrange in Ireland, one of the best examples of a corbelled tomb to be seen anywhere in the world, is an estimated 5,200 years old. Probably the finest example in Scotland, Maeshowe, is of a similar age.

A great deal of 'know-how' went into the construction of these magnificent structures. Many are intact and all are inclined to cause a sharp intake of breath on the part of the observer when they are seen for the first time.

Crannog

Crannogs are absolutely fascinating and represent one of the most long-lived of all prehistoric structures to be found in the British Isles. Imagine a small, artificial island, close to the shore of a lake and joined to it by a causeway or bridge. This is essentially what a crannog is. The earliest of these structures date back to around 5000 BC but many were used and recreated for many centuries.

Crannogs, which are to be found mostly in Scotland and Ireland (with only one example in Wales), seem to have been places of habitation, probably for an extended family. The merits of such a dwelling are easy to see. First of all the

Figure 8: A reconstructed crannog

Places to see crannogs:

Scottish Crannog Centre, Kenmore, Loch Tay, Perthshire, Scotland

LATITUDE: 56° 34′ 23.56″ N   LONGITUDE: 4° 4′ 43.6″ W

Crannogs are fascinating and at the Scottish Crannog Centre you can find out a great deal about them, as well as explore one.

Craggaunowen Crannog, Kilmurry, Co. Clare, Ireland

LATITUDE: 52° 48′ 32.34″ N   LONGITUDE: 8° 47′ 47.14″ W

This is a full-sized reconstruction of a crannog and is definitely worth a visit if you happen to be in the area.

The Welsh Crannog Centre, Lakeside Caravan Park, Llangorse Lake Powys, Wales

LATITUDE: 51° 56′ 06.61″ N   LONGITUDE: 3° 16′ 13.71″ W
                                                        4° 4′ 43.6″ W

A great reconstructed crannog set amidst stunning scenery – and in fact the only crannog in Wales of which I am aware.

people who lived in the crannogs were probably predominantly fisher-folk, so they were always close to their source of food, but the crannog was also fairly defendable, since part of the causeway or bridge could be readily removed if necessary. In order to create a typical crannog, many tonnes of stones were piled onto a lake bed, just offshore. Once it had reached the surface of the lake the structure would be covered with earth and turfs and the dwelling house or houses placed on top.

Not all crannogs were artificial. Sometimes natural small islands were utilized and these especially may have been continuously used by people for a tremendously long period of time – in some cases right up until the 17th century.

Cromlech

The word cromlech, which is Welsh in origin, is a more archaic form of description for a structure which would generally today be called a 'dolmen' (*see* Dolmen). Confusingly, the term is often used in France to describe stone circles but has never been used in this way in the British Isles.

Crop Marks (Parch Marks)

Until the advent of aircraft much of our lost archaeology remained just that – lost. But almost as soon as people began to soar above the landscape in the early part of the 20th century, they began to notice marks on the ground, especially in crops, that had never been noticed at ground level.

If, for example, a deep trench is dug in a particular field, and then is subsequently filled in again, either deliberately or through weathering, the 'fill' will be of a slightly different composition to the surrounding land which has not been disturbed. Its ability to drain surface water will be different and so crops growing in the area will behave in a slightly different way, either growing better or worse. Crop marks are often seen most readily in grassland, where they stand out as different-coloured patches within the landscape. The recognition of the value of crop marks or parch marks has led to a revolution in our recognition of the historical landscape and is no less useful when seeking prehistoric structures than it is for defining lost Roman settlements or medieval villages.

The picture that some crop marks betray is staggering and so easy to see that the shape of a structure is easy to determine. Others are less obvious, but all combine to give us a snapshot of the landscape as it once was. Many lost henges, enclosures, barrows and field systems have been relocated by studying crop marks and parch marks, and with the advent of Google Earth and other similar computer programs, the search for our prehistoric past is open to everyone. Together with my writing partner and friend, Christopher Knight, I have discovered henges on the landscape of North Yorkshire that are not marked on any map and which were previously lost to archaeology.

Unfortunately I cannot point the reader to any place they can go to see crop marks because of course they are invisible at ground level, but you can get a good idea of what you should be looking for on Google Earth by visiting the Google Earth Community Bulletin Board and going to 'Find the Archaeology'.

Cup and Ring Markings

Cup and ring markings represent part of the prehistoric graffiti that is to be found all over the landscape of the British Isles. You will never have to travel far to see cup and ring markings and they represent a fascinating, sometimes even spine-chilling, connection with people who lived at a very remote time, though inhabiting the same areas where we live today.

Cup and ring markings are petroglyphs, literally marks carved into rock – either rock built into structures or still present in its natural form in the landscape. The 'cup', which is the most common, is, as the name suggests, a circular indentation carved into sometimes extremely hard rock. Amongst the tools used to create cup markings Stone Age peoples may have used flint, or deer antler, though the absolute age of most cup marks is not known and some could have emerged after the introduction of bronze or even iron.

Cup marks vary in size but they are all quite distinctive and easy to recognize. Of course, because they are made in rock, they cannot be adequately dated. Sometimes, surrounding the cup is a ring, pecked out of the stone.

There are tens of thousands of cup and ring markings, spread all over the British Isles; so, do we have any firm idea about why they were made and what they mean? Unfortunately we do not. There are almost as many explanations for cup and ring markings as there are examples to be seen but no explanation is any more valid than the rest. We do know that a preponderance of such markings are to be found near cairns and burial chambers but they are also found on standing stones and stone circles as well as sometimes in totally isolated places where no other prehistoric activity is apparent.

Cup and ring markings, together with more elaborate abstract patterns that are rarer but still reasonably common, are a direct connection not only to the minds but also the creative hands of our ancient ancestors. Were they an invocation to the gods? Might they have been a simple message to say 'I was here', or do they serve some even more complex purpose, the realization of

Places to see cup and ring markings:

Achnabreck, Lochgilphead, Scotland

LATITUDE: 56° 3′ 39.32″ N   LONGITUDE: 5° 26′ 39.14″ W

These markings are approached via a short forest walk and are well signposted.

Kilmartin Glen, Baluachraig, Kilmartin, Scotland
(*See* Impressive Sites section)

LATITUDE: 56° 6′ 55.62″ N   LONGITUDE: 5° 29′ 15.75″ W

Most of the markings here can be found on a rocky outcrop and are in surprisingly good condition considering their age and weathering.

The Badger Stone, Ilkley Moor, Ilkley, West Yorkshire, England

LATITUDE: 53° 54′ 38.29″ N   LONGITUDE: 1° 49′ 51.63″ W

The Badger Stone is quite large, though not that easy to find amongst the many rocks on Ilkley Moor. It is, however, very impressive.

Bull Stone, Otley Chevin, Otley, West Yorkshire, England

LATITUDE: 53° 53′ 16.35″ N   LONGITUDE: 1° 41′ 11.56″ W

I have marvelled at the Bull Stone ever since I was a child of about six or seven when I was first taken to see it.

Llyn Du Carved Stone, near Harlech, Gwynedd, Wales

LATITUDE: 52° 51′ 14.4″ N   LONGITUDE: 4° 00′ 3.24″ W

There seem to be a multitude of rock carvings around this area, though many are extremely weathered and may be somewhat difficult to spot.

The Muff Stone, Ardmore, Co. Donegal, Ireland

LATITUDE: 55° 4′ 57.58″ N   LONGITUDE: 7° 15′ 36.42″ W

The Muff Stone is in a field, less than a mile north-northwest of the village of Muff. It carries over 40 different cup and ring markings.

which will open a completely new door onto the lives and mindset of ancient peoples? It's all part of the mystery but there is nothing more thrilling than coming across a cup and ring marking, in some sheltered spot, that is so clean it might have been made yesterday – and what is more you might be the first person to see it for hundreds or even thousands of years.

Cursus

Right back in the earliest days of archaeology, when the age of science was dawning and people began to look at our ancient landscape with genuinely wondering eyes, certain individuals began to notice earthworks on the landscape that were sometimes very extensive, but difficult to explain. Amongst these were structures that became known as 'cursus'. A typical cursus consists of a pair of parallel ditches and banks, anything up to 109 yards (100 metres) apart, but what is so strange and fascinating about them is that they can be anything from 40–50 yards (37–46 metres) in length, right up to 10 miles (16km).

A cursus is often straight, though not exclusively so, and many are extremely old. Some cursus could be well have been made over 5,000 years ago. We know this to be the case because later structures, such as the giant henges of North Yorkshire, are 'cut across' a pre-existent cursus, which logic asserts was already redundant by the time the henge was created, which itself dates to 3500 BC!

No practical purpose has ever been discovered for any of the hundreds of cursus that are known to exist (new ones are coming to light all the time) and it seems somewhat unlikely that they had a practical function. However, it has been suggested that they may have represented 'droving tracks' for moving livestock from one place to another, though this suggestion seems less than likely for a host of reasons – for example, many are too short to be of any practical use and there is little or no attendant archaeology to show field systems of settlements.

It might be more reasonable to look for a ritual or religious reason for the advent of cursus building, which represented a vast amount of effort to a small population of early farmers across the British Isles. A cursus could have

Places to see cursus:

Dorset Cursus, Blandford Forum, Dorset, England
LATITUDE: 50° 54' 40.92" N   LONGITUDE: 2° 2' 38.76" W

The Dorset Cursus is six miles long. It was originally quite wide with banks and ditches. Like all the cursus left to us it remains a great mystery.

Rudston Cursus, Rudston, East Yorkshire, England
(*See* Impressive Sites section)
LATITUDE: 54° 5' 35.57" N   LONGITUDE: 0° 19' 20.89" W

I have always found the Rudston Cursus difficult to spot but the location is well worth a visit on account of the huge standing stone in the churchyard.

Cleaven Dyke, Blairgowrie Road, Perth and Kinross, Scotland
LATITUDE: 56° 32' 50.21" N   LONGITUDE: 3° 21' 12.19" W

Probably dating to around 3600 BC, Cleaven Dyke was originally thought to be a defensive earthwork but is now referred to as a cursus.

Llandissilio Cursus, near Oswestry, Powys, Wales
LATITUDE: 51° 51' 28.37" N   LONGITUDE: 4° 43' 24.41" W

Wales is not abundant with cursus, and this particular one is mentioned in historical documents but not at all easy to find. However Old Oswestry is close by and also worth a visit.

Newgrange Cursus, Newgrange, Boyne Valley, Ireland
(*See* Impressive Sites section)
LATITUDE: 53° 41' 39.23" N   LONGITUDE: 6° 28' 20.25" W

What a wonderful place this is but it has to be said that the cursus is much less interesting than Newgrange chamber itself.

been a ritual avenue or a place of competition (after all, the name *cursus* is Latin and came about because those who first recognized the existence of cursus thought they were Roman athletic courses). One of the more plausible theories is that the longer cursus represented an athletic and ceremonial journey for young men from childhood to adulthood. The explanation is attractive but to my mind does little to explain the shorter cursus. A 50-yard journey to adulthood does not seem to be much of a rite of passage!

Maybe you have a better idea and the cursus represents one of those puzzles from the ancient past that is just as likely to be solved by an amateur as by a professional.

It is possible to walk along chunks of some of the known cursus across the British Isles and I list a representative selection on p.49, as well as covering one or two more specifically in the later stage of the book.

Dolmen

A dolmen is the remains of a single-chambered tomb, essentially the 'skeleton' of the structure. It is comprised of a number of large upright stones, usually angled inwards slightly, on top of which is one or more capstone. Most dolmens date back to the Neolithic period and they are widely distributed

Figure 9: A typical dolmen

Places to see dolmens:

Poulnabrone, Burren, Co. Clare, Ireland

LATITUDE: 53° 2' 55.76" N   LONGITUDE: 9° 8' 27.16" W

This is a wonderful and evocative dolmen in an elevated position and visible from quite a distance. It looks 'other-worldly'.

Pentre Ifan Dolmen, Nevern, Fishguard, Pembrokeshire, Wales

LATITUDE: 51° 59' 54.1" N   LONGITUDE: 4° 46' 10.29" W

This used to be known as 'Arthur's Quoit' but he must have been some sort of a man if he managed to throw this capstone into place.

Burnt Hill Dolmen, Chipping Norton, Oxfordshire, England
(poor condition)

LATITUDE: 51° 57' 20.53" N   LONGITUDE: 1° 36' 47.92" W

Unfortunately this dolmen is in a very bad state of repair but I mention it here because it is in such an evocative and history-rich location.

Chûn Quoit Dolmen, Madron, Penzance, Cornwall, England

LATITUDE: 50° 8' 54.98" N   LONGITUDE: 5° 38' 15.75" W

Not many of the dolmens in the area have retained their capstone but this one has. It overlooks the sea and is a truly impressive sight.

Legananny Dolmen, Slieve Croob, Leitrim, Co. Down, Ireland

LATITUDE: 54° 19' 22.57" N   LONGITUDE: 6° 1' 7.14" W

This is great but not for the faint-hearted. The capstone of this dolmen weighs an estimated 40 tonnes. Imagine the effort that was necessary in order to lift it into place.

Poltalloch, Kilmartin, Lochgilphead, Scotland

LATITUDE: 56° 6' 32.96" N   LONGITUDE: 5° 31' 9.56" W

Kilmartin is a feast of delights to anyone who loves prehistoric sites and any interested party could easily spend a week here in order to see everything.

across the British Isles. The word 'dolmen' comes from the Breton language, and there are indeed many examples in Brittany. Dolmen literally means 'stone table' and it's easy to see how these enigmatic structures got such a name. Doubtless those from later periods, who didn't understand what the dolmens had once been, thought they had been the dining tables of fabled giants.

Once the stones had been erected, forming the chamber at the centre, an earth bank was usually raised over them, so in the finished tomb the dolmen would not be seen from the outside. Some of the tombs in question also had passages, allowing for re-entry to the structure on what may have been a regular basis, whilst others were probably sealed.

There are few archaeological artefacts associated with dolmens, since the contents of the tomb would have been dispersed many centuries ago. Nevertheless, they are impressive structures and leave a sense of wonder as to how the capstones were raised into place. Doubtless some technique was employed similar to the one that must have been used to raise the trilithons at Stonehenge. (*See* Stonehenge in Impressive Sites section, and Trilithon.)

Druid

A Druid is self-evidently not a prehistoric monument but I thought the term was worth a mention, if only to dispel what is still a popular myth about Druids. A Druid was a Celtic holy man. They are mentioned repeatedly by Roman writers – Julius Caesar especially. Such men undertook long and arduous training in the ways of their people, sometimes spending up to 20 years learning the lore and oral traditions of the various tribes that inhabited the British Isles and the near Continent during the Iron Age. But that's the operative point – the Iron Age. The span of time between the creation of a cursus and the existence of the Celtic Druids was longer than the span of time between the Druids and ourselves. The structure of society must have changed immeasurably between the start of the Megalithic period and the Iron Age. Invasions, or at the very least, significant migrations had taken place on many occasions. There is probably very little direct connection between the lives and practices of a late Stone Age inhabitant of the British Isles and the people who were present in the Iron Age.

There is also a modern form of Druid, which appeared in the 18th century and probably bears no resemblance to the holy men of the Megalithic period. The people that created the fabulous henges, tombs, standing stones and stone circles, way back in the late Stone Age and the Bronze Age probably had holy men and women of their own, in fact it's an odds-on certainty that they did, but these people, about whom we know next to nothing, were not Druids.

The word Druid is associated with the word for 'oak' because they met in sacred groves in the forest. As wise and as clever as the Druids may have been, they had nothing to do with the doubtless well-intentioned but generally misinformed people who gather at Stonehenge at the time of the winter and summer solstice these days, wearing white robes and conducting somewhat dubious ceremonies. In my opinion these people are harmless; they add colour to our lives and they do reinforce the existence and importance of the ancient structures that still cover our landscape. However, nobody who wants to learn anything about our ancient forebears should be fooled into thinking that the modern Druids know anything more about these matters than anybody else.

Dun (*See* Stone Fort)

Earthworks

The word 'earthwork' is a general term that describes any group or distribution of banks, ditches, mounds or other structures created from the landscape.

Enclosure

An enclosure is a piece of land separated from the surrounding landscape by banks, ditches, walls or fences. Enclosures are one of the most common features of our ancient landscape and the vast majority of them probably had a very definite and practical purpose – they were designed and built in order to keep livestock safe or at least contained.

There are times in the farming year when it is necessary to protect and restrict livestock – for example during spring lambing, or with domestic stock at night in an environment where wolves and other predators exist. Many different types of enclosure were used by peoples throughout the late Stone Age, the Bronze Age and the Iron Age, but they all served more or less the same function if they were related to agriculture and animal husbandry.

Probably the most common sort of agricultural enclosure is known as a 'banjo enclosure' and was commonly used in the Iron Age. These were generally small circular areas, with a longish, straight track leading into them – hence the name banjo, because that is what they look like on aerial photographs.

Not all enclosures had an agricultural purpose and, in many cases, we simply do not know what their function was. A henge for example, which is a circular area with one or more ditches and banks, can be termed an enclosure but it seems quite unlikely that henges were a farming feature or ever had such a purpose.

Enclosures also surrounded dwelling houses and sometimes cemeteries; they can be almost any shape but they are always a sign that 'someone' was doing something in a particular place at some stage in our history and so they are always of interest to historians and archaeologists.

Flint

Flint is a stone and not a prehistoric monument, but its importance to our history here in the British Isles is so great, no book of this sort would be complete without a mention of it. Flint is an extremely hard sedimentary form of quartz. In colour it can be grey, greenish, black or white and (here is the important part) when shattered it can take on an extremely sharp edge that can be comparable with the honed edge of metal.

Flint is often found as nodules within chalk and limestone and is plentiful around the British Isles, but it doesn't appear everywhere, which is also another important factor in terms of our ancient past.

The first use of tools made from flint from the archaeological record in Britain comes from as long ago as 700,000 years; it is as a result of finding primitive flint tools, together with datable material, that we know what we do about humans at this remote time.

The fact that flint tools predominated in our part of the world right up until the Bronze Age (around 2100 BC) and that flint was also used long after this period, shows just how important it was to our species; in fact we have been utilizing metal tools for only a tiny fraction of the time that flint and other hard, sharp stones were of such importance.

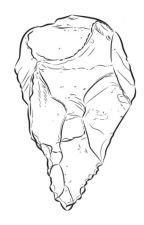

Experts have built up a good understanding of what sort of flint tools were used in any given period. They were created by a means known as 'knapping' in which pieces of flint are struck in a particular way (and with great skill) in order to achieve a particular objective. This technique differed throughout time and within specific cultures.

Figure 10: A flint hand axe

Flint was used for so many purposes it is hard to see how we could have advanced in the way we did without its presence, or at least something with similar properties. Flint was used to make hand axes, hafted axes, cutters, scrapers, knives and all manner of things that comprised the prehistoric work box.

Because of its overwhelming importance, flint was also one of the earliest commodities traded amongst ancient peoples. Because it does not occur everywhere, people undoubtedly undertook lengthy journeys in order to trade flint and doubtless this instigated a trade in other necessities that funded the beginning of a more cohesive society within our islands.

Flint was also extensively mined (*see* Mines).

Forecourt (*see also* Chambered Tomb)

Forecourt is the name archaeologists have chosen for the area immediately to the front of some chambered tombs. The forecourt was carefully defined by large stones, often semicircular in shape. It is thought to have been the site of ritual activities related to the tomb.

Foresights and Backsights

A foresight represents a particular stone within a stone circle and a backsight would be a remote stone or some significant marker in the distance that could be lined up with the foresight in order to track a particular astronomical happening, such as a sunrise.

Gallery Grave

A gallery grave is a Megalithic tomb similar to a passage grave (*see* Passage Grave) except that there is no size difference between the entrance passage and the burial chamber itself.

Henge

Henges are amongst the most fascinating of prehistoric structures in the British Isles. All henges are circular, or nearly so, and are defined by banks and ditches. In all henges there is at least one entrance, but more commonly two or four. These allow anyone entering or leaving the henge to access its centre without having to negotiate the ditch and bank.

Generally speaking, those structures defined as henges are over 22 yards (20 metres) in diameter, though they vary greatly in terms of size and also with regard to their other characteristics. Henges can be devoid of any other structure but are also often associated with standing stones, portal stones, stone circles, timber structures, other earthworks and also burials of one sort or another. Stonehenge, for example, is one of the most complex Megalithic structures ever created but it started its life as a relatively simple henge before later additions made it into the monument we see today.

Henges have gradually become classified into different types, so that those studying them know immediately what sort of henge they are dealing with. Class I henges have a single entrance, whilst Class II henges have two entrances, opposite each other. Class III henges have two pairs of entrances facing each other. Within these groups there are also subgroups, for example Class IIA henges.

Figure 11: Diagram of a
Class IIA henge

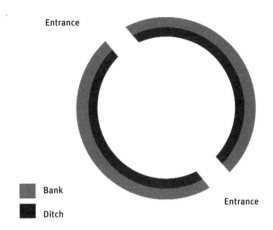

Entrance

Bank

Ditch

Entrance

The word 'henge' derives from Stonehenge, the name of which actually means 'hanging stones', so in a sense it is quite an inappropriate name for earthworks that sometimes have no stones at all. However, it was coined in 1932 and has simply stuck as the name for these extraordinary structures, of which there may once have been hundreds or even thousands across the British Isles.

A true henge has its ditch inside its bank, though there are exceptions, which include Stonehenge, where the bank is outside the ditch. In the normal arrangement for a henge the fact that the ditch is inside the bank makes it extremely unlikely that such structures ever had a defensive role. It would make no sense whatsoever to allow potential attackers to climb the bank and hurl stones and spears on the occupants. A much more common practice for defence would be to make attackers negotiate the ditch first, so that those defending the interior could rain down missiles and abuse on the attackers from the top of the bank.

It has sometimes been suggested that if the henge had no military role perhaps it was a device, like a banjo enclosure, for safeguarding and corralling domestic animals. This also seems rather unlikely, if only because the presence of a ditch inside the bank might be dangerous to such livestock in the dark of night, when they might easily fall into the ditches, which at the time they were made were very steep-sided. Once again in this situation it would make more sense if the ditch (which after all is the natural consequence of raising the mound) was on the outside of the structure.

So, if a typical henge was not for defence and had nothing to do with farming, what purpose did it serve? Faced with such problems archaeologists often fall back on the idea that such creations had a 'ritual' significance, or they may simply have been designated meeting places for extended communities. This idea may have become popular because later, for example during Anglo-Saxon times, areas *were* set aside where tribes would gather when local and regional decisions had to be made.

The idea of a ritualized meeting place seems fine when we think about some of the smaller henges dotted about the landscape, but what would we make of the super-henges, which are to be found especially in the north of England but with examples also in the south and in Northern Ireland? The best of these can still be seen in Yorkshire, at Thornborough near Ripon. These super-henges form part of a prehistoric landscape every bit as extensive and

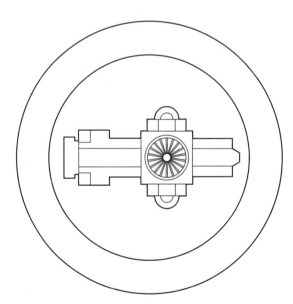

Figure 12: A representation of St Paul's Cathedral within one of the super-henges at Thornborough, Yorkshire

fascinating as that to be found on Salisbury Plain in Wiltshire. The term 'super-henge' could not be more appropriate.

Three henges survive more or less intact at Thornborough. They are in a line running roughly from northwest to southeast and each is so large that it would be quite possible to fit St Paul's Cathedral comfortably into any one of them. What is more, the Thornborough henges, like many of the henges that can still be recognized, are extremely old. Finds that have come to light from the ditches of the Thornborough henges shows them to have been created around 3500 BC, which means they are 5,500 years old! In other words they predate the major pyramids of Egypt by a full 1,000 years. Only the cursus to be seen in various places throughout the British Isles (*see* Cursus) have an older pedigree.

Henges date from the Stone Age, which means they were created using the simplest of tools. They were probably dug using deer antlers, with the shoulder blades of domestic or wild cattle being used as shovels. In the case of the largest examples the effort necessary to create such massive structures must have been colossal. We have to bear in mind that at this period the population of the British Isles would have been extremely small in comparison with today. This means that either the task took a very long time for a few individuals, or that people were drafted in from a great distance, probably in winter when the farming year was quiet, in order to dig the ditches and throw up the banks.

It was suggested some time ago that the Thornborough henges, and perhaps others in the district that are now largely ploughed out, may have had some cosmological component. Together with Christopher Knight I tackled this problem and you can find the result of our efforts in the Impressive Sites section of the book, where Thornborough is described in more detail. In the end this seems the most likely explanation for the henges. As meeting places the Thornborough henges, and others of their sort, would have been ridiculously large and it seemed to us that just about everyone in the British Isles during the Stone Age could have fitted into any one of them. It is therefore much more likely that they represented naked-eye observatories, in order to track stars and planets in the night sky and the Sun during the day. Although this idea remains contentious to many, we think there is ample evidence to bear out the suggestion.

Whilst there were once many super-henges in Yorkshire, as far as we know there was only one further south in England, at Dorchester-on-Thames, and there is another, slightly different example in Northern Ireland.

Even in the case of henges, large or small, that have been destroyed by farming during the intervening period, it is often possible to see them surviving as parch marks (*see* Crop Marks) in fields. How many more lie below urban areas or in woodland there is no way of knowing. What is more, the remaining henges are still in danger. The super-henge at Dorchester-on-Thames was destroyed very recently for gravel extraction and the examples at Thornborough are under threat for the same reason.

Really pristine henges are extremely hard to find. Natural weathering, as well as farming and building, have ensured that many have disappeared for good but there is no doubt that they were once a common feature on the landscape and they remain enigmatic and appealing to prehistory buffs. Henges were first erected before the idea of hauling great stones around the landscape became the norm, but as we shall see when we get to stone circles, the earlier henges may have been the blackboards that allowed places like Callanish, Stonehenge, Castlerigg or any of the great stone circles to be planned and built.

Henges may or may not be a specifically British structure. Debate still rages about this. Some experts think that henges simply developed from causewayed enclosures (*see* Causewayed Enclosures) and other features with ditches and banks that occur in continental Europe as well as in the British Isles. Others suggest that the henge is a uniquely British structure. The jury is still out on this argument.

It is possible not only to visit some henge sites but also to find ones that are not generally known about, or reported, by studying Google Earth. Nothing is more thrilling than stumbling across either a henge, or some other lost earthwork, that even the archaeologists and cartographers have missed. It's a great way to spend a few hours during the long, dark days of winter, when trudging across the heather and along river valleys is not quite so appealing.

Nobody knows for certain why henges were built or what they were used for and so your ideas on the subject are as good as anyone's.

Places to see henges:

Stonehenge, Amesbury, Wiltshire, England
(*See* Impressive Sites section)

LATITUDE: 51° 10' 43.87" N   LONGITUDE: 1° 49' 34.27" W

The most famous of all Megalithic monuments, but the henge itself is overshadowed by the stone circles that were built much later.

Avebury Henge and Stone Circle, Avebury, England (originally just a henge)
(*See* Impressive Sites section)

LATITUDE: 51° 25' 43.04" N   LONGITUDE: 1° 51' 14.66" W

The henge at Avebury is huge, as of course are the stone circles. In some ways this is my favourite because it is much larger than the one at Stonehenge.

Castlerigg Stone Circle, near Keswick, Cumbria, England
(*See* Impressive Sites section)

LATITUDE: 54° 36' 11.78" N   LONGITUDE: 3° 5' 46.08" W

What a wonderful place this is. So beautiful, so evocative and so remote. It has a grandeur that dwarfs many larger sites.

Mayburgh Henge, Penrith, Cumbria, England

LATITUDE: 54° 38' 53.46" N   LONGITUDE: 2° 44' 43.81" W

This henge is in relatively good condition and it contains only one, extremely large stone at its centre.

Castilly Henge, Bodmin, Cornwall, England

LATITUDE: 50° 25' 49.63" N   LONGITUDE: 4° 46' 21.82" W

Not everyone believes this to be a henge but there isn't much doubt in my mind.

Balfarg Henge, Markinch, Glenrothes, Fife, Scotland

LATITUDE: 56° 12' 53.9" N   LONGITUDE: 3° 9' 33.93" W

This one is easy to find. It is close to houses but still surprisingly impressive when seen for the first time.

Places to see henges (continued):

Llandegai Henge Complex, near Bangor, Gwynedd, Wales

LATITUDE: 53° 13′ 7.88″ N   LONGITUDE: 4° 6′ 21.81″ W

These henges lie at the centre of a landscape that looks as though it is going to turn out to be extremely important in terms of our ancient past.

Bryn Celli Ddu, Passage Grave and Henge, Llanddaniel Fab, Anglesey, Wales
(*See* Impressive Sites section)

LATITUDE: 53° 12′ 27″ N   LONGITUDE: 4° 14′ 8.89″ W

A double bonus here because in addition to a small henge there is one of the best passage graves to be seen anywhere in the British Isles.

Lismullin Henge, near Navan, Co. Meath, Ireland

LATITUDE: 53° 35′ 42″ N   LONGITUDE: 6° 35′ 15.57″ W

Some experts doubt that this is a henge and suggest that it is Bronze Age in date and may be an enclosure. For my money, it's a henge.

Castleruddery, Baltinglass, Co. Wicklow, Ireland

LATITUDE: 52° 59′ 29.93″ N   LONGITUDE: 6° 38′ 8.61″ W

There is no doubt about this being a henge. It also has stones and a rich tradition of local folklore to attest to its 'magic'.

Places to see super-henges:

The Thornborough Henge Complex, Near Ripon, North Yorkshire, England
(*See* Impressive Sites section)

LATITUDE: 54° 12′ 36.64″ N   LONGITUDE: 1° 33′ 46.68″ W

For my money this henge complex should be listed amongst the wonders of the ancient world. I am staggered that it is not internationally famous.

The Giant's Ring, Shaw's Bridge, Belfast, Ireland

LATITUDE: 54° 32′ 24.52″ N   LONGITUDE: 5° 56′ 57.87″ W

This henge has been much altered over the years. Very impressive.

Hill Figures

Our prehistoric ancestors began one tradition, especially in England, that is still very popular today. Choosing the side of a hill that could generally be seen from a very long way off, the prehistoric artists would cut through the natural turf, exposing what was often light-coloured stone below (especially chalk). By so doing they could create a visual representation, often of an animal but also frequently of a person. Some of the hill figures were extremely large and there could once have been many more such creations from prehistory than are available today. It stands to reason that if any such figure was abandoned for more than a few decades, the turf would once again grow over it and it would disappear for good.

Some care is necessary when dealing with hill figures because by no means all of them are prehistoric in origin. The White Horse on the Hambleton Hills in Yorkshire, for example, is Victorian, and there are many modern examples to be found across the length and breadth of the British Isles.

Perhaps the most famous examples of hill figures are the White Horse at Uffington, Oxfordshire, England, which is definitely prehistoric, and the Cerne Abbas Giant in Dorchester, England, which could be prehistoric but is just as likely to be much more recent. The former may well have been meant to

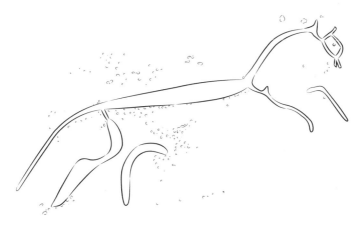

Figure 13: The white horse hill figure at Uffington

Places to see hill figures:

Uffington White Horse, Uffington, Wantage, Oxfordshire, England

LATITUDE: 51° 34′ 36.94″ N   LONGITUDE: 1° 33′ 50.92″ W

To catch a distant glimpse of this huge figure cut into the chalk is both impressive and slightly strange. Actually it is less impressive close up.

Long Man of Wilmington, Eastbourne, Sussex, England

LATITUDE: 50° 48′ 35.55″ N   LONGITUDE: 0° 11′ 25.22″ E

Some say this is ancient, and others suggest it is only a couple of centuries old at the most. Whoever is correct, this is art writ large and well worth a look anyway.

Cerne Abbas Giant, Dorchester, Dorset, England

LATITUDE: 50° 48′ 44.61″ N   LONGITUDE: 2° 28′ 21.75″ W

Again, this is probably not ancient but definitely worth a visit! An image to strike fear and doubt into the heart of any man who may already have a 'certain sort' of complex.

represent some sort of territorial boundary, whilst the latter, which shows a man with enlarged genitalia and bearing a club, may be a species of fertility symbol, or could equally well be an 18th-century joke.

Hill Fort

Hill forts are amongst the most common prehistoric structures left to us in the British Isles. As the name implies, they are generally areas of fortified upland, exploiting hill tops in particular, though not exclusively so. Some hill forts came into existence during the Bronze Age, though by far the majority were either created in the Iron Age, or much enlarged from earlier attempts.

Although there is some argument amongst experts as to how important hill forts were as true defensive structures, there is no doubt that they were sometimes used for this purpose. We know from the descriptions left to us by Julius Caesar and other Roman commentators that at the time of the two

Roman invasions (55 BC and AD 43), local resistance to the invasions was often centred in such structures. Nevertheless, since very remote times, and certainly since the introduction of farming and a settled life, structures had been created that offered an 'impression' of strength that might dissuade any would-be attacker from trying to seize a certain area.

When seen today, most hill forts comprise a series of banks and ditches, often flanking the top of a hill, or else in some position that allows natural topography to be used as part of the defensive structure. This might be a sheer rock face or a sea cliff. Obviously, to use such an area saved time and effort on the part of the fort builders. In lowland areas, where such natural fortifications were not to be found, the defences were built to be stronger but of course it is doubtful whether this sort of defensive camp could truly be termed a hill fort. Hill forts generally had more than one entrance.

There are over 2,000 hill forts in the British Isles, so anyone looking for a good day out and a fascinating glimpse into the mindset of Iron Age farmers in our islands will never have too far to go in order to see one. Many are extremely impressive, with numerous banks and ditches, together with other structures and earthworks that archaeologists are still struggling to recognize and name even today.

How often hill forts were used for their initial defensive purpose is hard to say. Archaeological evidence demonstrates that in many cases, and for much of the time, the forts were used to pen or corral animals. It is hard to imagine that communities actually 'lived' full-time within the confines of hill forts because although some of them are extremely large, the need for pasture, fuel and the extended use of farmland beyond the fort would have necessitated life outside the ramparts. This is not to suggest that nobody lived in hill forts because in many cases the remains of houses have been found, together with signs of continued habitation. This might be more likely in the case of extremely large hill forts, which can have a huge enclosure, sometimes more than 50 acres (20 hectares).

In order to understand the preponderance of hill forts we need to look at the structure of British society in the Iron Age. The British Isles were inhabited by a number of different tribes, many of whom did not see eye to eye with their neighbouring tribes. We know from Roman accounts that skirmishes and warfare between tribes was common (a fact that the Romans constantly exploited for their own ends). However, some of the larger hill forts are so massive that it is hard to understand how they could have been adequately manned at a time when populations were not high. One can imagine that the 'look' of impregnability may have sometimes been enough to deter a would-be attacker and, with bank tops protected by palisades and spiked logs, a frontal attack on such a structure would surely have been costly in terms of lives. The options at the time for anyone attacking a hill fort were limited because the British tribes did not generally possess the assault technology that is typified by the Roman invasion. Since we know that several British hill forts were successfully attacked and taken by the Romans, we can also be certain that they were not impregnable to a determined enemy, even when they were heavily defended.

The people living in Britain during the Iron Age are usually referred to as 'Celts'. This term can be slightly misleading because we are now beginning to understand that at least some elements of the British population had been around since extremely remote times, whereas the term Celt used to imply that the whole population of the British Isles arrived from continental Europe after the Bronze Age. What now seems more likely is that waves of immigrants – either peacefully or sometimes with more warlike intentions – entered the British Isles fairly frequently throughout history and that their languages, customs and technologies became suffused into the local population. Be that as it may, the people who lived in the British Isles during the Iron Age were naturally aggressive, quarrelsome and often warlike. It is within the mindset of these people that we find the need (either in reality or perception) for sometimes massive hill forts.

When danger threatened it is likely that everyone from a particular locality, together with their livestock where possible, would congregate in a local hill fort, ready to defend themselves and their livestock. How often this actually became necessary is difficult to say. One fact is certain; the amount of effort taken to create such impressive structures was colossal. Of course hill forts were not necessary created from scratch in a short period of time. We know that many of them became gradually more impressive as time passed but we can imagine that a great percentage of the available time for those who lived in the vicinity of such forts was spent on creating and maintaining the defences.

After years of looking at such matters I have my own explanation, or part explanation, about what such structures (and in fact much older ones such as henges and stone circles) may have represented. Early farming required a great deal of effort at specific times of year. The Bronze Age and Iron Age farmer was very busy in the spring, summer and autumn, but depending on the area where he lived, he did have time on his hands in winter. I think it was during the winter that common effort was expended on communal structures. To a widespread population in which people probably did not see each other on a day-to-day basis, several weeks of common effort would have welded family and clan bonds. It allowed people to sort out local issues and to pull together in a way that the farming of small plots by individual families did not. To some extent such efforts replaced the 'hunt', that had been so important during many thousands of years of much more communal hunter-gatherer life.

In this sense it can be seen that there was a very real benefit in creating a splendid hill fort, even if it wasn't strictly necessary and probably could not be adequately defended in any case with the number of people available. In its finished magnificence it also stood as a 'statement of intent' and it showed just how committed and determined a particular group or clan truly was. Society being what it was at the time, it is hard to envisage people being forced into digging huge ditches and raising massive mounds against their will. Tribal leaders were limited in the power they held and they could only rule with the sanction and goodwill of those around them. There were no standing armies, as would become the norm much later in history, and practically everyone in the Iron Age British community was, first and foremost, a farmer.

No matter how people were persuaded or coerced into creating many of the hill forts to be seen across the British Isles, a fair proportion of them still cause a sharp intake of breath when seen for the first time. They are literally massive and when one stops to work out just how much earth and rock must have been shifted to create them, the true worth of prehistoric people's determination and persistence becomes evident.

Some hill forts, especially examples along the Welsh Marches and in the south of England, seem to have been reoccupied and reused long after the Roman invasion of Britain. There are signs that at least a few were of pivotal importance in the Dark Ages, when the Anglo-Saxon onslaught began.

Places to see hill forts:

Old Oswestry, Oswestry, Shropshire, England
(*See* Impressive Sites section)

LATITUDE: 52° 52' 17.22" N   LONGITUDE: 3° 2' 51.06" W

This is my favourite hill fort. It is easy to access, though would not be suitable for people who have difficulty walking up slopes or a fair distance.

South Cadbury Hill Fort, Sparkford, Somerset, England
(*See* Impressive Sites section)

LATITUDE: 51° 1' 27.79" N   LONGITUDE: 2° 31' 49.71" W

Many people think that South Cadbury was the place that became famous as King Arthur's Camelot, though to me this seems entirely unlikely.

Maiden Castle, Dorchester, Dorset, England

LATITUDE: 50° 41' 37.32" N   LONGITUDE: 2° 28' 2.16" W

This is the largest and most complex hill fort anywhere in Britain and it would take quite a few hours to explore it fully.

Humbledon Hill Fort, Coldstream, Northumberland, England

LATITUDE: 55° 32' 50.49" N   LONGITUDE: 2° 3' 8.31" W

Take the longer route to the top because it is less difficult. This hill fort is not in good condition but it was once quite vast in extent.

Hambledon Hill Prehistoric Hill Fort, near Blandford Forum, Dorset
(*See* Impressive Sites section)

LATITUDE: 50° 53' 42.04" N   LONGITUDE: 2° 12' 12.07" W

This hill fort started its life as a simple Neolithic enclosure and went through many alterations before it assumed its final look.

Arthur's Seat, Edinburgh, Scotland (*See* Impressive Sites section)

LATITUDE: 55° 55' 59.87" N   LONGITUDE: 3° 10' 00.73" W

There isn't much of the hill fort here to see any more, and the climb is steep. But the view from the top makes the whole effort worthwhile.

Places to see hill forts (continued):

Norman's Law Hill Fort, Newburgh, Fife, Scotland

LATITUDE: 56° 22' 8.2" N   LONGITUDE: 3° 7' 30.85" W

This is not the best preserved hill fort but – oh the views! Take the route to the top that starts about a mile west of the village of Brunton. This was a superb defensive position for a hill fort.

Dinas Brân, Llangollen, Denbighshire, Wales

LATITUDE: 52° 58' 41.89" N   LONGITUDE: 3° 9' 31.81" W

Don't try this one unless you are fit. The hill fort is on a rocky crag, high above Llangollen and is spectacular beyond belief.

Dinas Emrys, Beddgelert, Gwynedd, Wales
(See Impressive Sites section)

LATITUDE: 53° 1' 4.52" N   LONGITUDE: 4° 5' 57.79" W

This hill fort is fascinating because it is not, strictly speaking, prehistoric. It was most likely built just after the Roman invasion of AD 43. Another hard climb but this site figures prominently in British folklore and history and has strong connections with the wizard Merlin.

Grainne's Enclosure, Hill of Tara, Dunshaughlin, Meath, Ireland

LATITUDE: 53° 34' 57.81" N   LONGITUDE: 6° 36' 49.47" W

The Hill of Tara is positively steeped in Irish history and folklore. It has been used by humanity as long as people have lived in Ireland.

Mooghaun, Newmarket on Fergus, Co. Clare, Ireland

LATITUDE: 52° 46' 59.69" N   LONGITUDE: 8° 52' 38.94" W

This site is suggested as a great place for a picnic. It may have been of both ceremonial and defensive importance. 'Look how great we are!'

Iron Age

For convenience's sake we use expressions such as Stone Age, late Stone Age, Bronze Age and Iron Age, as if there was a clear line of demarcation between any of them, which is clearly not the case. For example, flint tools were used well into the Bronze Age, whilst bronze tools and implements were common throughout the Iron Age. However, as a way of talking about an 'era' the terms do have some use. In the British Isles the Iron Age is generally considered to have begun around 800 BC and extended to the period of the Roman invasions of Britain, though of course the Romans were also an Iron Age culture.

Megalithic Period and Megalithic Structures

The word 'megalith' literally means 'large stone' and when we refer to Megalithic Britain, we are talking about that period of history during which peoples living in the British Isles found or cut large pieces of stone and dragged them around the landscape, before erecting them into sometimes extremely impressive structures. Generally one's mind is drawn to standing stone circles such as Stonehenge or Brodgar, but far more stones were used in other structures, such as dolmens (*see* Dolmen) or other tombs of one sort or another. Much of this stone remains hidden under mounds but if we take all of these structures together with stone circles, single standing stones, stone fans, avenues and the like, we can see that the amount of effort necessary to create such masterpieces was colossal.

Of course this did not take place in a single generation, or anything like it. The Megalithic period in Britain began in some places as early as 4500 BC and went on until around 1500 BC. It is therefore not a strictly defined period such as 'Stone Age' or 'Bronze Age' but extended throughout parts of both.

It is a fact that some of the earliest Megalithic structures in the British Isles were tombs of one sort or another. Perhaps those who first stood large stones upright and placed equally large stones on top of them, were trying to recreate the natural caves that they themselves frequented or which were frequented by their ancestors. Certainly many of the passage tombs give the impression of a cave and in many parts of the world cave burials were extremely common –

maybe as a way of sending the deceased back into the 'womb' of the Earth from which everyone originally came?

Megaliths are certainly not an exclusively British phenomenon. On the contrary, they are found throughout France, Iberia, along the Baltic coast and in the Mediterranean region. However, since few of them are significantly older than the first examples in the British Isles, it is unlikely that the technology necessary for moving such large stones came with the arrival of new people into our islands. In other words it seems to have taken place at around the same time wherever it occurred.

In the British Isles the situation was made slightly easier for the first stone shifters because of our topography and geology. Britain has many upland areas where retreating glaciers have left large, detached stones littered across the landscape. It is obviously easier to move a stone that one finds intact on the surface than it would be to cut stones from the living rock (though the Megalithic peoples did both).

All manner of different sorts of stone was used, dependent on what was locally available. Sometimes stones were 'bashed' into the rough shape required, using stone hammers or mauls, and great skill must have been used in the moving and erection of massive boulders. One can imagine that across the centuries literally hundreds or thousands of individuals must have been killed or maimed by stones that sometimes weighed many tonnes, and the necessity for wooden poles and lengthy, strong ropes must have required as much if not more man-hours than the finding or moving of the stones themselves.

We know that on some occasions stone was actually prised from rock faces, doubtless using a technique that involved constantly heating and cooling rock to make it split along natural faults, and it was also sometimes dragged many miles across undulating landscapes, bogs, rivers and even estuaries, to the spot where it was required. The purpose for the structures that resulted from all this effort is explained throughout this book under various headings but one point is worth making: people did not start to move stones around the British Isles specifically to construct standing stone circles. On the contrary, some of the tombs that incorporate huge stones are older than any of the circles. In other words the capability and the technology already existed before stone circles were considered (*see* Stone Circles).

Menhir (sometimes Monolith)

Menhir is the name given to a large standing stone, usually intended to be placed upright in the landscape. The word comes from two Breton words and means 'long stone'. Menhirs differ greatly in size but they would once have been a very common sight on the landscape across the whole of the British Isles. Sadly, both to rob the stone and for a wealth of other reasons, such as religious intolerance, probably far more menhirs have been removed over the centuries than have survived. Don't panic though, because there are still plenty to be seen and some of them are incredibly impressive.

Menhirs are often tall, usually squared off and they invariably, though not always, taper towards the top. They can be found as individuals or in groups. In Brittany, for example, there are extremely long avenues of menhirs, though if such ever existed in our islands they must have disappeared centuries ago.

There are many potential explanations as to why menhirs might have been erected, some of which are plausible and others that are downright ridiculous. Suggestions include boundary markers, memorial structures (intended as an epitaph to a deceased person), sexual symbols (*see* Sexual Stones) or that the stones were somehow associated with a study of the stars or the creation of farming calendars.

It used to be thought that the majority of the menhirs dated to the period of a people often referred to as the 'beaker people'. Their name comes from the particular sort of pottery found in the British Isles and dated from around 2400 BC. However, since it is now doubted by many that the beaker people actually ever existed as a tangible and separate entity, the idea has fallen into dispute. If the beaker people had been responsible for the menhirs, they could be dated to the very late Stone Age and early Bronze Age but many modern experts think the menhirs, or at least some of them, are far older. Dating stones of this sort is virtually impossible. Carbon dating techniques are available for any archaeological artefact that was once organic in composition, but unless there are samples of such evidence immediately below the hole in which a menhir is standing, the time at which the stone was erected is anyone's guess.

Menhirs are quite often found in extensive ceremonial landscapes, though this is not always the case. A good example is the Rudston Monolith in East

Yorkshire (*see* Impressive Sites section). This is Britain's tallest remaining monolith at 25ft (8 metres). The stone was quarried, or found, at least 10 miles (16km) away at Cayton Bay. The exercise of dragging a stone weighing in excess of 40 tonnes across such a distance must have been incredible. The Rudston Monolith is now in a churchyard, but long before churches existed, the monolith stood within a landscape scarred with cursus (*see* Cursus), various other earthworks and even a set of dinosaur footprints (which might explain why the site was considered sacred in the first place).

It is known that some cultures, amongst which were the Minoans who inhabited Crete from around 2000 BC, considered pillars of stone to be sacred and to contain within them the person of the Goddess. The same was broadly true in parts of the Levant and pillar worship is therefore not unknown in the ancient world. Something similar could have been taking place in the British Isles but since we know nothing of the religious beliefs or practices of people from such a remote period, we can only guess at the effort that was necessary to plan and create the menhirs.

Menhirs often contain prehistoric art and especially cup and ring markings (*see* Cup and Ring Markings).

Figure 14: A typical menhir

Places to see impressive menhirs:

Rudston Monolith, Rudston, East Yorkshire, England
(*See* Impressive Sites section)

LATITUDE: 54° 5′ 35.57″ N   LONGITUDE: 0° 19′ 20.89″ W

The biggest, and to me the best. Rudstone is picturesque and extremely impressive – if only they would remove its ridiculous metal hat.

The Devil's Arrows, Boroughbridge, North Yorkshire, England
(*See* Impressive Sites section)

LATITUDE: 54° 5′ 33.49″ N   LONGITUDE: 1° 24′ 7.62″ W

I took an Australian Aborigine to the Devil's Arrows. He was speechless. All he could do was hug the stones and cry. I know what he means.

Whitestone, Lee Bay, Devon

LATITUDE: 51° 11′ 37.45″ N   LONGITUDE: 4° 9′ 9.61″ W

This stone is about 10ft (3 metres) high and made of quartz. It is especially impressive when wet and must weigh a great deal.

Five Kings, near Alnwick, Northumberland, England

LATITUDE: 55° 17′ 41.4″ N   LONGITUDE: 2° 4′ 3.81″ W

Not too easy to find and quite unimpressive at a distance, but the biggest of the stones here is significant and must have taken a lot of grunt to put in place.

Callanish, Stornoway, Isle of Lewis, Scotland

LATITUDE: 58° 11′ 51.42″ N   LONGITUDE: 6° 44′ 38.5″ W

The stones of Callanish are understandably famous. Although they are arranged in a circle, each of the stones is a menhir in its own right and I could not resist including the site here.

Kempock Stone, Gourock, Inverclyde, Scotland

LATITUDE: 55° 57′ 38.93″ N   LONGITUDE: 4° 49′ 11.34″ W

This stone is very accessible, being close to the main street of the town. It has strong associations with witchcraft, which may be why it's kept in a cage.

Places to see impressive menhirs (continued):

Bwlch Farm Standing Stone, near Beaumaris, Gwynedd, Wales

LATITUDE: 53° 17′ 43.41″ N   LONGITUDE: 4° 9′ 1.23″ W

There are many standing stones and a stone circle close to here, though the going is quite tough and the weather often turns unseasonal.

Carreg Leidr, Llangefri, Anglesey, Wales

LATITUDE: 53° 19′ 56.75″ N   LONGITUDE: 4° 19′ 56.86″ W

This may have been a stone belonging to a cromlech. Anglesey is positively filled with Megalithic monuments and is a deeply atmospheric place.

Ballinskelligs, Iveragh Peninsula, Co. Kerry, Ireland

LATITUDE: 51° 49′ 22.49″ N   LONGITUDE: 10° 16′ 50.76″ W

This stone overlooks the sea in quite the most idyllic setting anyone could imagine. A real piece of old Ireland and quite unforgettable.

Lia Fail, Kilmessan, Co Meath, Ireland

LATITUDE: 53° 34′ 7.44″ N   LONGITUDE: 6° 3′ 44.57″ W

Known as the 'stone of destiny' this monolith is distinctly phallic in shape. It forms part of a deeply important historic Irish site.

Mines and Quarries

Long before the advent of metal, our ancestors required tools for all sorts of purposes. Although some animals can be observed using tools in a rudimentary way, it is the creation and use of specialized tools that first set our species apart. For most of our history such tools were made, almost universally, out of stone. In the British Isles that invariably meant flint (*see* Flint).

In many parts of the British Isles flint can be found occurring quite naturally in the landscape. It is often found as nodules in chalk, so it can be readily prised out of cliffs or can be found on the beaches below. But this is not always the case and there are parts of our islands where flint is harder to find. Chalk areas that are now well below the surface of the land due to geological activity do contain significant amounts of flint, but anyone requiring it will have to dig to get it. And that is just what our ancient ancestors did, in many different places.

A good example is Grime's Graves in Norfolk. There are an estimated 433 shafts at Grime's Graves, some of which were once up to 30ft (9 metres) deep. Work began to extract the flint around 3000 BC and continued well into the Bronze Age. Although chalk is fairly soft the only tools available to these early miners were deer antlers that could be used as pick axes, so the work would not have been easy. What is more, narrow tunnels connected the bottom of the shafts because what these miners were looking for was the best quality of flint, known as 'floorstone'. This was infinitely better than the sort of flints that could be found on the surface of the land, in river gravel or on beaches, and was obviously considered worth the effort and danger to exploit.

It seems likely that for generations a culture developed in such sites that was not dedicated to farming but rather specifically to mining and to trading the results of their efforts far and wide. Flint may have been one of the earliest commodities to be traded in this way and led to the degree of specialization that epitomizes more advanced societies.

With the arrival of the Bronze Age, copper ore and tin ore were both necessary prerequisites for a developing culture. Sometimes both could be found near the surface but increasingly people had to dig in order to find the veins of ore.

Chief amongst the earliest copper mines of Britain were those at Alderley Edge in Cheshire, England, where malachite (copper ore) was relatively easy to get at. Other reserves existed in parts of Wales but neither in Cheshire nor Wales could the miners obtain tin in the quantities found in Cornwall, which is in the far southwest of England. In Cornwall both copper and tin ore could be found, making this one of the most important parts of Britain, not just at the start of the Bronze Age but for many centuries beyond. Tin ore is not half as common as copper ore and so Cornwall's tin was in great demand. It may well have been traded, even abroad, in prehistoric times and it certainly found its way across the length and breadth of the British Isles.

Quarrying and, later, mining copper and tin ore was a hazardous business. Until the Iron Age, tools were primitive. Bronze, although a useful metal in

Places to see mines and quarries:

Grimes Graves (flint), Thetford, Norfolk, England
(*See* Impressive Sites section)

LATITUDE: 52° 28′ 31.43″ N   LONGITUDE: 0° 40′ 32.44″ E

Grimes Graves is extremely interesting and seems to fascinate children especially. It could form the nucleus of a good family day out.

Windover Hill (flint), near Folkington, East Sussex, England

LATITUDE: 50° 48′ 31.35″ N   LONGITUDE: 0° 11′ 19.10″ E

These are classed as 'alleged' Neolithic flint mines but there isn't much doubt in my mind that this is indeed what they were. The flint is of a very high quality.

Den of Boddam (flint), Stirling, Aberdeenshire, Scotland

LATITUDE: 57° 27′ 49.11″ N   LONGITUDE: 1° 48′ 47.85″ W

The Den of Boddom lies on what is practically the only reliable source of flint in Scotland and must have been of the upmost importance.

Alderley Edge (copper), near Macclesfield, Cheshire, England

LATITUDE: 53° 17′ 51.04″ N   LONGITUDE: 2° 12′ 36.28″ W

Copper represented a metal in its own right and, more importantly, a part of the composition of bronze. This site was extensively mined.

Great Orm (copper), Llandudno, Gwynedd, Wales

LATITUDE: 53° 19′ 51.83″ N   LONGITUDE: 3° 50′ 44.62″ W

This mine was not discovered until 1987 and proved to be a real archaeological wonder. Work is still going on to find its extent.

many ways, is fairly useless for making pick axes with which to work hard rock. Its surface blunts quickly and so for every worker chiselling away at the rock, others are needed to keep tools honed. Eventually tin was found in some of the deepest mines in Britain but in prehistoric times it would have to be located reasonably near to the surface, since technology did not allow for deep shafts that were subject to noxious gasses and to flooding.

Once the Iron Age arrived, supplies of ore could be found in many different places. In particular they occurred quite naturally on beaches, washed out from the cliff faces and looking for all the world like cannon balls. There were also places where iron occurred in Britain very close to the surface, so the deeper mines sometimes necessary for copper, and invariably for tin, were not really an issue in prehistoric times. However, some ancient iron mines did exist and must have represented a significant challenge to those exploiting the ore.

Stone was also regularly quarried in the prehistoric period, either for use around the farm in boundary walls or for more grandiose schemes, such as tombs, menhirs or standing stones, for circles and avenues. Finding ancient stone quarries is not easy, mainly because such readily available sources of stone were used long after the prehistoric period or because we fail to recognize them. It is also the case that surface sources of stone were exploited as a preference. These are legion in certain areas of Britain and, since they still exist in great numbers, they could never have been fully exploited in prehistory. So, except in very specific cases, nobody in those remote times 'mined' for general stone, they simply used what nature and geology had left them.

Monolith

A monolith is a rock structure that has been excavated and cut from the living rock of a particular location. There are few true monoliths in the British Isles, though the term is sometimes used (wrongly) to denote a tall standing stone. If such a stone has been dragged from the surrounding area and then erected somewhere else it is, by definition, not a monolith but a megalith.

Mounds (Natural and Artificial)

Apart from the various sorts of burial mounds, usually referred to as barrows (see Barrows), there are a limited number of other sorts of mounds in the British Isles that are not thought to have been intended for burials. The best example of all is Silbury Hill in Wiltshire, England. Silbury Hill rises 130ft (40 metres) above the surrounding countryside and was constructed, in stages, starting at about 2700 BC. Despite a number of excavations over the years nothing has ever been found within it, and its purpose remains something of a mystery. (*See* Impressive Sites section.)

Building artificial hills seems to have been a natural pastime for our species all around the world. In their most stylized form we call these pyramids and they may originally have been simply a way of approaching the gods, who inhabited the sky. The same may be true of a structure such as Silbury Hill.

In size and scale, Silbury Hill is unique in the British Isles and there is nothing else quite like it anywhere across our islands. However, our ancient ancestors do seem to have been particularly fascinated by regular, conical hills, such as Freebrough Hill, in Redcar and Cleveland, England. All manner of legends surround Freebrough which, quite naturally, looks like a giant version of Silbury Hill. Many such conical hills were created as the glaciers retreated after the last Ice Age and judging by burials that have been found dug into them, at least some were considered 'sacred' or 'special'.

A further example is Glastonbury Tor, Somerset, England. This is another natural, strange hill, that rises out of a generally flat landscape. Today its summit sports the ruins of a church but it seems to have been considered sacred for countless centuries.

It is possible that the existence of such significant hills across the British Isles is the reason that more structures such as Silbury Hill were not created. In other words, we have such a preponderance of significant-looking hills that could be utilized, there wasn't any real reason to create artificial ones.

Neolithic

The term 'Neolithic' is used to describe the New Stone Age, i.e. that period when farming began and human endeavour reached a stage from which it began to catapult forward. Although the Neolithic period is considered to have begun around 10,000 BC in some parts of the world, this is still incredibly recent in terms of our history as a species. Stone tools were being made and utilized in Africa as much as two million years ago, so 10,000 BC is more or less 'yesterday'. The Neolithic period is considered to have come to an end with the advent of metal in the Copper Age and Bronze Age.

Passage Grave

Passage graves or tombs come in a number of different varieties across the British Isles. What they have in common is that entry into the tomb is achieved via a deliberately created passage, which then usually opens out into a chamber or chambers beyond. The chambers and passage can be covered with cairns (*see* Cairn) or mounds, and can be constructed with large stone slabs or by corbelling.

Some passage graves or tombs are extremely complex and quite sophisticated in terms of their construction. In a number of cases it has been noted that the opening of a passage grave has been deliberately planned so that it faces some notable happening in the year, for example the midwinter sunrise. There must have been occasions, such as at Newgrange, Ireland, on which the builders of the tomb were obviously aware of this fact because they incorporated a 'light box' into the entrance. This allowed the light of the rising Sun at midwinter to flood down the passage and into the chamber beyond.

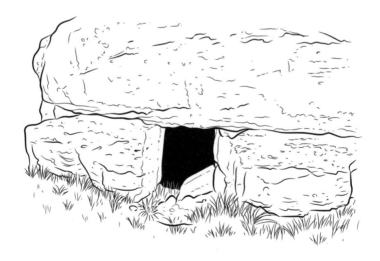

Figure 15: Entrance to a typical passage grave

Where to see passage graves:

Newgrange, Boyne Valley, Ireland
(*See* Impressive Sites section)

LATITUDE: 53° 41′ 40.69″ N   LONGITUDE: 6° 28′ 31.67″ W

Bryn Celli Ddu, Llanddaniel Fab, Anglesey, Wales
(*See* Impressive Sites section)

LATITUDE: 53° 12′ 27″ N   LONGITUDE: 4° 14′ 8.89″ W

Not a huge passage grave but extremely impressive and with mysterious components – including what we take to be a stone lens: a convex stone face that was once polished to amplify the reflection of any light that fell upon it.

Maeshowe, Stromness, Orkney, Scotland
(*See* Impressive Sites section)

LATITUDE: 58° 59′ 46.28″ N   LONGITUDE: 3° 11′ 13.55″ W

A tremendous tomb, set amongst incredible landscapes. The stonework in particular is so impressive. It could have been created yesterday.

West Kennet Long Barrow, Marlborough, Wiltshire, England

LATITUDE: 51° 24′ 30.78″ N   LONGITUDE: 1° 51′ 4″ W

The most famous English chambered tomb set in possibly the most intensively used prehistoric landscape. It is not classified as a chambered tomb but it is one.

Belas Knap Chambered Long Barrow, Gloucestershire, England
(*See* Impressive Sites section)

LATITUDE: 51° 55′ 35.83″ N   LONGITUDE: 1° 58′ 4.81″ W

This is a Neolithic long barrow that is in excellent condition. It has a false entrance and forecourt as many such tombs do.

Carrowmore Passage Tomb Cemetery, Co. Sligo, Ireland
(*See* Impressive Sites section)

LATITUDE: 54° 14′ 53.68″ N   LONGITUDE: 8° 31′ 6.88″ W

There are a number of passage tombs here, some in a better state of repair than others. There are also a significant number of stones.

Passage tombs are often found in clusters throughout Britain and Ireland and some date back to the New Stone Age. The purpose of the passages is unknown though it has often been suggested that they represent a 'birth canal' joining the world above with the 'womb of the Earth' within the tomb. This has to be conjecture but bearing in mind the importance of the rising Sun in terms of at least some of the more grandiose passage graves, this cannot be dismissed as a possibility.

Prehistoric Farms

Farming reached the British Isles around 4000 BC, after which a more settled existence became possible. This, in turn, led to the explosion of creativity that is still to be seen strewn across our landscape. None of the cursus, henges, standing stones or whatever could have been possible without the fact that people had sufficient time on their hands to think about doing something other than surviving. It stands to reason that when one is wondering where the next meal is going to come from, monumental creations in earth and stone must necessarily take a back seat.

We see wonderful structures such as Meashowe or Newgrange and we marvel at the effort that went into creating them, but we rarely take stock of the fact that behind all this effort, the land was tilled and planted each year, livestock was raised and land was carefully and often aggressively defended, especially in areas where the soil was very fertile.

Unfortunately, because ordinary dwelling houses in the New Stone Age and the Bronze Age were fairly flimsy structures, built mostly of organic materials such as wood, they don't tend to survive as anything other than a few postholes. Parch marks now offer archaeologists the chance to see where farmsteads and small villages once stood, and some work has been done on excavating such sites. In many ways these are more informative than the grand monuments because the minutia of life, abandoned in rubbish heaps or trodden into the floors of dwelling houses can tell us so much about the lives people led.

Even where such sites have been discovered and excavated, there is little for the visitor to see. What can be much more informative is to visit one of the

Places to see recreated prehistoric farms and farm sites:

Butser Ancient Farm, Petersfield, Hampshire, England

LATITUDE: 50° 58′ 37.45″ N   LONGITUDE: 0° 58′ 48.03″ W

A fascinating voyage of discovery and especially popular with children. Quite magically they can learn a great deal without even realizing it.

Flag Fen Causeway and Reconstructed Bronze Age Village,
near Peterborough, Cambridgeshire, England
(*See* Impressive Sites section)

LATITUDE: 52° 34′ 25.23″ N   LONGITUDE: 0° 11′ 31.74″ W

This is a very extensive site and one that would make a great family day out. It highlights the importance of the fenlands to our ancient ancestors.

Cinderbury Iron Age Farm, Coleford, Gloucestershire, England

LATITUDE: 51° 47′ 35.86″ N   LONGITUDE: 2° 36′ 57.98″ W

If you want to go back in time and learn what life was like in the Iron Age, take a trip to the wonderful Forest of Dean and look at Cinderbury.

Belderrig Prehistoric Farm Site, Co. Mayo, Ireland

LATITUDE: 54° 06′ 42.78″ N   LONGITUDE: 9° 09′ 26.51″ W

A lovely spot in County Mayo, with evidence of some of the earliest farming ever to take place in our islands. The sea is close by.

Dan-yr-Ogof Iron Age Village and Caves, Abercraf, Powys, Wales

LATITUDE: 51° 49′ 53.00″ N   LONGITUDE: 3° 41′ 15.77″ W

This is as much 'an experience' as a genuine historical excursion, but it is well worth a visit and for the family has much more than an Iron Age village.

recreated prehistoric farms, of which there are now quite a number throughout the British Isles. There the sum total of our acquired knowledge regarding ancient farming and life can be viewed at first hand. Such places are fascinating and make an especially good family day out.

Prehistoric Villages

In a general sense our ancient ancestors have left little to us that describes village life as it must have been lived. This is for the reasons listed above in Prehistoric Farms. Communities were widespread, usually small, and houses were built of materials that have not stood the test of time in the way that the tombs and standing stones have.

There are some exceptions and there are places where the ruins of villages originally built partly of stone have survived as foundations, especially in the uplands, and there is one example that is a virtual snapshot of life in the remote past. This is at Skara Brae on Orkney, Scotland, where an entire village

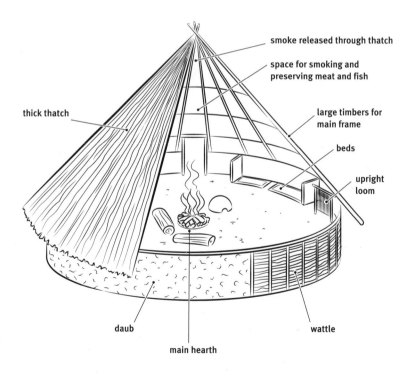

Figure 16: A reconstruction of a typical British Iron Age house

Figure 17: A reconstructed Iron Age village

of stone-built houses survived virtually intact because it was covered by sand dunes in very remote times. The village dates back to at least 3200 BC and is incalculably important in understanding late Stone Age life in the British Isles. All the same, it is not necessarily representative because stone used exclusively as a building material for dwelling houses was rare across Britain. (*See* Skara Brae in the Impressive Sites section.)

Places to see recreated prehistoric villages:

Skara Brae, Stromness, Orkney, Scotland
(The best of the best – *see* Impressive Sites section)

LATITUDE: 59° 2′ 54.78″ N   LONGITUDE: 3° 20′ 38.63″ W

Actually Skara Brae has not been recreated. It looks today very much the way it was found. This is genuine time travel at its very best.

Castell Henllys Iron Age Fort, Pembrokeshire, Wales

LATITUDE: 52° 1′ 5.82″ N   LONGITUDE: 4° 44′ 44.08″ W

Set within an actual Iron Age fort, the village here is quite fascinating and there are sometimes even 'hands on' projects for visitors.

As with prehistoric farms, there are a number of recreated prehistoric villages to be seen throughout the British Isles. Our knowledge of how people lived in the late Stone Age, Bronze Age and Iron Age is growing all the time and much trouble has been taken to recreate houses and styles of life that can be viewed by the interested visitor.

Rock-Cut Tomb

Rock-cut tombs are not only rare in the British Isles, they are like hens' teeth. In reality, and despite protestations from other places, there is probably only one to be found and that is on Hoy, Orkney Scotland. A rock-cut tomb, much more likely to be found in southern Europe and the Levant, is a tomb that is not constructed of separate stones, as most British examples are, but rather one that is carved into the rock in a particular location.

The example on Hoy is called Dwarfie Stane. It is cut into a massive piece of Devonian old red sandstone. It is similar in its internal design to other chambered tombs in and around Orkney and only its unique position as a rock-cut tomb sets it apart.

There are other places in Britain where rock-cut tombs have been claimed, though these are in some doubt. They may be modified natural caves or

Figure 18: A typical rock-cut tomb

Where to see a rock-cut tomb:

Dwarfie Stane, Hoy, Orkney, Scotland

LATITUDE: 58° 53′ 4.21″ N   LONGITUDE: 3° 18′ 42″ W

Since this is the only true rock-cut tomb in the British Isles, if you want to see such a structure you will have little choice but to visit Orkney – but what a place it is.

structures of a much more recent creation, but of the Dwarfie Stane there is no doubt whatsoever. For this reason alone it comes high on the list of 'must see' sites for prehistoric buffs.

Round Cairn (*See* Cairn)

Round Barrow (*See* Barrow)

Sexual Stones

Because archaeologists and others studying our ancient past are, of necessity, scientists, they try to avoid conjecture as much as possible. Whilst understandable this is somewhat restricting when dealing with structures the purposes of which are lost in the mists of time. Stone circles, tombs, forts and other structures don't come with 'instruction manuals', which means if we are going to make any sense at all of them we have to use every piece of evidence that is present. Sometimes that's as simple as using your eyes, which is definitely the case with sexual stones.

Because people all over the world are broadly similar in lots of ways, it is possible to use what we 'know' about one culture in order to make sense of another we know very little about. True, this can sometimes be quite misleading, but in the absence of other proof, at least it offers us a way forward. We know, for example, that many cultures in the past have made 'phallic' representations of one sort or another, often out of stone. The phallus is obviously of great importance because it is part of the mechanism by which our species has survived and flourished for so many thousands of years. And whilst talking about 'willies' might not be considered suitable for some company, we can't ignore them when we find them dotted about all over the prehistoric landscape. I am personally in no doubt whatsoever, and for a host of different reasons, that the sky and the earth were associated in the prehistoric British Isles with sex and birth and death. It seems as though these ancient peoples thought about a ritual 'coming together' of the sky god and the earth goddess, which allowed the world in which they lived to be fruitful. Each year the seasons turned, bringing potential famine and death in the winter months, hope in the spring, and bounty in the summer and especially the autumn. That they equated these cycles with the cycles of human fertility, together with life and death, seems self-evident.

Buried in the deepest recesses of the chamber at Knowth, Ireland, was found an exquisite red stone phallus, which is really quite unmistakable. That it was found in association with burials seems to indicate, as we can be sure was the case, that the people who built Knowth, and the other prehistoric tombs, fully expected the deceased to be born again into some other sort of reality – or else to be reincarnated into their own world.

Now let us look at much bigger stones. A great example is that of a stone contained in the circle at Aikey Brae in Aberdeenshire, Scotland. If this particular stone is not fully intended to be a phallus I will eat my hat (and I often wear a very big and quite unappetizing hat). If you can get there, go and see it for yourself. The symbolism is glaringly obvious. There are other examples in Aberdeenshire, for example at Whitehill, where at several sites a deliberate and obvious phallus stone is included.

It looks as though the Scots (or at least their prehistoric equivalents) were particularly keen on this sort of thing. There is another great example at Cnoc Fillibhear Bheag on the Island of Lewis. Callanish also has phallic stones. In fact it might be suggested that all tall standing stones, single or in circles, may well be intended to represent the male member and male fertility, whilst other stones, invariably lozenge-shaped or diamond-shaped, are representative of female sexuality (the diamond in particular has been a symbol for the feminine since time out of mind because it has vaginal connotations). Often the tall stones and the diamond stones are alternately placed in a standing stone circle, as is the case at Avebury, and this is surely intended to indicate both genders as being part of the 'fertility game' exhibited both by people and by nature as a whole.

Nor is this use of obvious phallus stones and vagina stones restricted to just a couple of locations. It can be seen on Bodmin Moor at the Hurlers stone circle, in the trilithons at Stonehenge and especially at Men-an-Tol in Cornwall, England. Here the builders have gone one stage further because there is a very wide, roughly circular stone with a large hole through its centre. This has been associated with procreation and childbirth as long as memory goes back but it is also quite definitely equated with sexual penetration, which I am certain it was intended to be since it was carved and put up. This stone may also be associated with the Moon, which because of its 28–29-day cycles has always had a connection with the female menstrual cycle.

Neither can we forget that burial mounds and tombs of one sort or another have often been equated with 'wombs of the Earth' and that certainly seems to be what most of them are meant to represent. There is so often a chamber that represents the womb, together with a passage that is clearly meant to be the birth canal. Whether the deceased were meant to be reborn into this world or into some other existence we can't possibly know, but of a belief in an afterlife there is no doubt – or else why would the dead be supplied with grave goods of an entirely practical or status-related nature?

I have deliberately avoided giving specific examples of places where readers can see sexual stones, apart from the examples quoted above. This is because I am personally so sure that sexuality, life and death, together with the cycles of nature, are so closely allied to all our prehistoric structures, that I think they are obvious in all of them. It only takes a moment to look at a host of daily newspapers or magazines, at television, films or the internet, in order to see just how obsessed with sex we still are. A leopard doesn't change its spots, and nor do humans. In many cases, it isn't a matter of searching to find out what is sexual about particular prehistoric sites, and especially standing stones; what is more to the point is recognizing what isn't.

Standing Stone

There is nothing mysterious about the term 'standing stone'; it simply refers to a stone that has been found or quarried, taken to a chosen site and then erected in an upright position. There are literally tens of thousands of standing stones across the British Isles, some of them standing alone (*see* Menhir), in groups, or as part of circles and other arrangements.

Some standing stones are very crude, in fact little altered from the state they were in when they were found in the landscape, whereas others have been carefully worked to achieve an obviously desired shape and size (a process that sometimes must have taken weeks of hard work with stone mauls).

Standing stones can be extremely small or massively large (up to 40 tonnes in some cases!) and the purpose for their existence probably varied from place to place and across a long period of time.

Doubtless some standing stones were simple, territorial markers, defining the extent of the property of a clan or tribe, with others clearly of a more ritual or religious nature. Britain is far from being unique in possessing standing stones; they are found in a wide arc down the western seaboard of Europe, in the Mediterranean, down into northern Africa and, in fact, in so many places they seem to be the norm rather than any sort of exception.

Figure 19: A typical standing stone

Figure 20: Stonehenge

We can only guess at the mindset of the people who chose to select such stones, hammer them into shape and drag them sometimes great distances across the landscape, before erecting them, often with great care, in specific shapes and designs. Some standing stones may have been used as waymarkers – as they still are in some upland areas of Britain where they stand out well against a background of snow – and not a few unknown standing stones that have been brought to my attention over the years turned out to be medieval and made as gate posts (though the reverse is sometimes true because there are many gate posts that used to be standing stones).

No particular sort of stone seems to have been of specific importance to the majority of our ancient ancestors. In most cases they simply used whatever was at hand. There are exceptions (*see* Stonehenge in Impressive Sites section) because it appears that on rare occasions particular types of stone from a distance were chosen, even if local stone was readily available.

Some standing stones seem to have a self-evident purpose (*see* Sexual Stones) and it is true that some stone circles have alternate long stones and diamond-shaped stones (which, as mentioned before, it is often suggested represented the alternate male and female principle).

Local standing stones always attract their own myths (*see* The Devil's Arrows in the Impressive Sites section) but most of these have simply been attached to stones that have occupied a particular spot on the landscape for so long that nobody has any idea why they were really put there. Many attract local superstitions, which can only be seen as a good thing because it has preserved them. In the 17th and 18th centuries in parts of Britain there was a religious fervour that caused some people to deliberately destroy standing stones, which were said to be the work of the Devil. This was less likely to happen on the Celtic fringe, in Wales, Scotland and Ireland, where local legends warned people not to damage the stones, which were thought to be of a different supernatural origin.

Figure 21: A standing stone

Places to see really impressive standing stones (*see also* Menhir):

Stonehenge, Amesbury, Wiltshire, England
(*See* Impressive Sites section)

LATITUDE: 51° 10' 43.87" N   LONGITUDE: 1° 49' 34.27" W

There are all manner of standing stones at Stonehenge and some of the outlying ones are especially large and truly impressive.

Avebury, near Marlborough, Wiltshire, England
(*See* Impressive Sites section)

LATITUDE: 51° 25' 43.04" N   LONGITUDE: 1° 51' 14.66" W

I really love Avebury. The stones here are huge and most were not carved into shape but look much as they must have done when dragged from the earth.

The Bull Stone, Otley Chevin, West Yorkshire, England

LATITUDE: 53° 53' 16.35" N   LONGITUDE: 1° 41' 11.56" W

The Bull Stone is not especially large or impressive but it is a feast of cup and ring markings and a true survivor across a vast period of time.

Ballinaby Standing Stone, Islay, Hebrides, Scotland

LATITUDE: 55° 49' 0.54" N   LONGITUDE: 6° 26' 18.74" W

Tall, gaunt and weathered, this slim stone has been watching over the island of Islay for so long it looks as though it truly belongs to the landscape.

Gelligaer, Cefn Bugail, Mid Glamorgan, Wales

LATITUDE: 51° 43' 17.86" N   LONGITUDE: 3° 17' 55.42" W

The Gelligaer standing stone stands drunkenly beside a track that is so old our very earliest ancestors must have walked along it.

Maen Llia, Brecon, Brecon Beacons, Wales

LATITUDE: 51° 51' 34.55" N   LONGITUDE: 3° 33' 45.62" W

Maen Llia stone looks like a giant's tear, frozen into solid rock. It's fat and squat and somehow especially friendly to travellers.

> ## Places to see really impressive standing stones (continued):
>
> **Ballycrovane,** Sneem, Co. Cork, Ireland
>
> LATITUDE: 51° 42' 45.3" N   LONGITUDE: 9° 56' 36.09" W
>
> The stone here is in such a prominent position and is so large that it may have been a marker for those coming into shore at the nearby harbour.
>
> **Punchestown,** Ballymore, Eustace, Co. Kildare, Ireland
>
> LATITUDE: 53° 11' 27.85" N   LONGITUDE: 6° 37' 40.46" W
>
> The age of this stone is in some doubt but few would deny that it has kept its vigil for a very long time indeed. There are other stones in the area.

Some standing stones are the remnants of half-destroyed tombs but most remain as silent sentinels, spanning the ages and linking us directly with people whose religion, social structures and motivations we can only guess at. But at least we can see what they saw and touch what they touched, in this way at least completing a connection that is strong at a genetic level but all too distant in terms of understanding.

Stone Age (Old and New)

The term 'Stone Age' covers a fantastically long period of time, in fact from the very first period at which people in Africa started to use primitive stone tools. Since some of our primate relatives also use stone tools for specific tasks, for example chimps use stones to crack nuts, our use of such technology clearly goes back a very long way.

It is estimated that humans first used stone tools as much as two and a half million years ago (though opinions vary) and what is generally referred to as the Stone Age continued until the advent of metal smelting with the arrival of the Copper Age and then, fairly quickly, the Bronze Age. During the majority of this period very little altered as far as humanity was concerned. True, stone tool technology improved and more specialized tools were created in different places by different groups. It also has to be remembered that Stone Age hunter-gatherers used a wide variety of other substances, such as wood, bone, antler and the like, but examples such as these do not survive well in the ground and so it is stone tools that are most likely to be found.

For convenience's sake the vast period that was the Stone Age is split into 'Old Stone Age' and 'New Stone Age', though there are more technical terms, which are Palaeolithic, Mesolithic and Neolithic, all of which serve to confuse ordinary people but which are of tremendous use to experts.

The term Stone Age, 'Old and New', is quite useful in Europe but less so when considering the entire world, in which some cultures were still technically in the Stone Age until their discovery by and contact with technologically superior peoples from elsewhere (as recently as the last century in some cases). However, for the purposes of this book the Old Stone Age is that period before farming and a more settled life came to the British Isles, whilst New Stone Age refers to the period of time between the onset of farming and the first smelting of metals in our islands. The New Stone Age therefore began in the British Isles around 4000 BC. This is the period also known as the Neolithic, as opposed to the Mesolithic, which preceded it.

Stone Avenue

A stone avenue is the term given to a series of parallel standing stones marking a ritual pathway of some sort. The very best stone avenues are not to be seen in the British Isles, but rather in Brittany, where there are long rows of stones that extend for kilometres across the landscape.

Some of the more grandiose Megalithic structures, for example Stonehenge, once had wide ceremonial avenues leading to them from other locations in the landscape and some of these once had timber or stone sentinels to mark their course. In most cases these have survived only in part, if at all, though the telltale holes where stones once stood can still be located. True stone avenues are rare in the British Isles but Brittany and the region around Carnac are the places to go in order to see just how persistent and determined our Neolithic ancestors could be when it came to finding and erecting standing stones. It has been suggested, perhaps fairly, that in the long avenues such as those in Brittany, each successive stone represented one person or generation within a long-lasting culture that inhabited the region.

Stone Circle

Stone circles represent what are generally thought of as being the primary legacy left to us from Megalithic times. They are extremely numerous and many more than a thousand have been noted in the British Isles and across parts of the western seaboard of Europe. There were probably many more originally and some unknown ones doubtless still exist below peat or within heavily wooded areas, whilst others have been removed for farming or urban development.

As to the age of stone circles, we have to be quite careful. Stone can only be dated geologically, which of course is of no use whatsoever when trying to establish when it was collected and dragged to a particular location. I have personally recreated a stone circle in the extensive back garden of a friend. The stones had originally formed part of a stone circle that was destroyed in the 20th century and I used measurements that were common in the Megalithic period. In a few hundred years it might be difficult for an archaeologist to date the stone circle I designed, which merely serves to highlight the dilemma regarding the age of some stone circles.

Even excavations within the confines of stone circles may not prove to be particularly useful when dating the erection of the stones themselves. Material that can be carbon dated or shards of pottery may well have been placed in the ground long after the circle was first built, since it seems that ancient stone circles have always been held in awe, by successive generations and even entirely different peoples. Thus, when dealing with almost any circle that has been the subject of an archaeological excavation, a range of dates has been achieved.

A slightly more reliable yardstick is to date artefacts that have been found under erected stones, as in the case at Stonehenge when stones have been occasionally removed for realignment or because they were in danger of falling. It stands to reason that anything placed, or lost, immediately below a massive stone that has not been moved since it was put in place is likely to date from the time of the erection of the stones.

Figure 22: A typical stone circle

There is no absolute convention regarding the size, shape and distribution of stones in stone circles throughout the British Isles and this has led experts to conclude that each was created locally and independently. All the same, there are similarities in many cases. For example, there are a whole series of stone circles, especially in Scotland, that are not true circles at all but various types of ellipses. It has been suggested that the makers of these stone egg-shapes were attempting to square the circle, in other words to define pi as an integer '3'.

Circles can contain many stones or very few and the stones can be massive or tiny. Many of the very small 'fairy rings' as they are sometimes called are doubtless lost in the vegetation of the British uplands, whilst other circles are so massive they can be seen from a great distance.

As to the purpose of all the stone circles, there is great conjecture. Doubtless they had some ritual or religious function but one famous researcher, Professor Alexander Thom (*see* Thom, Alexander), a Scottish engineer who taught at Oxford University, solved the problem regarding many Scottish circles. He discovered, as a result of very careful surveying and a good knowledge of astronomy, that these circles were designed to study and track the positions of the Moon on the horizon. The Moon, though going through regular and repeatable phases, has a relationship with the horizon that is tortuously difficult to understand and predict. For whatever reason, it appears that our Megalithic ancestors (or at least some of them) were interested enough to build 'machines' that could work out where the Moon might be at any given time.

Astronomical alignments have been suggested for many stone circles, with specific stones lining up with natural objects on the horizon. These might indicate the position of midwinter or midsummer sunrise or sunset, or the rising or setting of particular stars. The problem is that the sky is extremely complicated in terms of what *can* be tracked and unless a relationship between stones in a given circle and celestial happenings can be proved, there will always be people who shout 'coincidence'. One can imagine that in a circle as complex as Stonehenge, which is actually a number of circles within each other, the possibilities are endless. Add to this the fact that many circles have outlying stones at some distance from the circle, which could have been used as backsights – additional stones or other markers that line up with one of the circle stones and point to a part of the horizon – and the situation becomes almost unworkable.

My own research, together with my colleague and writing partner Christopher Knight, tends to add weight to the idea that stone circles were primarily for astronomical observation. We showed in our books *Civilization One* and *Before the Pyramids* that the earlier henge monuments were used as

Figure 23: A stone circle

astronomical observatories, in which the parameters could be changed repeatedly using wooden stakes instead of fixed stones. Under such circumstances it could be the case that the later stone circles were 'fixed' observatories, 'set' to particular happenings in specific sites. The frequency of midsummer and midwinter observations from many stone circles adds weight to the astronomical theory.

The earliest stone circles are most likely to be around 5,000 years old, whilst the last phase of Stonehenge took place between 2000 and 1500 BC, so a large span of time encompasses the building at such sites. In most examples local stone was used, though even in these cases it may have been moved a number of miles in order to get it to the desired site. Rarer are situations, such as at Stonehenge, where some of the stones came from as far away as Wales, a considerable journey when local stone was readily available. (*See* Stonehenge in the Impressive Sites section.)

The stone used in stone circles was sometimes left as rough as it must have been when it was found lying in the landscape, but in other examples it has been carefully crafted to form graceful megaliths or the diamond shapes that are also fairly common.

Perhaps the most contentious issue of all regarding standing stone circles also relates to Professor Alexander Thom, mentioned above. In addition to his work on lunar circles, for which he has been repeatedly praised, he made another discovery that is less well accepted. Working on mathematical evidence from hundreds of sites, Thom came to the unavoidable conclusion that common units of measurement had been used in the construction of nearly all of them. He named the most regularly found unit the Megalithic Yard, which he showed was 2.722ft (82.966cm). There was also the Megalithic Rod, which was 2.5 times the length of the Megalithic Yard, and the Megalithic Inch, of which there were 40 to the Megalithic Yard, and 100 to the Megalithic Rod. I personally have no doubt that these units did exist and that they were used across vast areas for a very long time. However, many experts doubt the existence of the Megalithic Yard, Rod and Inch, and Thom has had a bad press because of them.

Many people of a 'New Age' bent congregate at stone circles at specific times of the year, in particular midsummer and midwinter sunrise. Whatever they do at such times has no relationship whatsoever to the intentions of the builders of such sites (as far as we know). It might all be good fun but nobody should be under any illusion that these revellers, as good as their intentions may be, have any idea what they are doing or why – at least in connection with the original intention of the circle builders. The fact is that we just don't know, though much can be extrapolated from sky patterns that existed when the various circles were constructed, and this sort of research goes on.

It appears that stone circles were first built in coastal areas, but by the later Neolithic period they began to appear inland and also became more complex. This period marked the high point of stone circle building and accounts for by far the majority of examples.

Circles can be single or double. Some, such as Avebury, have an epicyclical feel and many were extremely difficult to work out from a mathematical point of view. All the stone circles are fascinating and there is a wealth of potential for research in the case of each one. Some circles also have 'recumbent' stones, which appear to have been laid down lengthwise from the time they were installed. Often these attract the legend of being 'sacrificial stones', though there isn't the slightest shred of evidence that this was their intended purpose.

In some cases there was almost certainly a 'fertility' aspect to stones used in circles (*see* Sexual Stones) but that does not preclude the astronomical explanation for the circles. We are dealing with a period at which the line of demarcation between religion and science simply did not exist – even in the Middle Ages it was more or less the same thing. Only in the last two or three hundred years have specialists disassociated the power of the gods and the natural forces of physics.

Perhaps we cannot entirely blame those individuals who suggest that stone circles are places of mysterious 'earth power', which they cannot define but insist they feel. I for one never fail to get a tremendous thrill when I stand inside one of the many impressive stone circles that still point to the sky across so many areas of the British Isles. The stones do seem 'alive' with energy, and maybe that's the way they were meant to feel. Certainly the amount of work that went into planning and creating many of them was colossal, so they were clearly of great importance. The larger ones must have represented a great deal of communal effort, so there is little doubt that, like a parish church or a

Places to see stone circles:

Stonehenge, Amesbury, Wiltshire, England
(*See* Impressive Sites section)

LATITUDE: 51° 10' 43.87" N   LONGITUDE: 1° 49' 34.27" W

Surely the grandfather of all stone circles. True, it's quite commercial but it is still the most impressive structure our ancient ancestors left us.

Stanton Drew Stone Circle, near Keynsham, Somerset, England

LATITUDE: 51° 22' 0.5" N   LONGITUDE: 2° 34' 28.73" W

Stanton Drew is a charming double circle and one that especially fascinated those antiquarians who first began to look at our ancient past.

Avebury, near Marlborough, Wiltshire, England
(*See* Impressive Sites section)

LATITUDE: 51° 25' 43.04" N   LONGITUDE: 1° 51' 14.66" W

In comparison with almost all stone circles Avebury is massive. It is also complex and must have been a nightmare to devise and build.

Castlerigg, near Keswick, Cumbria, England

LATITUDE: 54° 36' 11.78" N   LONGITUDE: 3° 5' 46.08" W

This has to be my own personal favourite of all England's stone circles. It is set amidst a huge landscape and yet is not lost within it.

Long Meg and her Daughters, Penrith, Cumbria, England

LATITUDE: 54° 43' 43.12" N   LONGITUDE: 2° 39' 52.81" W

Long Meg herself is a large piece of red sandstone, and her daughters dance around her. The site is looked after by English Heritage.

Rollright Stones, Chipping Norton, Oxfordshire, England

LATITUDE: 51° 58' 31.06" N   LONGITUDE: 1° 34' 13.73" W

This is a delightful site, suffused with both history and legend. Oxford is a beautiful county and the Rollrights are set in the best of it.

Places to see stone circles (continued):

The Hurlers Stone Circles, Bodmin Moor, Cornwall
(*See* Impressive Sites section)

LATITUDE: 50° 30' 56.89" N   LONGITUDE: 4° 27' 26.83" W

Not only is the stone circle on Bodmin Moor very impressive, but it is set amidst the very best of what the West Country has to offer.

Arbor Low Henge and Stone Circle, near Hartington, Derbyshire, England
(*See* Impressive Sites section)

LATITUDE: 53° 10' 8.13" N   LONGITUDE: 1° 45' 42.18" W

All the stones here are recumbent, which means someone pushed them over at a remote time in the past. They look as though they are sleeping.

Callanish, Isle of Lewis, Scotland

LATITUDE: 58° 11' 51.42" N   LONGITUDE: 6° 44' 38.5" W

Impressive or what? The north of Scotland has some of the best prehistoric monuments anywhere in the world and Callanish is right up there with them.

Ring of Brodgar, Orkney, West Mainland, Scotland
(*See* Impressive Sites section)

LATITUDE: 59° 0' 7.5" N   LONGITUDE: 3° 13' 44.7" W

This site is haunting and very beautiful, especially at dawn or dusk.

Dyffryn Syfynwy, Rosebush, near Fishguard, Pembrokeshire, Wales

LATITUDE: 51° 55' 12.72" N   LONGITUDE: 4° 49' 26.18" W

Some stones here are recumbent and some still standing. This is not strictly a circle because it is elliptical in shape – though clearly deliberately so.

Gors Fawr, near Narberth, Pembrokeshire, Wales
(*See* Impressive Sites section)

LATITUDE: 51° 55' 52.76" N   LONGITUDE: 4° 42' 46.85" W

The circle stones are not large but there are a couple of taller stones close by that seem to have been erected to mark an important path or far-off view.

Places to see stone circles (continued):

Druids Circle, Penmaenmawr, Conwy, Wales
(*See* Impressive Sites section)

LATITUDE: 53° 15′ 9.58″ N   LONGITUDE: 3° 54′ 51.53″ W

This circle stands close to what was once a polished hand-axe factory. The locals were probably wealthy by the standards of their day and were clearly keen to show their skill.

Drombeg Stone Circle, Ross Carbery, Co. Cork, Ireland

LATITUDE: 51° 33′ 52.32″ N   LONGITUDE: 9° 5′ 9.73″ W

There are 17 stones in this circle. You will have to watch carefully for the signs as you approach the place.

Beltany Stone Circle, near Raphoe, Co. Donegal, Ireland

LATITUDE: 54° 50′ 59.12″ N   LONGITUDE: 7° 36′ 16.29″ W

Beltany sports a very large circle, one of the biggest in Ireland, with 64 stones. Sometimes referred to as 'the Stonehenge of Donegal'.

cathedral, they 'belonged' to society as a whole. What took place within them we can only guess, but they do speak of 'specialization' and of people who had sufficient time on their hands to undertake a great deal of effort that had little or nothing to do with sowing the seed and bringing in the grain.

Stone Rows

The best stone rows to be seen are not in the British Isles but rather just across the sea in Brittany. There the puzzled visitor can see literally hundreds of stones, marching off across the landscape like some frozen army. The stone rows that occur in Britain are less impressive in terms of numbers but sometimes significant regarding their size. It takes three or more stones to comprise what is known as a 'row' and they tend to be aligned on the same axis. Unlike a stone avenue (*see* Stone Avenue) which tends to mark a path or ceremonial route and which can curve, stone rows are always straight.

Stone rows can be found on Dartmoor, in the south of England, in Co. Cork, Ireland, at Caithness in Scotland and at various other locations. One of the best examples is not far from the impressive super-henges of North Yorkshire. These are the 'Devil's Arrows' at Boroughbridge, a row of three (and possibly once four) extremely large stones, the tallest of which is over 22ft (7 metres) in height. They don't form a perfect row but they are often considered as such and are well worth a visit.

Stone rows are as mysterious as stone circles. They are often quite isolated, though are equally likely to form part of a Megalithic sacred landscape. They may have an astronomical association, though in isolation this is difficult to prove, or they might have been some sort of boundary marker.

As with stones in circles, stone rows often contain prehistoric art, such as cup and ring markings (*see* Cup and Ring Markings) but since these cannot be dated it is unknown whether they date from the time of the erection of the stones or if they were a later addition. It is thought that most of the stone rows were erected late in the New Stone Age or in the Bronze Age and they may have been part of a cult or a religious diversion that began at that time.

Figure 24: A typical stone row

Places to see stone rows:

The Pipers, Trewoofe, near Penzance, Cornwall, England

LATITUDE: 50° 30′ 56.78″ N   LONGITUDE: 4° 27′ 31.9″ W

These two stones are said to be two revellers that made a mockery of the Sabbath by dancing. As a result they were turned to stone.

Mayburgh, Penrith, Cumbria, England

LATITUDE: 54° 38′ 53.46″ N   LONGITUDE: 2° 44′ 43.81″ W

Only one stone out of four survives here but there is an impressive henge and this site must once have been extremely important in its district.

Merrivale Stone Rows, Princetown, Devon, England

LATITUDE: 50° 33′ 9.37″ N   LONGITUDE: 4° 2′ 34.24″ W

This is one of 60 known stone rows on Dartmoor, and there are other impressive structures not far off. Merrivale is easier to get at than most.

Saith Maen, Brecon Beacons, Powys, Wales

LATITUDE: 51° 49′ 28.25″ N   LONGITUDE: 3° 41′ 36.68″ W

These stones are certainly impressive, but visiting is not for the faint-hearted or anyone who is not in good physical shape.

Carreg Wen Fawr y Rugos, Wern, Powys, Wales

LATITUDE: 51° 51′ 0.79″ N   LONGITUDE: 3° 15′ 41.63″ W

Remote and brooding, this is Wales at its sombre best. Once again you will need to be quite agile to get there and find all the stones.

Ballymeanoch Stone Row, near Slockavullin, Argyll, Scotland
(*See* Impressive Sites section)

LATITUDE: 56° 6′ 39.8″ N   LONGITUDE: 5° 29′ 2.73″ W

There are two rows here, one with two stones and the other with four. They are to be found in the Kilmartin valley, maybe the best of Scotland's prehistoric areas of note.

Souterrain (Fogou or Earth House)

Souterrains, the name for which derives from the French for 'underground', are tunnels dug into the earth or bedrock of many parts of Britain during the late Iron Age. They were originally lined with timber or large stones and some of them may well have been used as storage places, though it is equally likely that they had some ritual or religious significance. It has been suggested that they could have been a place of retreat in times of danger, though it hardly seems credible that when faced with attackers someone would willingly crawl down a hole that generally only had one entrance, and therefore one exit!

Some of the Irish souterrains may well not be prehistoric at all but could date to the 6th or 7th centuries AD. This should not prevent visitors from looking at any of the souterrains that are open to the public. Most of us like crawling around in mysterious galleries and passages and even if we don't know what they were used for it is fun to speculate. Fogou is the name given to the specific sort of souterrain to be found in Cornwall, England.

Figure 25: A typical fougou

Where to see souterrains and fogous:

Carn Euny Fogou, near Newlyn, Cornwall, England

LATITUDE: 50° 6' 6.17" N   LONGITUDE: 5° 38' 0.78" W

This is a fascinating site but to get to it you have to walk through fields that become extremely muddy when the rain falls.

Halliggye Fogou, near Mullion, Cornwall, England

LATITUDE: 50° 4' 13.94" N   LONGITUDE: 5° 11' 42.09" W

There are plenty of fogous in Cornwall but this is certainly one of the best. The reason for such structures remains a secret held by the past.

Chrichton Souterrain, near Dalkeith, Midlothian, Scotland

LATITUDE: 55° 50' 47.29" N   LONGITUDE: 2° 57' 30.06" W

Wear your waterproofs because Scottish souterrains tend to be even wetter than Cornish fogous. A bit of a walk but well worth the effort.

Culsh Souterrain, near Ballater, Aberdeenshire, Scotland

LATITUDE: 57° 8' 12.67" N   LONGITUDE: 2° 49' 10.53" W

There is a lot of red granite here, but you will still need a good torch, as is the case at all fogous and souterrains.

Castletown Souterrain, Carran, Co. Clare, Ireland

LATITUDE: 54° 0' 48.94" N   LONGITUDE: 6° 25' 48.35" W

This site is as mysterious and uninformative as any of the others. What were souterrains created for? Maybe you are the one who will come up with an answer.

Finnis Souterrain (Binder's Cove), near Dromara, Co. Down, Ireland

LATITUDE: 54° 19' 22.57" N   LONGITUDE: 6° 1' 7.14" W

You will have to be truly intrepid to get to this souterrain, but if you are fit and healthy and like a walk and scramble, this one could be for you.

Spirals

Spirals are found almost anywhere that our ancient ancestors lived and worshipped. The spiral seems to have had a special significance for prehistoric people and all sorts of explanations have been put forward to suggest why this might have been the case. Spirals can be found pecked into the stone of some Megalithic structures and at the entrance of some tombs (*see* Newgrange in the Impressive Sites section).

Alexander Thom (see Thom, Alexander) showed that considerable mathematical know-how was used in the creation of some of the spiral carvings, which are a geometric construct that is not easy to replicate. This is not true of all prehistoric spirals, some of which are obviously freehand constructs and intended to give an 'impression' rather than to be totally accurate.

Some people have suggested that the spiral was somehow designed to signify the behaviour of the Sun across the horizon throughout an entire year, or the Moon during a month. These theories are somewhat difficult to understand but do make sense. Spirals occur repeatedly in nature, such as in

Figure 26: A triple spiral carving at Newgrange

the case of a snail shell or the seeds in a sunflower, and our ancient ancestors cannot have failed to notice their presence. Spirals are by no means restricted to British prehistoric art and are to be found all over the world wherever people have made carvings into rock or undertaken art on cave walls or cliffs. It is a symbol that seems to be endemic to our species and it is impossible to say when it was first used in a pictographic sense. Be that as it may, the spiral is one of the commonest symbols from prehistory. Most spirals carved onto rocks in the British Isles are difficult if not impossible to see these days, mainly due to weathering, but the example at Newgrange is probably the best of all. Spirals can be single or double in nature.

Temple

The word temple can be slightly misleading when applied to prehistoric monuments. This is because temple implies a place where some sort of religious worship was taking place and although this is almost certain to have been the case at many British prehistoric sites, we cannot be absolutely sure of it. Therefore, although we might call Stonehenge, Avebury or any of the ancient stone circles 'temples', this might be an inappropriate description. As far as I am aware, although some sites across the British Isles are referred to as temples, there is no absolute proof that this was their intended function, which may well have been totally astronomical or social.

Thom, Alexander (1894–1985)

Alexander Thom was a Scot who came from farming stock but who grew to become an engineer. By the end of the Second World War he had gained the title of Professor of Engineering at Oxford University.

Thom was interested from childhood in both astronomy and history and had a particular fascination for stone circles and stone rows. As soon as his academic career allowed it, Alexander Thom began carefully surveying sites, both in Scotland and eventually right across Britain and down into Brittany.

Thom was able to prove that many of the sites, especially the Scottish ones, had been used to track the movements of the Moon and he contributed greatly to our understanding of the astronomy used by our ancient ancestors. A more contentious discovery was the fact that most, if not all, of the Megalithic sites had been laid out using a common unit of measurement. Thom called this the 'Megalithic Yard' and declared it to be 2.722ft (82.966cm) in length. He also claimed there was a Megalithic Rod, which was equal to 2.5 Megalithic Yards and a Megalithic Inch, of which there were 40 to the Megalithic Yard.

Some experts have dismissed Thom's findings on the grounds that no such accurate units could possibly have been maintained or passed on across such a huge area, and maybe over 2,000 years, without having deviated or changed. However, together with fellow writer and researcher Christopher Knight, I have been able to show how the Megalithic Yard was calibrated through astronomical observation and the use of a simple pendulum. In my opinion Alexander Thom deserves far better than he has received from a number of supposed experts who eulogize him in one way but vilify him in another.

Trackways

A trackway is merely a path that has been formed by the continued passage of people across a period of time. We tend to think that roads only came into existence in the British Isles with the arrival of the Romans but this is far from being the truth. People had to get about and they did so amidst a landscape that was fraught with danger and difficulty. Even by the Iron Age much of the British Isles was either heavily wooded or was covered by bogs and marshland; places where one could easily fall prey to wolves or sink without trace.

There is strong evidence, even from the most remote times, that a great deal of trading was going on across our islands. Commodities such as flint for tools and salt for human and animal consumption had to be taken from places where it could be readily found to areas where it could not. In addition there was trade in gold, amber, various sorts of ornamental stone and many other items. All of this meant people undertaking significant journeys and, over a period of time, the best way to get from A to B in any case would be established using local knowledge.

Ancient trackways do still exist, though it's amazing how often they were utilized later by the Romans and thence became some of the busiest roads we have today. The A1 is a good example, because for much of its route it follows a ridge and high ground, so although it is credited to the Romans and became the Great North Road, it is doubtless extremely ancient as a trackway.

Sometimes parts of ancient trackways are discovered because they pass or once passed through marshy ground and so were supplied with a causeway, generally made of wooden planks fastened to poles driven into the ground. Not all such tracks are still used and their discovery allows archaeologists a glimpse into the past, particularly since our ancient ancestors seem to have been fond of throwing votive offerings into marshes and streams.

Such sites are rarely open to the public and even when they are for short periods there isn't a great deal to see. However, you probably walk or drive along ancient trackways on any given day of your life. A diligent look at large-scale maps, which carry contours, shows how frequently roads and paths stick to ridges and high ground, and how responsive they are to field boundaries that sometimes don't exist any more. In this sense trackways and even modern roads have a great deal to tell us about the remote past.

Tumulus

Tumulus is the all-encompassing name for a burial mound. Although the term is still used, such sites are now split into their various types, such as barrows, passage graves etc.

Unspecified Structures, Odd Sites and Extensive Areas

The prehistoric people of the British Isles were certainly busy and across a vast period of time they were responsible for creating a wealth of structures, many of which can still be seen on the landscape. Most of what they have left us falls into one or other of the categories described in this section of the book but there are some that defy any direct comparison with others. I therefore decided on the heading Unspecified Structures, so that I could mention a number of sites in the second part of the book that did not belong in any other listing. All are well worth a visit and some are mightily impressive.

Where to find unspecified, 'odd' or just plain impressive structures and areas:

Dane's Dyke, near Bridlington, East Yorkshire, England

LATITUDE: 54° 8′ 24.08″ N   LONGITUDE: 0° 8′ 34.7″ W

Dane's Dyke is a massive earthwork. It must have taken countless thousands of hours to complete and yet it remains a mystery.

King Arthur's Round Table, near Penrith, Cumbria, England

LATITUDE: 54° 38′ 53.46″ N   LONGITUDE: 2° 44′ 43.81″ W

This strange saucer-shaped circle appears to be a very unusual henge and it once had at least two sizeable standing stones at the entrance. Nothing to do with King Arthur.

Isle of Haxey, Doncaster, South Yorkshire, England

LATITUDE: 53° 29′ 18.73″ N   LONGITUDE: 0° 50′ 10.75″ W

A strange, enigmatic area, filled with folklore and tradition, doubtless based on a prehistoric past. There is a celebration here every January known as the Haxey Hood, which I think is a hangover from a very remote and quite spooky period.

Glastonbury and **Glastonbury Tor**, Somerset, England

LATITUDE: 51° 8′ 38.48″ N   LONGITUDE: 2° 41′ 46.54″ W

Apart from the Tor (*see* Mounds) Glastonbury just oozes its ancient past. There are sacred wells here, as well as sites to please all visitors and a wealth of history that is unparalleled in Britain. The Tor is well worth a climb and you don't have to be a mountaineer, though it is very steep and you may have to take it slowly.

Kilmartin area, Lochgilphead, Argyll and Bute, Scotland
(*See* Impressive Sites section)

LATITUDE: 56° 07′ 58″ N   LONGITUDE: 5° 29′ 13″ W

I have given the longitude and latitude for Kilmartin itself. This is an extensive area, with more ancient remains than one could shake a stick at. A visitor could spend days here and never see the same thing twice. I strongly recommend this area for a holiday, but take your waterproofs.

Where to find unspecified, 'odd' or just plain impressive structures and areas (continued):

Salisbury Plain, Salisbury, Wiltshire, England

LATITUDE: 51° 10′ 43.87″ N   LONGITUDE: 1° 49′ 34.27″ W

I have given the longitude and latitude for Stonehenge. Probably the most famous prehistoric sacred area in the world, and certainly in the British Isles. As with Kilmartin, expect to be here for a long time if you want to see everything.

Silbury Hill, near Marlborough, Wiltshire, England
(*See* Impressive Sites section)

LATITUDE: 51° 24′ 56.79″ N   LONGITUDE: 1° 51′ 27.33″ W

Surely the most impressive man-made hill in the British Isles. You can't climb it these days but just to stand beneath it is mind-boggling.

Boyne Valley, Ireland

LATITUDE: 53° 41′ 40.69″ N   LONGITUDE: 6° 28′ 31.67″ W

Here I give the longitude and latitude for Newgrange but the Boyne Valley is filled with mounds, tombs, sacred enclosures and much more. I can't think of a better area to spend a few days (and the porter in the evenings is very good too!).

The Thornborough Henge Complex, Nr Ripon, North Yorkshire, England
(*See* Impressive Sites section)

LATITUDE: 54° 12′ 36.64″ N   LONGITUDE: 1° 33′ 46.68″ W

I have taken the liberty of mentioning Thornborough again because it is just so overwhelmingly impressive. Each structure of the three is so big it could swallow a large cathedral. You may have to climb a few fences and you will be astounded at just how ignored this site is but you are bound to be staggered by the proportions.

The Gop Cairn, near Prestatyn, Denbighshire, Wales

LATITUDE: 53° 18′ 34.56″ N   LONGITUDE: 3° 22′ 13.57″ W

This may well have been one of the most extensive prehistoric areas of note in what is now Wales. Sometimes, when you stand and look at a landscape you just get a 'feeling' about it. Not very scientific I know, but it's certainly true of the area around the Gop Cairn.

Vitrified Fort

Vitrified forts are at one and the same time absolutely intriguing and deeply mystifying. Imagine a hill top, protected by a stone wall that is sometimes many feet thick and up to 12ft (3.7 metres) high. Now ask yourself how, in the days before mortar of any sort was invented, it would be possible to lock all of the stones together, to make one solid whole? The answer is that the builders would have heated the stones so much that they fused together. Sounds unlikely? Well, that's what vitrified forts are and they exist in significant numbers in Scotland, with a few examples also in Ireland.

Exactly how such a procedure was possible has been discussed for generations. Clearly it would take extremely high temperatures to vitrify most rocks. It has been noted that in some cases small rocks of a type that would melt relatively easily were introduced into the ramparts of the forts, but high temperatures would still be required and the heat would have to be somehow 'directed' to the right place. In the case of some of the French examples of vitrified forts, high concentrations of natron have been found. Natron is a form of salt and this may have been used as a sort of 'flux' in order to get the process started.

Not all vitrified forts are totally vitrified. In many cases it tends to be the inner walls, with the larger, outer ramparts left untouched by fire. In other cases parts of the structure have been subjected to intense heat, whilst other sections have been left alone.

We know little about the people that created vitrified forts, except that they were probably a maritime culture and that the forts were constructed around 1000 BC or slightly earlier. What makes the whole situation even more puzzling is that rather than strengthening such defences, vitrifying would invariably make them weaker because it would cause the stones to crumble more readily. It is therefore likely that it wasn't the strategic benefits of melting rocks together that was of the utmost importance, but probably rather the 'look' of the finished product or the sense of 'power' inspired by the ability to perform such a feat. Another explanation is that the forts were ritually 'destroyed' by fire after having been captured by an enemy. This seems quite unlikely to me for a whole host of reasons, not least of which is the physical

Places to see vitrified forts:

Dunnideer, near Huntley, Aberdeenshire, Scotland

LATITUDE: 57° 20′ 33.75″ N   LONGITUDE: 2° 38′ 40.96″ W

How on earth did they get the stones hot enough to vitrify? It's a great puzzle.

Dun Deardail, near Fort William, Highland, Scotland

LATITUDE: 56° 47′ 4.92″ N   LONGITUDE: 5° 3′ 59.18″ W

This is an excursion for the summer, and even then you need to be a good walker, fit and well prepared if you want to see Dun Deardail.

Barry Hill, near, Alyth, Perth and Kinross, Scotland

LATITUDE: 56° 38′ 19.24″ N   LONGITUDE: 3° 12′ 12.14″ W

There are many legends surrounding this scenic site. Many are linked with King Arthur and, in this case, his queen, Guinevere.

effort necessary to collect enough wood and to supervise a burning that must have taken days.

Vitrified forts remain a great puzzle. There are over 50 examples in Scotland but only a handful in Ireland and none at all in England or Wales. There are also many vitrified forts elsewhere in Europe.

Wedge Tomb

This seems to be a peculiarly Irish type of tomb (though other examples may have different classifications elsewhere). As the name implies, this is a wedge-shaped mound that tapers along its length and is entered by a passage. There are often antechambers within the tomb, separated from the main burial area. These tombs are very evocative, they date back to between 2500 BC and 2000 BC. They are a form of gallery grave (*see* Gallery Grave).

Places to see wedge tombs:

Giant's Grave (Burren), Blacklion, Co. Cavan, Ireland

LATITUDE: 54° 15′ 26.52″ N   LONGITUDE: 7° 51′ 42.79″ W

There is no wonder this is called the Giant's Grave. The stones used are massive and it boggles the mind even to contemplate the task.

Caherphuca, near O'Briensbridge, Co. Clare, Ireland

LATITUDE: 52° 45′ 10.44″ N   LONGITUDE: 8° 32′ 31.62″ W

It is probable that the designation of a 'wedge tomb' would be lost on most of us, but County Clare is wonderful and the porter is especially good.

Carrowcrom, near Ballina, Co. Mayo, Ireland

LATITUDE: 54° 5′ 21.74″ N   LONGITUDE: 9° 2′ 49.05″ W

Not easy to find but there is plenty of this tomb that can still be seen.

Figure 27: A wedge tomb

PART II

Impressive Sites

The Background

For the last three to four decades I have made it my business every year to get to a few prehistoric sites I haven't seen before, as well as often visiting those that have already captured my imagination. As with most people, I have my own particular fascinations. Since I am especially interested in ancient astronomy I have spent a great deal of time looking at stone circles and stone rows. Apart from my own personal favourites, the sheer number and type of prehistoric monuments has always amazed me and I am so grateful to the many thousands of people who toiled away to create all the amazing structures that are dotted around every part of the landscape of our lovely islands.

What Is Prehistoric?

In a way the word 'prehistoric' is a little unfortunate because it is a 'catch-all' word and merely relates to anything that happened before written records were available to us. So, for example, a standing stone circle, a Scottish broch or a Neolithic passage grave are all prehistoric, but they are about as different in terms of form and function as a croft is from a city skyscraper. The intentions of those who built these structures were not the same and in many cases they would have been from different backgrounds and probably did not even speak the same language.

It has to be remembered that to the comparatively recent broch builders, those who created passage graves and long barrows appeared almost as ancient and as mythical as they seem to us today. This is surely why structures of vastly different ages often occupy adjacent sites. At Dorchester-on-Thames in Oxfordshire, England, for example, there was once a super-henge of the sort that can still be seen in North Yorkshire, but at the present time, as I write these words, significant numbers of Anglo-Saxon burials are being dug by archaeologists in the same area. Doubtless the Anglo-Saxons of the immediate post-Roman period looked at structures such as the super-henge and assumed that whoever had built it were either gods or had been in close communion with gods. As a result, they felt reverence for the site and chose the area to become a deeply reverential place for their own culture. They did not understand the motivation of the henge builders, and would have had little in common with them. They came from a culture that was probably dramatically different, but there was still a sort of instinctive understanding and an empathy that transcended the many centuries that divided them.

The Arrival of Christianity

It is often the case that the Christian Church chose to build its own places of worship on sites that were already ancient before Christianity even came about. The suggestion that the building of a church on a pagan site was a sensible expedient, in order to bring pagans to the Church, is surely only a part of the reason. By the time the present church was built at Rudston in East Yorkshire, the huge standing stone that gives the place its name was already so old that surely nobody in the district could have had the slightest clue why it had been put there. Whatever ceremonies took place around this giant stone immediately before the Christians arrived probably had nothing at all to do with the reason for the stone's presence; but someone had gone to the trouble of marking out this spot and logically it was somehow sacred to them, and successive generations simply built on something mysterious but obviously in some way 'holy'.

Less scientific observers have suggested that certain sites have been marked by stones, stone circles and even graves of one sort or another because they were already considered 'special' in some way. The emergence of underground streams has been one explanation – in other words a meeting of the world below and the world above. Doubtless this was sometimes the case, but it is certainly not always so. Really adventurous thinkers suggest that the Earth has 'channels' of energy, which are known by various names, and that it is where these channels, said to be similar to the meridians in the human body used in acupuncture, cross that people have felt a particular atmosphere and an affinity with the planet. As a result, they chose to place their most sacred structures in such locations.

I have to admit that I stand firmly on the fence in this regard. I well remember entering the crypt of an ancient church near Rosedale in my own county of Yorkshire. In a moment I was overwhelmed by a feeling of energy and an insistent power that I have sometimes encountered in some of our most magnificent cathedrals. I just knew for certain that the site of this crypt had been held in awe and reverence long before the church was even thought about. Don't ask me how I knew, and certainly don't ask me to prove the fact.

This is not science of course but we have to remember that although our Stone Age and Bronze Age ancestors were excellent engineers and good mathematicians, they didn't even know what science meant. To them the world was far less clear-cut than it seems to us with our modern way of thinking. They understood the patterns of stars above their heads and built many of their structures to either copy the patterns they saw, or to point to astronomical events that could be observed from such sites. But surely their motivation was more religious than scientific?

Even modern science cannot answer all our questions, no matter how advanced it considers itself to be. Where did we come from? Where will we go to when our life is over? How can I best live my life so that whatever forces rule the universe will take care of me? What can I do to better 'own' or 'control' my environment, or at least live in such a state of harmony with it that the crops will keep growing and the Sun will return north each spring?

Some of these questions appear archaic to us these days, but they are still being asked, all over our planet. The truth is that we are animated bits of the Earth and we are inextricably linked to it at every stage of our lives. Would it be so extraordinary if, for some reason we don't understand, some locations on the Earth were somehow relevant or special to us in a way we still cannot answer directly?

For me the sites mentioned below have a historical fascination, and most of them also have that 'something else' that I have been trying to track down for nearly four decades – but I don't expect I ever will. Nevertheless, to stand and look at the largest standing stone in the British Isles or to crawl into the shady depths of a 3,000-year-old burial chamber is probably enough.

ENGLAND

CONTENTS

Stonehenge

Stonehenge, Amesbury, Wiltshire

LATITUDE: 51° 10′ 43.87″ N   LONGITUDE: 1° 49′ 34.27″ W

Stonehenge is to be found in southern England on Salisbury Plain in Wiltshire. Salisbury Plain was clearly an extremely important ritual landscape for many centuries and a visit to Stonehenge also offers the opportunity to take in an impressive cross-section of prehistoric structures in a relatively small area.

Those who have not visited Stonehenge before, but who have been brought up on photographs or film of the structure, are often quite surprised when they actually view it for the first time. Set amidst such a wide and flat landscape, and especially viewed first from a distance, they often report that it is smaller than they expected. But once the edifice is approached on foot and seen close up, its impressive nature becomes immediately obvious.

The British Isles are filled with standing stones and stone circles but there is nothing quite like Stonehenge to be seen anywhere else. Here, the Megalithic art was brought to its zenith in a complex monument that spanned over 2,000 years and which was altered and refined on several occasions.

The Building of a Henge

Around 3100 BC people in the area decided to build a henge – a circular ditch and bank with two entrances, though even this was slightly different from henges that were being constructed in other parts of the British Isles at the same time. At Stonehenge the ditch is on the outside of the bank, as might be expected in a defensive structure, whereas true henges have their ditches on the inside of the bank. This henge is around 300 metres in circumference and at more or less the same time as it was constructed the Aubrey Holes came into existence. The Aubrey Holes comprise 56 chalk-filled pits, each about a metre across and arranged in a circle just inside the henge. It is thought unlikely that they ever contained wooden posts and their purpose has always been something of a mystery. It has been suggested that they were used as a sort of

Figure 28: Stonehenge is the only standing stone circle in the British Isles with cross stones above its uprights

calculator or prehistoric computer, in order to calculate some of the longer lunar cycles – and possibly eclipse cycles. If this is the case, coloured stones could have been placed in the pits and moved at regular and prescribed intervals. The theory is fascinating but remains in doubt in the minds of many experts. It is generally accepted that after the construction of the henge and the Aubrey Holes (incidentally named after John Aubrey, a 17th-century antiquarian, pseudo-historian and self-styled Druid), the site was abandoned for about a thousand years. What this broadly means is that no datable evidence has been found that covers the period, but that may not be surprising because few henges reveal all that much in the way of datable evidence. It is true that this could be because the site remained unused, but could equally be a reflection of the fact that it was only used for ritual purposes and perhaps only on a few occasions during the year.

Welsh Bluestones

Whether or not the site was truly abandoned for a millennium, around 2150 BC something dramatic took place at Stonehenge. Around 82 stones were brought to the henge and erected in an incomplete double circle – more like a giant horseshoe in a way. What makes this part of the Stonehenge story quite remarkable is where these stones – known as bluestones – actually came from. It is now generally accepted that they came from the Preseli Mountains in South Wales, a location 143 miles (230km) away to the west. Clearly disbelieving that stones, some of which weigh as much as 4 tonnes, could have been brought such a vast distance, people suggested for decades that the bluestones may have been brought to Salisbury Plain by glacial action in the remote past. This suggestion has now been cast into doubt and it does look as though each and every stone was hauled down from its mountain, carried on rafts along the south coast of Wales, before being brought by the River Avon and then the Frome, to be finally hauled overland to the site of Stonehenge.

Why on earth would anyone have gone to such tremendous trouble to obtain stone when there was plenty to be had on and not far from Salisbury Plain? It remains one of Stonehenge's most enigmatic mysteries. The bluestones are dwarfed by the later sarsen stones but their quarrying and transportation surely ranks as one of the wonders of the Megalithic period. It is known that they were brought to the site in a fairly rough state and then beaten into shape using stone mauls because chippings of the bluestones have been found on site.

At this time the entrance to the henge was widened and a couple of other stones were erected. These are known as 'heel stones'. Stonehenge would eventually be approached by a wide 'avenue' or ceremonial route and the first part of this was completed at the same time as the bluestones were erected.

Bigger and Bigger

About a century and a half later the site underwent another great transformation. Around 2100 BC huge stones were brought from the Marlborough Downs, about 25 miles away, and the Stonehenge we all know today began to take shape. The largest of the sarsen stones weighs around 50 tonnes, so

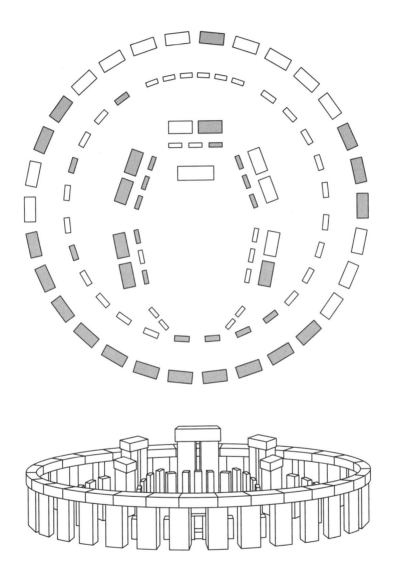

Figure 29: Stonehenge from the air (above), and reconstructed (below).
In the aerial view, grey stones mark those still present, and white stones show
where originals once stood.

although the journey they took to Stonehenge was significantly shorter than the one enjoyed by the bluestones, the feat was none the less impressive. It must have taken great ingenuity, not to mention a massive amount of muscle power, to drag such huge stones across an undulating landscape, though this pales into insignificance at the thought of not only standing some of them upright, but managing to balance other, equally massive stones, on top.

Once again the stones underwent a great deal of preparation both before they began their journey and again when on site. They had to be pounded into shape and this time they were carefully designed with pegs and sockets so that a continual run of stones could sit on top of the outer circle and also on top of the horseshoe of five so-called trilithons nearer the centre of the henge.

Finally, around 1500 BC, the position of the bluestones was altered. They were made into a circle, with another horseshoe within the trilithons, creating the monument which, allowing for wear and tear and the great passage of time, is what we see at the site today.

The Ultimate Purpose

So, what was the purpose of Stonehenge? Why was it revered and altered over such a long period of time, and why should prehistoric farmers, most of whom would be struggling to stay alive through at least some parts of the year, invest so much time and effort into something that offered them nothing concrete in return? It's a fair question, but one might just as well ask why the poor citizens of the small village of Southwell in Nottinghamshire should have taken it upon themselves to build one of the finest cathedrals in Britain during the Middle Ages? After all, most of those who built the great gothic masterpieces were living in squalid little dwellings and eking out the best existence they could under difficult circumstances. What on earth did they want with a massive and generally useless cathedral?

It is a fact that can be observed all over the world that human beings will do wonderful things and sacrifice almost anything for the sake of 'belief'. The same was surely just as true for the Bronze Age farmers of the British Isles as it was for the peasants of Egypt or those living in pre-Columbian America – societies that created massive and enduring pyramids. Undoubtedly then, at the back of those who carefully planned and executed the various stages of Stonehenge's development lay a need to placate and worship gods and goddesses. True, we don't know much about the deities, or what practices were expected to keep them happy, but the thought of Stonehenge without a deep and abiding belief in a religion of some sort is plainly ridiculous.

Is Stonehenge an Observatory?

There have been many commentators over the years who have suggested that Stonehenge is actually a working astronomical observatory, and that it was used exclusively for tracking the Sun, Moon, planets and stars on their journeys around the sky. Certainly there seems to have been a very definite fascination for the winter and summer solstice, as well as the spring and autumn equinoxes. I, for one, think it certain that this was the case. I have shown, together with my colleague Christopher Knight, that the henges, long before any stones were erected on the sites, were naked-eye observatories of tremendous power and potential, as well as being recreations of certain parts of the observable sky translated onto the ground. If the bare henges allowed 'experimentation' (because moveable wooden stakes could be used instead of permanent stones, in order to learn about the heavens) then the finished stone circles were all 'fixed' observatories, where the foresights and backsights of specific stones and markers on the horizon allowed known and repeatable events in the heavens to be tracked on a regular basis in that geographical location. (The presence of outlying stones at Stonehenge, such as the Sentinel stone bears this out.)

The idea that science exists as a distinct and quite separate subject, totally divorced from religion and superstition, is very new indeed. Apart from a brief flirtation with logic during the ancient Greek period, in the main a consideration of the natural universe as distinct from the will of the gods was not really considered until the age of the European Renaissance. So, throughout most of human history, science and religion went hand in hand. In other words, to fully understand the pattern of the changing seasons or to comprehend the complex interplay of planets and stars were merely ways of getting into the minds of the gods.

Figure 30: The so-called Sentinel, an outlying stone close to Stonehenge standing stone circle

Christianity was no different, and did not willingly relinquish its hold on a large section of humanity until it was forced to do so by the arrival of the age of reason. It is therefore surely preposterous to see Stonehenge or indeed any of the other henges, circles or tombs as being places of religion or places of observable science – they were obviously both!

Controlling the Population

Just as an example, working out when a solar eclipse is likely to take place is a complicated business. It was attempted in ancient times, sometimes with great success and for a very sensible reason. People have always been fascinated by the sight of the Sun being swallowed by some unseen monster. In addition to this fascination, and in the absence of knowing what was really taking place, they were probably also terrified by such events for most of our history as a species. After all, nobody expects a cloudless world to suddenly go pitch black in the middle of a bright and sunny day. This can only be the work of the gods! Anyone who can predict when such a horrifying display is likely to take place is clearly very special, and probably in direct communication with the deity – or at least that's how it would look to the ignorant majority. Knowledge is power. Put at its simplest, I say to a fairly primitive community with little mathematical or astronomical knowledge: 'The Sun is going to be swallowed tomorrow. I will make it happen because I know God well. But don't worry, because I will make sure that the Sun shines again.' Everyone in the community turns out and, sure enough, the sky goes as dark as night and then, after a few minutes, light floods again into the world. What a powerful person I am and this little demonstration should make sure that everyone does more or less exactly what I tell them to do for the foreseeable future.

I might decide to create a machine that will make future predictions of eclipses more certain and accurate. So, whilst the fear is still upon them, I convince my fellow prehistoric farmers to build the machine I design. Of course they don't know it's a machine – to them it's a sort of temple, a place where the gods and goddesses of nature are worshipped at certain parts of the year. The effort of creating the machine builds social cohesion, and it can take place in the winter, when there isn't much to be done on the farm and when physical effort keeps people warm and more cheerful. Everyone wins – but of course I win most of all because I get my eclipse calculator, making my future predictions more certain and further increasing my power in the community.

This is just a single example. By putting stones in the right place I can ensure that the rising Sun at the time of the shortest day of the year (the winter solstice) emerges from the horizon and climbs up the northern side of a stone, strategically placed for the purpose. I tell everyone that the rising Sun will go no further south than this – that the days will get no shorter and that thanks to my intervention and my relationship with the gods, the Sun will now start to move north along the horizon at dawn, bringing warmer days and fruitfulness to the land. This is only one of a thousand tricks I can accomplish once I learn the natural patterns of the sky and the seasons, and I have plenty of time to do so because I am now a specialist. I don't have to work long hours every day tilling land and planting crops. I am held in such reverence and awe that people for miles around are more than willing to cater for my every need, just so I can concentrate on being close to the gods. I have become a priest – the forerunner of every shaman and ultimately clergyman that has inhabited human societies.

So, how did I learn all of this in the first place? I inherited the knowledge from other priests who had spent generations at the henges, placing and replacing wooden poles around the bank tops, measuring angles and defining planetary cycles, until I was confident enough to make my observatory into something much more durable than wooden poles – I could build it in stone.

This is surely the story of Stonehenge. As knowledge grew, power also grew amongst the priestly class. Cultures came and went, influencing local populations and slowly changing belief patterns, but the priests remained. The more they understood, the greater the power they had over society and the more they could push for ever more grandiose monuments, for both observation and worship. It's all a little simplistic, but I'm sure you get the picture. I don't really see how the fantastic evolution of a site such as Stonehenge can be interpreted in any other way. The population of the British Isles at the time of the Megalithic era was incredibly small. Farmers might have some time on their hands in winter, but they could surely find better things to do with it than to risk injury or death dragging massive stones around the landscape.

Rites of Passage

On the other hand, what of rites of passage? Might not these almost superhuman feats of strength and endurance have been a very real part of the culture that created the henges and stone circles? Perhaps a boy could not truly become a man until he had taken part in the epic journey to Wales to collect a bluestone or until he had helped to haul a massive sarsen stone upright.

In other words there is not one but probably dozens of reasons why the Megalithic revolution took place, but we will find all of them within the realms of an acquisition of knowledge, a search for power, and the desire to be part of a cohesive culture – if only because in an uncertain world that is a much more comfortable objective.

Unfortunately, except on rare occasions, it is no longer possible to stand amidst the great stones of Stonehenge, as I was privileged to do as a child. The great numbers of people who come every year to see this masterpiece are now kept at a safe distance by a low, and it has to be said, generally not too intrusive fence. But it is a shame nevertheless because Stonehenge is part of our heritage and for some, possibly deluded souls, to be kept away from the stones is the same as being denied access to a great church or cathedral.

Such was not the case for visitors to Stonehenge until fairly recent times, though it seems to have attracted interest and awe in equal proportions for a long time. Early antiquarians thought it might be Roman, or even Greek, and it was often thought to be the remnants of a temple of Apollo, which, bearing in mind Apollo was a solar deity, may be quite an accurate description. The name of Stonehenge means 'hanging stones', an allusion to the way the trilithons sit atop the sarsen uprights. Some of these have been put back where they belong, having toppled over the centuries, though there are still examples on the ground that show the mortise-and-tenon joints used to make sure the hanging stones stayed in place. In fact woodworking techniques seem to have been used extensively by the Megalithic builders, demonstrating that they had already had plenty of experience in handling timber.

A Tremendous Achievement

It has been estimated that as much as 30 million man-hours of labour went into the various stages of Stonehenge. To me this somehow seems quite excessive but of course it was expended across an extremely long period of time and in many different stages.

Because various burials and cremations have been found within the confines of the structure, especially from the period around 3000 BC, it has been suggested that the site should be defined as an enclosed cremation cemetery, but to my way of thinking this is like declassifying the major cathedrals from being churches and redefining them as charnel houses. After all, many worthy people have been buried in churches and cathedrals, but this is not the primary function of the buildings. It might be done as a mark of respect, for example the lords of a manor, or in the case of the great cathedrals, a statesman or even a poet, and the same is probably true in the case of Stonehenge. Permanent priests, planners or even chieftains may have had their cremated remains interned within Stonehenge but that does not make the place some sort of ornate cemetery.

It has always been a great fascination to me to try and work out exactly how stones in general, but especially those as large as the examples to be found at Stonehenge, were quarried, shaped and brought to a particular site; though in the case of the sarsen stones at Stonehenge, a further complication arises when we consider how the stones were lifted into a vertical position. Even more remarkable is the way the capstones were lifted into place, high above the ground.

A possible explanation of how some stones were prised from a naturally occurring rock face is that a mixture of brute force and ingenuity was used. Natural faults were found in the rock and these were exploited by the alternate use of heat and cold. Fires were built along the faults and kept burning until the rock was hot. At this point the burning brands were swept aside and cold water was poured onto the fault. The sudden change in temperature, with attendant contraction, would eventually have caused the rock to fracture. Large pieces could then be prised out with poles. The process is tried and tested but not entirely reliable and certainly time-consuming.

Many rocks used in stone circles, and particularly for large standing stones, have clearly been shaped, since it is very unlikely a useable stone would be achieved by the hot-and-cold method of quarrying. It seems evident that stones were sculpted using 'mauls', which are simply other large stones, but ones light enough in weight for people to lift. These were repeatedly pounded against the would-be standing stone until, after very much effort, it began to assume the desired shape. Again this would have been a long and laborious process and in the case of a large project a great number of people would have been involved.

It has been suggested that the sarsen stones used at Stonehenge were probably found as individual boulders, strewn around the landscape. If this was the case they would have needed a great deal of pounding into shape because they have clearly been worked a great deal. This may have taken place wherever the boulders were found, and before they were moved to the site. It is known that the smaller bluestones were worked on site, because significant numbers of bluestone shards have been found buried within the circle, but presumably such large stones as the sarsens would have been easier to handle if they were already a regular shape.

A Winter's Tale?

So, how were these huge stones carried across up to 25 miles (40km) of admittedly fairly flat but still undulating terrain? It is now generally accepted that they were placed on stout wooden sledges and hauled along using brute force. The land in front of the stones would have had to be cleared of major vegetation and the presence of streams, outcrops and wooded areas would have significantly added to the problem.

Many years ago, when I was still a teenager, I came across a remarkable, though sometimes contentious archaeologist by the name of Thomas Charles Lethbridge, who was also an explorer and a parapsychologist. About the slightly whacky side of T C Lethbridge I will remain silent, but despite the fact that he infuriated orthodox archaeologists, he did have some ideas that seem to me to be well worth exploring. Amongst these is Lethbridge's theory that the moving and erection of many stone circles and standing stones took place in winter and that the main agent used to facilitate an easy passage for the stones was snow.

First of all we have to remember that the men and women who erected structures such as Stonehenge were farmers. Their first duty, to themselves and their communities, was to grow sufficient crops and to rear enough animals to keep everyone fed. Outside of this there would be plenty of jobs to do around the farmstead but during the coldest days of winter there would probably not have been a great deal to do. So, as I have indicated elsewhere in this book, it is in any case most likely that communal civil-engineering jobs such as the creation of stone circles would have taken place in winter.

As is the case today, some winters in the late Stone Age and Bronze Age would have been more severe than others but there is little reason to suggest that the climate then was much warmer than it is today – even though some people suggest this is the case. At times it would have snowed heavily, and this, according to Lethbridge, was the period chosen to move and erect stones. Snow could be packed down and used as a track upon which to move the sledges containing the stones. Small undulations in the landscape could have been evened out and streams might well have been frozen. In reality hard-packed snow would have made an excellent track upon which to haul the sarsen stones to Stonehenge. True, it would still have been extremely difficult but it *was* done somehow, and this seems to be a likely explanation.

Building the Trilithons

Another puzzle regarding the sarsen stones is trying to work out how they were hoisted upright, and an even greater problem is how the capstones were put in place. Many suggestions have been put forward. Undoubtedly the large stones, once prepared, would have been slid into place and a substantial hole would have been dug at one end (where the base of the stone was intended to be). The other end of the stone would then have been gradually prised up and packed with timber until it quite naturally fell into the hole. It could then be hauled into a fully upright position using ropes and wedges.

It has been suggested that the capstones could have been brought up to the level of the uprights by using an ever-increasing platform. Each end of the capstone would be levered up and timbers placed under it. The construction would gradually have got higher and higher until the capstone could be levered off the platform and onto the uprights. It is very unlikely that an earthen bank would have been employed for this purpose, because such large structures of earth would undoubtedly have left some trace of their original presence. But why bother going to the trouble of chopping down what must have amounted to many hundreds of trees when the same job could have been achieved using hard-packed snow? Little by little the capstone could have been levered up at each side and propped in position, whilst snow was used to fill the gap, before the procedure was repeated at the other side until the capstone stood level again. True, it would have taken a long time and it could only have been achieved during the depths of winter but snow is very cheap and is easy to move. It has the added advantage of conveniently disappearing again once summer comes.

I have absolutely no idea whether this is the way Stonehenge and maybe many other stone circles were built. One might ask the question 'Would the snow last long enough for a capstone to be lifted into place?' The only evidence I have to address this perfectly rational question is to think back to a particularly snowy winter during my childhood. Together with a number of friends I took part in the creation of the largest igloo I have ever seen. It was made not with blocks of snow, as is the case in the Arctic Circle, but with innumerable snowballs, packed tight together and with all the gaps filled in with more snow.

Long after the weather had improved and the spring flowers were painting the meadows, a large remnant of our igloo remained on the grass where we built it and the last trace did not disappear until well past the middle of May.

No doubt everyone involved not only worked extremely hard but also had fun. Everyone loves snowball fights and I see no reason why our ancient ancestors should have been any different. The exercise would have kept them warm and cheerful, and the cohesion of a society would be improved by such communal activity. Since there was nothing else that could be done towards subsistence at this time of year, one might as well take part in a grandiose scheme that would still be wowing people several thousand years later.

Reconstruction

Much smaller stone circles would not have been such a problem as the giants of Stonehenge, and in fact moving even relatively large stones is not as difficult as might at first seem to be the case. I well remember designing and helping to build a stone circle about one-tenth the size of Stonehenge, using a collection of stones that had once been either gateposts or marker stones of one sort or another. True, we did not have to quarry the stones and they were brought to the site on a flatbed truck, but we still had to move them into place – a job for which we left ourselves three days.

There were upwards of 12 stones to move and after having marked out their eventual positions we dug through the turf and then created holes for sockets. There were only four of us present, two men and two women.

We moved the stones partly by brute force or in many cases standing them on end and 'rocking'-'walking' them along slowly but surely to their intended positions.

The whole job was finished by just after lunch on the first day and the circle, now well over a decade old, looks as if it has been there forever. I mention this exercise not as a means of belittling our ancient ancestors, who were superb engineers and strong and vigorous people, but merely to demonstrate that moving large stones, if approached properly, is not quite as difficult as it might at first seem. Even a project such as Stonehenge probably did not require hundreds of people at any point in time. Doubtless there were occasions when a great deal of manpower was required but the employment of strategy and know-how can often be worth a great number of people who are all working against each other.

Nevertheless I am stunned when I look at the finished project. Doubtless any stage of Stonehenge took a long time to complete and in the case of the sarsens maybe only one or two stones were brought to the site during each winter. It could have taken several generations before the capstones were all in place and it is quite possible that relatively few family groups or villages, assisted by others on occasion, did most of the work. The fact is that we really don't know, though with a population for the whole of the British Isles that was incredibly small compared with today, brain would have been just as important as brawn when it came to completing such a gargantuan task.

Myths and Legends

As befits a place of such antiquity there are many myths and legends associated with Stonehenge. One Arthurian tale claims that the bluestones came originally from Africa (which they patently did not) and that they were then brought to Ireland and only later to their present site. People also used to believe that if water was washed over the stones, and then used to bathe parts of the body, it could cure all manner of ills. Bits of the stones have been chiselled off for centuries and carted off heaven knows where (which is one of the reasons why people are generally kept outside the circle these days).

On a couple of occasions each year Druids and other New Age types are allowed to enter the circle. Midwinter and midsummer attract great crowds for ceremonies led by modern Druids. As I explained in the A–Z section, these new Druids have little to do with their ancient counterparts and nothing whatsoever to do with the builders of Stonehenge. For all their white cloaks and incantations they know no more about the true history or original functions of Stonehenge than you or I do. All the same, they add colour to the site, do no damage, and are genuinely concerned about its preservation.

If you take my advice you will choose to visit Stonehenge on a quiet weekday, maybe even in the middle of winter. That way, although having to wrap up warmly, you will be less troubled by the constant flow of tourists, all of whom have their own reasons for being there but few of whom are particularly interested to know the details of this fabulous human creation.

There are other works of prehistoric genius and strength that far surpass Stonehenge in terms of planning and building but none that are identical. The use of lintels was common in dolmens and is seen as 'T' stones in some of the Mediterranean islands but there is no other Megalithic standing stone circle in the British Isles that is half so impressive in a technical sense than Stonehenge (even though many are more beautiful). Salisbury Plain does have its own natural grandeur but Stonehenge cannot compare with the mountain circles, or those overlooking the sea and magnificent lochs, in Scotland, Ireland or Wales. All the same, you probably cannot call yourself a true Megalithic or prehistory buff until you have stood and marvelled at over 2,000 years of planning, effort and pure ingenuity.

For my money, Avebury, just 17 miles (27km) to the north is grander, so try to take both in during the same visit.

Avebury

Avebury, near Marlborough, Wiltshire

LATITUDE: 51° 25' 43.04" N   LONGITUDE: 1° 51' 14.66" W

Avebury is my favourite stone circle in the south of England, partly because of its beauty but mostly because of its scale. John Aubrey (*see* Stonehenge) once said that if Stonehenge could be said to represent a parish church, Avebury was the greatest of cathedrals. Avebury isn't simply large, it is massive in scale. True, it doesn't have the trilithons and lintels of Stonehenge but some of its stones are incredibly large and heavy and in terms of its geometric planning it far surpasses its southern neighbour.

The henge within which the stones of Avebury were erected is not simply large, it is colossal. It is not strictly circular and Alexander Thom demonstrated the method used to create it using poles and ropes. He maintained that it was constructed around two foci and that it was never intended to be a perfect circle. At its widest the henge at Avebury is around 460 yards (420 metres) in diameter, making it many times bigger than all henges in the British Isles (except the super-henges in Yorkshire and Oxfordshire which, for all their massive dimensions, are still not as large as Avebury).

A Massive Ditch

When it was first dug, the ditch at Avebury was 36ft (11 metres) deep and a probable 69ft (21 metres) wide, though, as with other henges, it was never meant to be a defensive structure since the ditch lies within the banks, which would make it hopeless for defensive purposes. It can only be described as 'ritual' in intention and it was a feat of engineering that beggars belief, especially since it was dug out of natural chalk using nothing more than deer antlers for picks.

The spoil was most probably removed from the site in baskets of the sort we know to have been used in the construction of the nearby Silbury Hill, and I suppose it isn't out of the question that much of the material removed from the huge ditches of Avebury is presently to be found incorporated into Silbury Hill. It would have made great sense to use this material, rather than spreading it across the landscape. Even the contemplation of removing all this earth and chalk is so daunting it is hard to imagine how anyone in that remote period could have planned such a task, let alone carried it out. However, this presupposes that the builders of Avebury were somehow inferior to us in terms of brain power, which they most certainly were not. Their technological achievements may not have been so great as ours are but the evidence shows they could and did get things done.

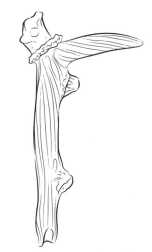

Figure 31: A red deer antler of the type used to dig the extensive ditches around Avebury

Such a monumental amount of chalk and earth had to be shifted to make the henge at Avebury that it must have taken years, if not generations, to complete. It is staggering that such a plan was brought to fruition and that the place was then peopled by huge stones, one of which weighs an estimated 100 tonnes.

The stones at Avebury are all relatively local and few, if any of them, were substantially altered before they were dragged into place and erected. Rather, it seems that the planners chose the stones very carefully for grace and form, and probably to achieve objectives we can now only guess at.

Avebury stands on a slight chalk ridge, a little higher than the surrounding countryside and it is part of a significant ritual landscape that may tie it in with Stonehenge, and which certainly associates it with nearby Silbury Hill and West Kennet Long Barrow. Some disturbance of the land prior to the building of the monument (as early as 3300 BC) shows post holes to have existed, indicating that either there was a timber ritual site already in place or that people had been surveying the site for its astronomical possibilities for some time. In the case of Avebury, both the henge and the stones were completed at more or less the same period and certainly within a few hundred years of each other.

Figure 32: Avebury ring now encompasses part of the village of Avebury within its massive area

The Circles

Within the henge the remnants of the once 99 massive sentinels that stood around its periphery are a reminder of the physical effort that went into building Avebury. And as if it wasn't enough to create such a massive henge and outer circle, the builders then went on to create two separate stone circles within it. These were both roughly the same size, the southernmost one having a diameter of 118 yards (108 metres) and its northernmost partner being 107 yards (98 metres) in diameter. (Actually, some experts think that the smaller circles came first.) Both of these inner circles have suffered from the ravages of time. This is partly because within the henge of Avebury lies the village that bears the same name. Not only was stone taken for use in building but after the 14th century the Church decided that such structures must be the work of the Devil and therefore the stones should be toppled, buried, or if possible destroyed altogether. As a result the inner circles contain few stones now and the village has ensured that the southern one is all but gone.

The West Kennet Avenue

Also associated with Avebury is an avenue of stones, the West Kennet Avenue, that begins at the southern entrance of Avebury. It was 27 yards (25 metres) wide, flanked by standing stones, and it was originally 1.6 miles (2.5km) in length. The West Kennet Avenue ran from Avebury to another structure known as the Sanctuary. Probably 100 pairs of standing stones flanked the Avenue, which, according to the most recent dating of finds associated with it, was completed around 2200 BC. The Sanctuary is a rather puzzling site. It once contained six rings of timbers and may have been a large building with a turf roof. Its association with Avebury via the Avenue shows it to have been part of the same ritual landscape, and no doubt processions of one sort or another took place between the two sites. There are signs of domestic habitation at the Sanctuary because animal bones and pottery have been found there, which is rarely the case inside henges. The Sanctuary was altered around 2100 BC, when two stone circles were created at the site. Alas for the visitor, the stones at the Sanctuary were destroyed or used elsewhere in 1723, though concrete markers show where many of the stones originally stood. In any case, the site was never of the same scale as that of Avebury.

Extending from the western entrance of Avebury is what remains of another avenue, this one known as the Beckhampton Avenue. This once led to the Longstones of Beckhampton and, before its stones were broken up and removed, it would have looked very much like the West Kennet Avenue. It has been conjectured that the two avenues together would have had the appearance of a giant snake, with its head at West Kennet, its tail at Longstones, and with Avebury in the centre of its sinuous body. I remain open-minded about this but since any winding path on the landscape could be said to resemble a snake, not many experts are all that enthusiastic about the possibility.

Avebury's Revenge

Such destruction fell upon this magnificent site in the 18th century that it is almost poetic justice that the crushed body of a man was found under one of the fallen stones in the 1930s. This giant of a rock is now called the Barber Stone because the unfortunate individual found beneath it was carrying on his person a lancet and a pair of scissors, the tools of a barber surgeon of the 18th century. It seems that, no doubt together with other villagers, he was trying to topple the stone when it fell on him. Whether out of superstition or simply because the stone was too large to move, his body was left where it lay. This is not the only instance of a megalith that 'fought back' because similar discoveries have been made in Scotland.

In the A–Z section of the book, under Sexual Stones and elsewhere, I mentioned the theory that alternate tall stones and squat, diamond- or lozenge-shaped stones in circles, are often said to represent the male and female genders. Whether or not this is the case, such an arrangement is definitely to be seen at Avebury. With the exception of some of the giant standing stones, such as Rudston and the Devil's Arrows, the sheer bulk of the stones lining the henge at Avebury makes them amongst the largest ever to be hauled about and erected during the Megalithic period.

Both Avebury and Stonehenge are linked together as a World Heritage Site and although this is gratifying, because it means they will be looked after well into the future, it is something of a pity that other, even more extensive, sites elsewhere in the British Isles do not get the same treatment. Avebury is supervised by the National Trust but since the henge lies within an established and living community it has been impossible for the authorities to rope off the site, in order to either charge people to visit or make sure nobody touches the stones. This means you can go there at any time. However, to compensate, there is a museum and gallery, together with a shop and the restaurant at which the National Trust will be more than happy to divest you of your hard-earned cash.

Early Visitors

I am willing to bet that if you have not been to Avebury before you will be singularly impressed by its scale and its timeless atmosphere. Through the eye of the imagination it is possible to see the site as it must have once looked, with its sinuous avenues leading off into the distance and with the bulk of Silbury Hill close by. In its own way this may once have been as important as Canterbury Cathedral would one day become and it is likely that people from all over our islands came to view it during its finest phase. People travelled about much more in prehistoric times than we have often given them credit for, and with DNA evidence now giving us so many answers, we are starting to realize that a good percentage of the population moved about the landscape readily. Avebury could have been a place of pilgrimage and it would certainly have been impressive – even before the National Trust came along to make sure it keeps astounding people well into the future.

No photograph or drawing can offer a true impression of just how large some of the stones at Avebury actually are. It is only when one stands close to some of them that the real effort involved in moving them into place becomes obvious. Even with a great deal of manpower the effort seems staggering. For example, countless ropes would have been needed and all of these would have had to be made by hand, probably across many months or years. The scale of the job is breathtaking.

We have no comprehension of the sort of ceremonies that may have taken place at Avebury, though it stands to reason that such a massive effort to create such a site means it must have been of the greatest importance to people in the vicinity, and probably from across Britain as a whole.

It used to be thought that our Stone Age ancestors were brutish, ignorant savages, with little intelligence. Anyone who spends even a short time within the stones of Avebury will quickly realize that it took real intelligence and perseverance to create such a massive structure. The level of organization necessary was quite definitely equal to that involved in major civic undertakings today.

Silbury Hill

Silbury Hill, near Marlborough, Wiltshire

LATITUDE: 51° 24' 56.79" N   LONGITUDE: 1° 51' 27.33" W

Close to Avebury and easily seen from the henge is the extraordinary bulk of Silbury Hill. In my estimation Silbury Hill doesn't get the press it deserves. For starters it is the largest man-made hill in Europe and the only example on such a grandiose scale in the British Isles. It is deeply shrouded in mystery and probably represents one of the single most time-consuming projects ever to be completed in a relatively short place of time during prehistory anywhere in our islands.

As seen from the landscape today Silbury is a large, conical hill. It is 44 yards (40 metres) high and its base covers around 5 acres (2 hectares). These days the top of the mound is flat, though it is suggested by archaeologists that this was not always the case. It is estimated that the rounded top of the mound may have been flattened off comparatively recently, possibly for defensive purposes. Until quite recently the age of Silbury Hill lay within the realms of conjecture. However, in 2002 during remedial work, a red deer antler was found in situ. This had once been used as a pick to move the chalk necessary to create the hill. A reliable carbon dating showed that the second phase of the hill, during which the antler had been used, took place around 2500 BC.

More than a Pile of Earth

Silbury Hill is far from being a simple mound of earth. On the contrary, it was well planned, was built in two (or perhaps three) separate stages, and it may once have been surrounded by a very impressive water-filled ditch. When work started on the project, Silbury represented a small and fairly insignificant natural hill. For the first stage of the building a gravel core was created, within a kerb of stakes and large stones. Onto this were piled turfs, followed by basket after basket of loose chalk rubble and earth that had been dug from the surrounding area. Most of the early material came from a ditch that may have

Figure 33: Silbury Hill

formed a water-filled moat, but this was later filled in again when it was decided to make the hill even higher.

At this time, not only all the material necessary to enlarge the hill was required, but also a significant amount to backfill the ditch. This leads us to an interesting point. It is estimated that, in total, the creation of Silbury Hill consumed 18 million man- (or woman-) hours of labour. Bearing in mind that the population of the British Isles at this period was extremely small, we have to find ways to justify the amount of effort necessary, for what were essentially subsistence farmers, to contemplate such an undertaking. Did the people concerned willingly give their spare time for months, years or more than a generation, or were they somehow coerced into the project? Of course there is no way of knowing, though ideas do change. It used to be thought that thousands of slaves had been used to build the pyramids of Egypt but we now know that this was not the case and that people from all over Egypt willingly co-operated in such projects at times of year when their farming allowed them to do so. To them it was a matter of religion and pride to participate in something so crucially important and it is probable that the same was true for the people of what is now southern England when Silbury Hill and the other local monuments were planned and constructed.

Modern Excavations

All sorts of tunnels have been driven into Silbury Hill across the last 200 years. Doubtless the earliest searchers were looking for what would surely be a magnificent tomb if the hill was merely a giant burial mound, though they didn't understand that the burial practices at such a remote time were somewhat different. In any case, no such interment has ever been found. It seems that the hill is exactly what it appears to be – a very carefully constructed mound of stone and earth, the function of which was not funerary but rather ceremonial in some way. So cleverly did these prehistoric engineers plan the final hill that it is estimated that the centre of the top of the mound is less than 3ft (1 metre) away from the centre of the original foundation at the bottom. The mound was originally built in steps – it only weathered into its conical shape over a vast period of time. Even more significant is the fact that, because it was made primarily from chalk, it would have glistened in the Sun when it was first built and would have been seen from many miles away.

Evidence of purpose for structures from such a remote period often relies on frequency. There are, for example, very many long barrows and round barrows (albeit from a different period to the creation of Silbury Hill). Because so many have been excavated and so much material has come to light, it has been possible for us to reach some fairly definite conclusions about how the barrows were made, and even more importantly – why. In the case of Silbury Hill we have only this one example. Silbury is absolutely unique – a tour de force of prehistoric effort for which there is no apparent explanation that would make sense to us. In a worldwide sense it is far less unique. Building earth pyramids and artificial hills has been popular for our species across much of the planet's surface and since time out of mind. If something such as Silbury Hill had been found in Central America, North America, in Asia or a host of other locations, it would hardly have raised an eyebrow. There are, after

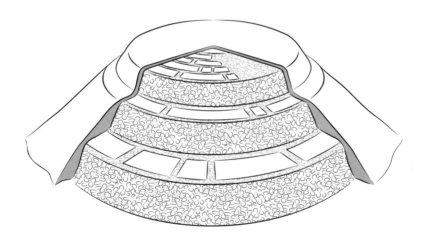

Figure 34: Silbury Hill is thought to have been originally built as a spiral of flat banks

all, artificial mounds in various parts of the world that make Silbury Hill look like a pimple in comparison. But for us, here in the British Isles, it is a one-off and certainly not part of any evolutionary tendency that can be seen elsewhere.

Making a Mountain

This makes Silbury Hill all the more compelling. Of course in islands such as ours we are used to seeing hills, and archaeologists are also used to finding that our ancient ancestors were drawn to natural mounds, unusual hills and mountains, for a host of different reasons. What we are not used to is when, in a place replete with natural mounds, people should take the decision to create one of their own from scratch. Silbury remains an enigma. It is a curiosity and a substantial work of art – as well as a gift to us from our remote ancestors. It might be best in future to stop trying to destroy it by tunnelling through its bulk but rather to enjoy it and to scratch our heads in wonder.

Just as it was possible for me to walk amongst the uprights and touch the stones at Stonehenge when I was a child, I also had the privilege of climbing Silbury Hill – a joy you will not be allowed to experience these days. Maybe that is as it should be but it seems a pity all the same. The view from the top is spectacular and may have been part of the reason Silbury Hill was built in the first place.

Castlerigg Stone Circle

Castlerigg, near Keswick, Cumbria

LATITUDE: 54° 36′ 11.78″ N   LONGITUDE: 3° 5′ 46.08″ W

Set high within a landscape of towering hills and a location that is heart-achingly beautiful at any time of year, Castlerigg is probably my personal favourite amongst the English stone circles. It is located in Cumbria, within the area of England known as the Lake District and is not too far from Keswick (where you can get an excellent lunch or tea).

It is a mark of respect to the remoteness of this particular circle that it has remained so intact across such a vast period of time. Local superstition, together with a preponderance of building stone all around these rocky slopes, mean that Castlerigg has been left more or less totally unmolested – except by the weather, which can be ferocious in these parts.

A Flattened Circle

Presently there are 38 stones to be seen, all unworked and local, and of varying sizes; though originally there were probably nearer to 41 stones comprising the circle. Actually, the term 'circle' is not absolutely appropriate in this case because Castlerigg is one of those mystifying circles that has a flattened side. Some people think this reflects the inability of its planners to create a true circle, but for my money this is a preposterous suggestion. The people who say such things have clearly not created a large circle for themselves, which by way of a number of different techniques is really quite simple. People who, as Alexander Thom shows, were capable of dabbling in Euclidian geometry would have had no trouble at all creating the most perfect of circles, which they did quite regularly in other places.

A more likely explanation is that the planners of Castlerigg, and other flattened or egg-shaped rings, went to great trouble to make certain that the finished result *was not* a true circle. Why would they have done this? One possible answer is that they were trying to 'square' the circle. These early

149

Figure 35: Castlerigg in Cumbria – undoubtedly one of the most beautiful of all Britain's standing stone circles

engineers and mathematicians must have been very aware that the perimeter of a circle is 'three and a bit' times the length of its diameter. Perhaps this annoyed them to such an extent that they decided to create some of their circles in such a way that the perimeter was a true '3' times the diameter. This is certainly close to being the case at Castlerigg, though of course in the absence of a true circle, definite knowledge of the diameter is a complicated thing!

Christopher Knight and I have shown just how interested prehistoric site planners were in the relationship between the diameter and circumference of circles. From the very early henge builders onwards they appear to have been aware that although a true circle cannot be squared, it can be made to *apparently* fall in line with logic. For example, any circle that has a diameter of 233 units must have a circumference of almost exactly 732 of the same units. (Actually it's 731.99.) This might not appear to be all that obvious or significant but they used this rule of thumb time and again. For example, it is reflected in the henge that underpins Stonehenge and in all the super-henges of North Yorkshire.

However the engineers that planned and built Castlerigg decided to deal

with the incongruity of pi, they definitely did choose one of the most spectacular sites possible on which to place their circle, which as far as anyone can tell
was completed around 3200 BC, though dating has been difficult due to a lack
of datable artefacts from the site.

Like many of its Scottish counterparts, Castlerigg is quite remote. Doubtless
the early farmers lived in the locality and it would have been them, or perhaps
a peripatetic priesthood, that decided to gather the stones for the ring and
place them in this most picturesque of settings. It's so wonderful at Castlerigg,
especially on a fine day, that the casual visitor might assume the circle was
placed here simply so that those utilizing it, in whatever way they did, could
also appreciate the ever changing view. In fact this is almost certainly not the
case and it is much more likely that the landscape played a part in the site
chosen for Castlerigg for reasons that had nothing to do with natural charm.

When one stands at the centre of Castlerigg it can be seen that the
landscape all around, and especially the horizon, is replete with natural
markers that are bound to remain the same throughout hundreds or
thousands of years. These can be clefts in hills, hill summits, natural crags or a
host of other features that may have been 'incorporated' into the working
matrix of the circle.

Using Foresight

Alexander Thom suggested, and it seems to be eminently reasonable to think
he is correct, that if one wishes to track stars, planets, the Sun or Moon along
the horizon, a whole series of foresights and backsights will be necessary (*see*
Foresights and Backsights in A–Z section). The backsight can either be placed
in the landscape artificially, or it might be possible to use what nature has
already provided on the horizon as an 'aide-memoir' for continued observation. If, for example, when seen from the centre of the circle the Sun at the
winter solstice always rises through a particular cleft in a hill, one can always
know that when the Sun *does* rise through that cleft as seen from the same spot,
it *must be* the time of the winter solstice. In other words it is a way to
understand the true length of the year and to plan sowing times and other
farm tasks accordingly.

This is a relatively simple example. We now know that our ancient ancestors were tracking the Sun and Moon, as well as gaining a knowledge of planetary movement, and that they could achieve a tremendous amount with naked-eye observation, just as long as the rules always remained the same. So, with stones for foresights and natural marks on the landscape for backsights, they could, after many generations of observation, gain a tremendously good knowledge of the workings of the sky and therefore establish much about the day and year. All of this may have been studied in a religious or ritual context but the result would have been the same – knowledge.

This, I am certain, was part of the reason for building circles such as Castlerigg where we find them today. We are also dealing with a period during which light pollution was as good as nonexistent, and even now the sky when seen from Castlerigg is stunning, with the stars seeming to be so close it appears to be perfectly possible to reach out and grab some.

The Cove

Like many stone circles in the British Isles, Castlerigg has not been extensively excavated. Even if it was there is little likelihood that we would learn a great deal more. Just inside the circle, at the eastern end, there is a group of 10 stones forming a rectangle known as the 'cove', the purpose of which is completely unknown. It is amazing just how little archaeology is found within stone circles, though this offers its own clues. People certainly did not live or apparently even eat inside the circles, which is a good indication that they were 'special' and 'apart' from everyday life. There is a slight exception in the case of Castlerigg in that quantities of charcoal were found buried within the circle.

As befits such a mysterious place, there are local legends associating Castlerigg with strange lights that are often seen in the locality. These have been fairly reliably reported for a hundred years or more and they may even be related to the local rock strata and general geology of such a rugged spot. Perhaps it isn't entirely out of the question to suggest that these strange floating lights might have inspired the Megalithic people to put their calendar/observatory/temple/meeting place, in this lovely, remote spot.

Thornborough Henges

Thornborough Henges, near Ripon, North Yorkshire

LATITUDE: 54° 12' 36.64" N   LONGITUDE: 1° 33' 46.68" W

Thornborough Henges is the only site mentioned in the Impressive Sites section of this book at which the visitor, rather than being encouraged to visit one of the most important places in the British Isles, will find that he or she is less than welcome and actually discouraged. Despite this, few people could argue that Thornborough Henges does not rank amongst the most important prehistoric structures in the world, let alone in our small islands.

The scale of the undertaking at Thornborough was immense, especially when we realize that these three massive henges were not alone on the landscape. There are at least three other super-henges in the immediate locality – all of which only exist now as parch marks in the fields and crops of North Yorkshire. Thornborough itself has fared better, but the whole site lies on private land with no recognized access for visitors and, what is worse, its environs are under constant threat from gravel extraction.

A Family of Henges

What remains are three super-henges, each around 263 yards (240 metres) in diameter and each in a slightly different state of preservation. The henges lie in a line, on a roughly northwest–southeast axis and the distance between the centre of the northernmost henge and that of the southernmost member of the group is just under 1 mile (1.49km). The area that includes these henges has been called 'The Stonehenge of the North' and English Heritage describes it as the most important ancient site between Stonehenge and the Orkney Islands of Scotland.

The best of the three henges in terms of access (though prospective visitors should be aware that the site is on private land) is the central henge. It still retains very impressive banks and some semblance of the massive ditch from which the banks were thrown up. These are known as Class IIA henges and so

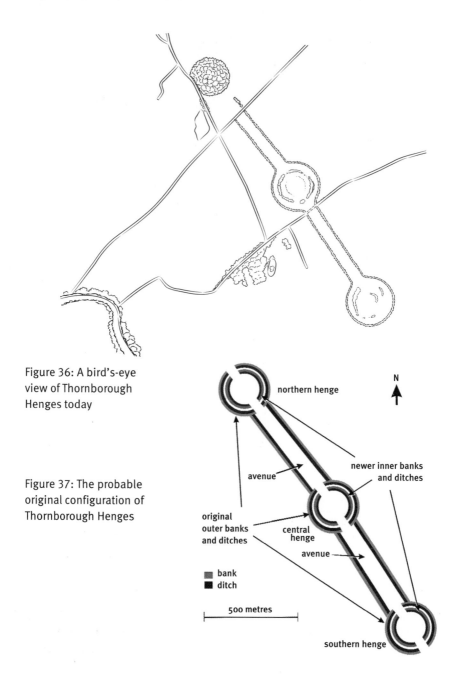

Figure 36: A bird's-eye view of Thornborough Henges today

Figure 37: The probable original configuration of Thornborough Henges

each has two entrances and exits, which follow the orientation of the group, being in the northwest and the southeast. In the case of the central henge it appears that there was originally an outer bank and ditch, which could have made the structure even larger. This was levelled early in the henge's existence and the present structure created.

Now comes the incredible part. Each of these henges, and all those that once accompanied them in and around the Vale of Mobray, were built around 3500 BC and just to get this into perspective, this date is a full 1,000 years before any of the pyramids in Egypt were constructed! Even more remarkable is the fact that the site of the central henge at Thornborough also contains a cursus (*see* Cursus) which was 'overbuilt' when the henge was constructed and which therefore has to be older than 3500 BC. This is a truly ancient site and was already around 500 years old before a deer antler was swung at

Figure 38: Part of the remaining bank of Thornborough central henge

Stonehenge. On these grounds alone the fact that it remains in obscurity and teeters on the brink of possible destruction is beyond belief.

The Purpose of the Super-Henges

There are many theories as to why such huge henges were built and what they might represent. It has been the tendency of many experts to see them as important meeting places, where a generally small and dispersed population could get together or where trading could take place. Though a reasonable suggestion, it becomes slightly ludicrous in the context of the size of each of the Thornborough henges. At the time they were constructed it would have been possible to fit every man, woman and child in the entire British Isles into any one of these structures – so if they really served the purpose of a meeting place, why would three such large henges be needed? (As I pointed out, there are at least three such additional super-henges in the immediate vicinity apart from the Thornborough group.)

The other, and to my way of thinking far more likely explanation, is that the henges had a religious, ceremonial or practical purpose. But whatever the reason for their planning and construction, the amount of work necessary to create them must have been mind-blowing. Whilst Thornborough Henges has no stone circle, it should be remembered that the physical effort of digging a ditch and creating a bank on the scale we see at Avebury, and especially at Thornborough, is far more time-consuming than moving a few stones around the landscape, no matter how large they might be. I am not a sufficiently competent mathematician to work out just how long the Thornborough project would have taken but in total it must surely have been just as great a time span as the creation of Silbury Hill, which is estimated to have taken 18 million man-hours (though in reality the task at Thornborough could have been twice or three times as great).

Gypsum Banks

When the banks at Thornborough had been thrown up, they were then covered with a mineral called gypsum. This would have made them shine brightly in the Sun and it has been argued that they could have been seen from a great distance. This is something of a misnomer because a henge bank, no matter how impressive, would not present a good target from a distance when viewed at the same level, and the ground around Thornborough is actually fairly flat. It seems more likely that making the henges so bright was actually for the benefit of the gods, rather than for visitors to the locality.

Orion's Belt

It was suggested (surprisingly enough by an archaeologist) that the arrangement of the three henges at Thornborough made them look strikingly like the three stars of the constellation of Orion known as Orion's Belt. This comment, together with research that Christopher Knight and I had been undertaking regarding these early structures on the British landscape, led to an intensive phase of study into Thornborough on our part. The results of our efforts can be read in full in our book *Before the Pyramids* but in brief we came to the conclusion that Thornborough was not simply an approximation of Orion's Belt, it was an *absolutely* faithful copy of it. What is more, the dimensions of the Thornborough henges, both individually and in terms of their relationship to one another, fully vindicates everything Professor Alexander Thom (*see* Thom, Alexander) observed regarding the standard units of measurement used in the late Stone Age and Bronze Age British Isles. Finally, we were led to a realization that henges such as those at Thornborough had been built as extremely efficient naked-eye astronomical observatories, though they undoubtedly also had a religious significance because, as I have stated elsewhere, science and religion at this early date were one and the same thing.

Of the three henges at Thornborough the real treasure is the northernmost henge. It is covered by trees, which seems to have been the case for a very long time. Because of this it has survived in quite remarkable condition – in fact it is the best-preserved henge to be found anywhere. Walking through it is something akin to taking an excursion in the Amazon rainforest, but if one really wishes to get an impression of how high the banks of these early henges were and how deep the ditches were dug, the northern henge at Thornborough is a perfect example (though of course, once again, anyone who goes there should know in advance that the henges are on private land, and are rarely open to the public).

Safeguarding the Site

A dedicated group of people, known as the Friends of Thornborough Henges, have worked tirelessly over many years in order for the site to get the recognition it deserves and to be fully protected by law and open to visitors. The wider area has barrows, burials of other kinds and all sorts of features on the landscape that are not understood. Working out what has already been destroyed by gravel extraction is impossible, and it is probably just as well because it would make any history buff weep in the knowledge of what we have already lost.

As Thornborough Henges are absolutely not open to the public (except on the odd day now and again) there is no museum, gift shop or café, and nothing to tell you where you are or what you are looking at. You will find plenty of fences and padlocked gates to keep you out, together with a lingering sense of indignation left behind by all those visitors who avidly believe that nobody should be able to divorce us from our common past and heritage.

The land around Thornborough is rich with gravel. It is partly the presence of the gravel that has allowed the banks of the henges to remain in place for so long. The site is also massive and that means that the thought of levelling it later for farming may always have been so daunting that nobody bothered to do so.

The northernmost henge at Thornborough is heavily wooded and seems to have been so for a very long time. Although the tree roots do some damage to the banks, in the main they tend to have protected the site. As a result it is probably the most intact henge in Britain. It has probably been left this way for so long as cover for game birds.

Old Oswestry

Old Oswestry, Oswestry, Shropshire

LATITUDE: 52° 52' 17.22" N   LONGITUDE: 3° 2' 51.06" W

On the borders of Wales, and very close to the modern town of Oswestry in Shropshire, is the remarkable hill fort known as Old Oswestry. Before you think about going there take a look at it on Google Earth, which gives a tremendous view of this Iron Age project and which shows the scale of the undertaking in a single glance. There are many higher hill forts in England than this one, but Old Oswestry is unique in a number of ways and has a charm and a grandeur that makes it second to none. 'Charm' might not be quite the right word to use when one considers that hill forts of this sort were designed to keep people out and to act as a deterrent to any would-be attacker, and indeed they were very efficient at doing so. Even the might of the Roman legions sometimes had difficulty dealing with British Iron Age forts which were impressive feats of engineering and which must have taken a great deal of time and effort to create.

An Early Settlement

Old Oswestry was once little more than a scattered group of huts on top of a natural hill. Then, around the 6th century BC, a double ditch and bank were created around the top of the hill. Later, more ditches and banks were added, probably because the hill upon which the fort is located is not especially high and its sides are not particularly precipitous. As a result, better defences were necessary.

Considering that Old Oswestry is so close to a thriving modern town, it has survived in a quite remarkable state. This is often the case for earthworks that are not ultimately subjected to agriculture because nobody has anything much to gain from disturbing them.

Apart from being a very healthy walk and a good insight into Iron Age life, especially in terms of the fighting that took place between various tribes at the time, Old Oswestry has a past filled with fabulous legends, all of which add significant colour to the experience. In Welsh (and after all you can see Wales from the top of it) Old Oswestry is called Caer Ogyrfan. In some of the earliest Arthurian legends Ogyrfan was a giant and also the father of Guinevere, famed wife of King Arthur. There may be a tiny grain of truth to be teased out of this legend. It is thought that Old Oswestry was abandoned after the Roman conquest of Britain but that it was reoccupied a few hundred years later, around the time the Roman legions withdrew from Britain and when the Saxon hoards began to pour into the islands.

Legends of King Arthur

This is precisely the time when King Arthur, or some Celtic warlord who ultimately 'became' King Arthur in the legends, was active in this part of the British Isles. As the rampaging, invading Saxons gradually extended their hold upon what is now England, the Celtic British were forced west into what we now know as Wales. (Interestingly enough the word 'Welsh' is Anglo-Saxon and means 'foreigner'.) Arthur, a tribal chief, ex-Roman officer or mercenary general hired by the Celts, fought the Saxons up and down the Welsh border and also up into the Lake District and possibly as far south as Cornwall, trying to keep at least the west of the British Isles in Celtic hands.

Old Oswestry would have made a likely base for such a warrior, or one of his cohorts, and Ogyrfan could easily have been one of them. If he was a really good fighter and maybe of above average stature, Ogyrfan could easily have gone down in history as a giant. It is also possible (if you will allow me to stretch credibility) that Ogyrfan had a daughter that Arthur (or whatever he was really called) chose to marry – hence the legend. It is amazing how often there is a grain of truth supporting any legend, no matter how old or far-fetched it might seem to be.

Impressive Vistas

The views from the top of Old Oswestry are impressive, looking in one direction into Wales and in the other out across the beautiful county of Shropshire.

If you do decide on a day out to Old Oswestry, make certain to look at a very strange set of depressions in the ground, just to the north and east of the main entrance (they are easy to see on the Google Earth image). These depressions are a great mystery and they don't seem to be part of the original defensive structure of the Iron Age fort. It has been suggested that they may have been of later construction and that they could have been the area where Dark Age chieftains (and for all we know King Arthur) stabled their horses, though they could equally well have been food storage pits of some sort.

If you are fit and healthy, take a run up the path that leads to the top of the fort. Now imagine that you have to cross each ditch and bank, which would also have sported sharpened stakes at their summits. At the same time, you would have been bombarded with both missiles and insults from above, whilst

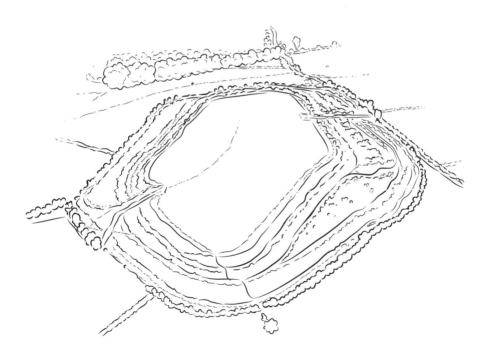

Figure 39: A bird's-eye view of Old Oswestry

representing a sitting target when in the bottom of the ditches. On the western side of the fort there are an impressive seven ditches and banks. All things considered, it might have been better to stay at home. Fortunately you won't have to take a spear with you these days but if the weather is fine this is an excellent place for a picnic.

It is very unlikely that manpower at the time would have allowed the Iron Age builders of hill forts such as Old Oswestry to guard the entire area of banks and ditches on the site. Rather it is likely that the finished structure was meant to be so impressive that it would make any would-be attacker think twice about the veracity and power of anyone who could have conceived of or created such a structure.

Old Oswestry seems to have always been a place of strategic importance. It is close to the site of a major battle between the petty kings in early Anglo-Saxon Britain and in later times it came to mark the boundary between England and Wales. The view from the top is quite magnificent and the hill has been used as a place from which to view the Welsh Marches for many hundreds of years.

Rudston Standing Stone

Rudston Standing Stone, near Bridlington, Yorkshire

LATITUDE: 54° 5′ 35.57″ N   LONGITUDE: 0° 19′ 20.89″ W

Rudston is a small village in the East Riding of Yorkshire, not far from the east coast seaside resort of Bridlington (where the fish and chips are amazing). The name Rudston is taken from Old English *'rood stane'* which in this context means 'stone of the cross'. That is because a little way out of the village, in the churchyard of the parish church to the east, is the tallest and most impressive standing stone (megalith) in the British Isles.

It is mighty to say the least. These days it is 25ft (7.6 metres) tall but it is thought that it was once a further 3ft (1 metre) taller. There is no stone of the sort from which the megalith is made to be found in the immediate vicinity and it probably came from around 10 miles (16km) away, at the coast near Cayton Bay. Since the stone is estimated to weigh in the region of 40 tonnes, getting it to its present site was no mean feat. There is another, much smaller stone of the same type in the churchyard, though this probably does not occupy its original site and could itself have been very much taller at one time.

Standing Stones and Churches

To find a standing stone in a churchyard or in close proximity to a church is not at all extraordinary. It was a deliberate policy of early Christians in Britain, and indeed everywhere else, to build their churches on sites where religious practice of one sort or another was already taking place. That way those visiting the sites were more likely to eventually become Christian. The church at Rudston today, All Saints, is Norman in foundation, though its dedication gives a clue that it may occupy the site of an earlier church. Many of the 'All Saints' churches of the north of England stand on Saxon, Celtic or sometimes even Roman foundations.

The site of Rudston is not famous in prehistoric circles simply for the standing stone. On the contrary, it seems to have been the centre of an

Figure 40: Rudston standing stone, the tallest standing stone in Britain

important ceremonial landscape in prehistoric times. Not one but four cursus (*see* Cursus) pass through the locality and there are significant earthworks also close to the church. Some of the cursus are extremely long and were found to contain burials of beaker people. Since cursus tend to be amongst the very oldest of prehistoric structures they almost certainly predate the erection of the standing stone, which estimates put at around 1600 BC. I have no reason to argue against this except an instinct that it is probably considerably older, maybe in the range of 2500 to 2000 BC.

Dinosaur Footprints

Why this area should have been of such significance – and let's face it, the place must have been important in order to convince locals to drag such a large stone so far – is not known but a possible clue is the discovery in the churchyard of dinosaur footprints. I have personally never seen these, though other commentators assure me that they are or were present. If they were very apparent in the Bronze Age it might have been assumed that some sort of dragon or an equally powerful creature had once occupied the place. It's a tenuous clue but a possibility.

You can visit the standing stone at Rudston at more or less any time, though of course it is in a churchyard so a little decorum is appreciated. The stone appears to have cup and ring markings, though these are not especially distinct. Was there originally more than one stone here? The presence of the stump of a similar type of stone close by tends to indicate that this may well have been the case. I am unaware of any stone of a similar kind incorporated into the body of the church but I would not be in the least surprised if it was. However, for some reason this large specimen has survived. It now wears a slightly ridiculous metal 'hat', which seems somehow to emasculate it, but the sheer size of the stone makes a journey to Rudston a must (and of course there are those excellent fish and chips only a few miles away).

The Devil's Arrows

The Devil's Arrows, near Boroughbridge, Yorkshire

LATITUDE: 54° 5' 33.49" N   LONGITUDE: 1° 24' 7.62" W

If you have ever travelled up the A1 in England, maybe going from the south up to Scotland, you would have passed close by the Devil's Arrows, though without necessarily realizing that you did. The Devil's Arrows are three massive standing stones, roughly aligned in a row and running nearly parallel with the line of the A1 as it passes close to Boroughbridge in North Yorkshire. It is thought that there could originally have been five or more stones forming the group and it is known for certain there were once at least four. The tallest of the stones is over 22ft (6 metres), making it second in height only to Rudston, though it is considerably broader in girth.

The companion stones are 22ft (6 metres) and 18ft (5 metres) respectively. Two of the Devil's Arrows are in a farmer's field and the other is by the pavement and adjacent to a house.

There is a rumour locally that the Devil's Arrows once formed part of the periphery of a gigantic henge, which must have been over a mile in diameter. As far as I can tell there is no substantiation for this assertion. It is much more likely the stones date to around 2000 BC and formed the southern part of a ritual landscape that encompassed an area stretching well up beyond Thornborough (*see* Thornborough Henges). They could also have been erected to mark the southernmost passage of the Moon.

Millstone Grit

The stones are composed of Millstone Grit, a local common sandstone and it is not likely that they were worked much, if at all, before their erection on the site. They are now considerably weathered and fluted by the rain but this is a perfectly natural process for Millstone Grit that has been left unprotected for so many centuries. The stones probably came from around two miles away, at Plumpton Rocks, where such large rocks would have been readily available. All

Figure 41: Two of the three Devil's Arrows near Boroughbridge

the same, it must have taken significant determination and effort to get the stones to the site and then erect them – especially if there were once many more than three. Further proof that this was indeed the case comes from the fact that pieces of exactly the same sort of stone have been found in the garden of a house adjacent to the site.

The name Devil's Arrows comes from a story that in remote times the Devil had taken offence at the old settlement of Aldborough, which is close by, and fired three enormous stone arrows at the settlement. Thanks to the general piety of the people thereabouts the Devil's arrows fell short and landed where we see them today. Aside from colourful legends it certainly seems a pity that we cannot know for sure why so much effort was expended at a site that was probably extremely impressive in its day. The tallest of the stones extends 6ft (2 metres) into the ground. Its base was carefully sculpted and smoothed and packed around with stones to ensure it retained its position, which it has successfully done until today, at least 4,000 years later!

The Hurlers Stone Circles

The Hurlers Stone Circles, Bodmin Moor, Cornwall

LATITUDE: 50° 30′ 56.89″ N   LONGITUDE: 4° 27′ 26.83″ W

Just a short walk from the village of Minions and close to Bodmin Moor in Cornwall is a very impressive site where not just one but three stone circles can be seen. These are arranged in a line, running roughly north-northeast to south-southwest. The central stone circle is slightly oval, indicating another attempt on the part of our ancient ancestors to square the circle. It is just over 44 yards (40 metres), in diameter on average and retains 14 stones. These are by no means giants but the presence of three aligned circles of this sort is quite rare and must have made the site significant. The southern circle is smaller and now has only 9 stones remaining, whilst the northern circle has a diameter of about 38 yards (35 metres) and retains 15 of its original stones.

It looks as though significant effort went into getting the stones that were ultimately used to look right. They all reach to a similar height, even though they may extend to different depths, and significant finds of pieces of the same stone within the circle tends to offer evidence that they were hammered into shape with mauls prior to being erected. This seems to have been a common procedure because pieces of bluestone were found within the circle at Stonehenge. Perhaps the unused stone was considered of no value but it is equally likely that it was deliberately left within the circle as a mark of respect to its sacred nature.

The Hurlers probably date to that period around 2000 BC when so many of the standing stones of the British Isles were being erected. It is also likely that they had significant outlying stones to allow for astronomical sightings of one sort or another.

As far as the name is concerned, the term 'hurlers' meant something like dancers or musicians and it is said locally that there was once a group of such people taking part in revelries on the flanks of the moor, on, of all days, the Sabbath. The Good Lord took offence and turned the cavorting dancers to stone.

Arbor Low

Arbor Low Henge and Stone Circle, Derbyshire

LATITUDE: 53° 10′ 8.13″ N   LONGITUDE: 1° 45′ 42.18″ W

Arbor Low, in the wonderful Peak District of Derbyshire, is a fine henge and stone circle but it has at its heart a mystery that has never been fully explained.

This is another spectacular site and it was probably chosen because it stands on a limestone plateau. I never cease to marvel at the capacity of our ancient henge-building ancestors for finding the most spectacular locations to erect their monuments but then, since they were no less intelligent than we are, perhaps their appreciation of natural beauty was just as great as ours can be.

Arbor Low is an oval rather than a circular henge, with two entrances, within which the stone circle was intended to stand. 'Intended' seems to be the appropriate word in this case because although at least 50 limestone sentinels wait patiently on the grass, and in a carefully arranged circle within the henge, all but one of them are recumbent. It is apparent that some of the stones have been broken, so there were probably originally less than 50 stones intended for the circle but there seems to be no doubt that when they were found or quarried, they were specifically chosen to stand upright.

For some time it was suggested that the same zealous Christians who tried to destroy other sites, and who in some cases succeeded, had toppled all the stones of Arbor Low, but this cannot be the case for one important reason. Search as they may, nobody has ever been able to find sockets that the stones once stood in, and no matter how much time elapsed since they were upright, these would not disappear altogether.

It is estimated that the stones were brought to the site around 2000 BC and the henge is almost certainly slightly older. Later in the Bronze Age some of the material from the bank was used to create a cairn burial close by. This was excavated in the 19th century and found to contain a cremation burial.

Recumbent Stones

There seems to be no satisfactory immediate answer to the puzzle of why a complete set of stones was manhandled to this site and then left, lying in the grass. Perhaps the builders were subjected to a natural calamity, such as plague or famine, and so decided that it was not the will of the gods that the stones should be erected. Is it possible that they were caught up in some sort of tribal struggle that left so many of them dead there were not enough able-bodied locals around to erect the stones? It seems likely that we will never know, but this site does seem to have a strange atmosphere – a sort of brooding stillness that I haven't registered at other henges and circles. If you happen to be close by or fancy a little excursion into one of the most picturesque parts of England, Arbor Low is definitely worth a visit.

Derbyshire is part of the uplands of the North Midlands of England. Much of the land is moorland and some is extensively wooded. There are many prehistoric monuments of one sort or another to be found across the county and some which still await discovery. Scanning Google Earth is a good way to start looking, especially on rainy days or during winter.

South Cadbury

South Cadbury Hill Fort, Sparkford, Somerset

LATITUDE: 51° 1′ 27.79″ N   LONGITUDE: 2° 31′ 49.71″ W

Down in the southwest of England is the county of Somerset, famed for its cider and the home of what must be one of the most charming English dialects to be found throughout our islands. There is no doubt that this area was well populated throughout prehistory though much of it, and especially the Somerset Levels, was flooded for large parts of the year. Glastonbury is in Somerset – a town steeped in history and a place well worth a visit, whilst nearby Glastonbury Tor, a natural hill that rises well above the low-lying ground around it, is also fascinating. It is said that the Tor, which until relatively modern times would have been an island amidst lakes and marshes, was the famed Avalon of Arthurian legend. In truth there are many ancient sites to see in Somerset but probably the best of them, and another with Arthurian connections, is the hill fort of South Cadbury.

South Cadbury must have risen out of the southern edge of the Somerset Levels in a very impressive way, back in the time when late Stone Age people chose to live there. It would have made a good base because it is quite high compared to the surrounding countryside (the summit is 500ft (152 metres) above sea level) and an ideal location to live for those engaged in wildfowling and hunting in the marshes.

Britain becomes Warlike

Archaeological finds indicate that the site was also occupied during the Bronze Age, though probably in a domestic rather than a defensive capacity. The date at which South Cadbury started to take on the look it has today seems to have been around 400 BC. This was a warring period in the British Isles and certainly seems to have been a time when almost everyone was rushing to build defensive structures of one sort or another. We know that the various tribes living throughout our islands did not always get along happily together. Proof of this comes from the way the invading Romans were able to use old enmities between certain of the Iron Age tribes of Britain for their own purposes. Had Britain been defended by a single people under an all-powerful king it is far less likely that the Romans could ever have successfully invaded or occupied the place.

Around 400 BC the locals in the district got together, presumably under their tribal king, and began to make the hill at South Cadbury into a fairly impregnable fortress. 'Fairly' is an appropriate word because there is archaeological evidence that great destruction took place here even before the Roman invasion and the legions managed to storm the place successfully soon after the conquest of AD 43.

The fort at South Cadbury involved the creation of four sets of banks and ditches, on a hill that was already fairly steep. These banks would have been defended by stockades and there may well have been sharpened stakes driven into the ditch bottoms and bank sides. The result was the best-known and probably one of the most impressive of the British hill forts of the Iron Age.

For Living or for Fighting?

There have been arguments about the extent to which hill forts were used as places of regular habitation. Back in the 1950s and 1960s I was taught at school that hill forts were usually empty and that only during times of threat was everyone, together with their livestock, herded into the hill forts and the gates firmly shut against an enemy. Archaeological digs at South Cadbury show that the picture is not quite so clear-cut. Evidence of constant occupation has been found within the banks and ditches, to the extent that a smithy existed there, together with a significant number of houses and even a structure that could well have been a temple. This seems reasonable enough because the amount of land within the hill fort is quite substantial.

What now seems much more likely is that some people did live within the hill forts on a more or less permanent basis. Perhaps they held the equivalent of markets, where people from the outlying communities could come to buy and sell their goods, and with a more cohesive tribal structure developing in the Iron Age, it is likely that chieftains or petty kings spent a considerable period of time in such strongholds. Iron Age culture in the British Isles was quite advanced, well before the Roman conquest. Some of the tribal areas were large and powerful – even minting their own coins and trading heavily with other tribes and also other countries.

South Cadbury has been a treasure house for archaeological discoveries. In the second half of the 1960s the site was extensively dug by Leslie Alcock and many of the finds that he and his team made can still be seen in the Somerset County Museum in Taunton.

The Arthurian Connection

King Arthur has little to do with a book about prehistoric sites but not to mention him in connection with South Cadbury would be a pity. If Arthur ever did exist, he is most likely to have been around in the 4th or 5th century AD, though stories associated with him are clearly much older and go back to the pre-conquest Iron Age. It is suggested, not just by folklorists, but also by some expert historians, that Arthur may have had one of his headquarters at South Cadbury. It is known that the site was reoccupied during the Dark Ages and so, in deference to a legend that is as good as an invitation to print money, the place is now often referred to as 'Cadbury Camelot'.

For a really great day out it might be good to visit South Cadbury and then maybe to take in Glastonbury and the Tor, which are 12 miles (19.3km) to the northwest. Make sure you are wearing stout footwear, and especially so if the weather has been wet. It should also be borne in mind that whilst South Cadbury is lovingly maintained it isn't always easy going and parts of the journey to the top are quite steep – though nowhere near as steep as Glastonbury Tor.

Belas Knap

Belas Knap Chambered Long Barrow, near Cheltenham, Gloucestershire

LATITUDE: 51° 55' 35.83" N   LONGITUDE: 1° 58' 4.81" W

It is not all that common to find a good example of a chambered tomb in England. Though there are examples to be seen in this part of the British Isles, the best of the chambered tombs are in the Celtic heartland, in Wales but especially in Scotland and Ireland. It is for this reason that I have included Belas Knap in my list of interesting sites to visit. True, Belas Knap is a complete recreation – in other words it probably does not look *exactly* as it once did, but to my way of thinking it has been sympathetically restored and it does give a good impression of what the tomb must have looked like when it was first created.

Before you go racing off to the Cotswolds, which is where you will find Belas Knap, south of Winchcombe in Gloucestershire, do be aware that to get to the tomb you will have a very steep climb. The effort is definitely worthwhile though, because what greets you on arriving is a stunning example of a type of tomb known as a 'Seven-Cotswold' chambered long barrow, a type of structure confined to this region of England. There is a lay-by in the Humblebee Woods where you can park, and the steep path to the tomb is around the side of the woods.

Outside the entrance to the tomb is a typical courtyard, showing just how proud the builders of these tombs were of their handiwork. In the centre of this is a massive false entrance, which once again is typical of this form of tomb. The widest part of the barrow is this northern end and it then tapers off significantly towards the south. It is actually trapezoid in shape and is a good size, being around 77 yards (70 metres) in length. It was, and is, entirely covered in a carefully created mound – the long barrow.

The burial chambers, of which there are four, are located around the sides and the back of the mound. The false entrance was, as its name indicates, purely for show, or perhaps to discourage grave robbers (though this doesn't seem all that likely because anyone who really wanted to get at the burials simply had to dig into the mound). We don't know what the roofs of the chambers look like. It is entirely possible that they were corbelled, though they could have been covered with stone slabs. Some of them now have concrete roofs which, although not at all convincing, do at least offer an impression of what the chambers must have looked like when first created.

Elegant Walling

Extensive dry-stone walling was used at the site and it has been described as far from random in construction, since great care went into getting the courses right and creating a solid structure that would truly stand the test of time. To the west is one chamber, with another two on the eastern side of the mound. At the rear is a further cist-type chamber.

So much has been learned about the builders of these tombs and about the period during which they were active, that it is a wonder that Belas Knap is not much better known. The tomb was first excavated in the 1860s and it seems with greater care than usual. On hand were specialists in human anatomy, which led to some fairly startling conclusions about racial types living in and around the area when the barrow tomb was created.

A Cemetary

Upwards of 40 bodies were found in Belas Knap and one or two of them gave great pause for thought. This is because of a rule of thumb introduced by an interested professional who worked for Wiltshire county asylums in the 1860s. His name was John Thurnam. He had a good knowledge of anatomy and a fascination for ancient tombs. After extensive analysis of bodies found in all manner of burials from the Neolithic period and later, Thurnam came to the conclusion that long, narrow human skulls are usually found in long barrows, whilst those found in round barrows are generally less long and much rounder. In the main, Belas Knap lived up to his expectations in that most of the skulls found in the tomb were long. There was one exception because a round skull was present. It was an isolated example and it is now generally accepted that this belonged to a young man of a different race who was captured by those who built Belas Knap and probably sacrificed – or per-haps he was killed in battle. This is a puzzle that will probably never be solved but it is fascinating all the same. Curiously enough, the long, narrow skulls are usually associated with the Neolithic period, whilst the rounder skulls are commonly found to be of the Bronze Age – and may fall into the culture known as the beaker people. It seems self-evident that the two groups did coexist at some level, or the round skull could not have been associated with the other burials at Belas Knap.

Most of the bones found at Belas Knap were randomly placed, and had probably been de-fleshed at some other location, though one whole skeleton was found, which is apparently not unusual for tombs of this class – almost as if one really important individual was placed there in entirety for a very specific reason. Perhaps this was the person who supervised the creation of the tomb or maybe a local chief?

Although most of the bones were discovered long before carbon dating was possible, many were carefully retained and they have been dated since. They are all from roughly the same period, between 4000 and 3700 BC.

I can almost guarantee that nobody with an interest in things prehistoric will be disappointed with what they are able to view at Belas Knap. Incidentally, nobody really knows where the name came from. It could be ancient but it may equally be medieval in origin.

It should also be borne in mind that Belas Knap is situated in the Cotswolds, an area of great charm and many picturesque villages. And without wanting to make it sound as though I think of little else but my stomach, the various country cafés of the Cotswolds offer some of the best cream teas I've ever tasted.

Grimes Graves

Grimes Graves Flint Mine, near Thetford, Norfolk

LATITUDE: 52° 28′ 31.43″ N   LONGITUDE: 0° 40′ 32.44″ E

It cannot be doubted that the technical innovation that brought us from the rank of simple hominids to the place we hold in the world today was our use of tools of various sorts. High on the list of such aids to mastery of our environment were stone utensils and, in this part of the world for sure, flint. Everyone knows that prehistoric man used flint tools extensively and most people may also have learned that the quality and usefulness of flint tools changed and improved across a vast period of time.

What might not be so obvious is that flint cannot be found in every location across the British Isles. On the contrary, although an inferior type can be found in river beds or often on beaches, the best flint comes from the ground and then only in very specific areas. Since throughout the whole of the Neolithic period flint was an indispensable source of tools, for everything from hunting and chopping down trees to scraping animal skins, it stands to reason that all Neolithic people in the British Isles had to get hold of flint from somewhere. It is now generally accepted that flint was heavily traded across our islands, and from an extremely early date. This made its finding and transhipment one of the earliest professions, and way back in our history there seem to have been cultures that specialized in digging out flint, sometimes from significant depths and at great potential personal danger.

One such place is Grimes Graves, which is located on the border between Norfolk and Suffolk near the town of Brandon. At this site, between around 3000 BC and 1900 BC, many hundreds of tonnes of flint nodules were brought up from deep underground – so much in fact that it cannot simply have been intended for local consumption. The work at Grimes Graves was extensive, well organized, and obviously undertaken by men who were specialists – even if they were also local farmers.

There are a known 96 acres (39 hectares) of shafts at Grimes Graves and even allowing for the long period of time the site was in use, this is an incredible area. There are at least 433 known shafts, though many others could exist under more modern structures. This is partly because once they were fully exploited, each shaft was very carefully and comprehensively back-filled with the same earth that had originally been dug out of it – clearly to avoid the whole area collapsing because flint is found predominantly in chalk, which is not the hardest or most resilient of stones by a long way.

In order to get at the flint they wanted, the Neolithic miners dug through two other layers of less refined flint. They had to get down as deep as 40ft (14 metres) and it must have taken them a long time just to get to the required depth. Once they had done so they would come across the layer of superior flint they were looking for and then they would dig horizontal shafts, following the seam of flint as far as they realistically could, before backfilling the holes and starting again somewhere else.

Red Deer

The work must have been extremely cramped and was undertaken predominantly with red deer antler picks. It is possible that the farmers responsible for the mining kept herds of red deer because the antlers would not have lasted long and would have had to be replaced on a regular basis. The deer, when killed, could also have supplied leather for the bags they would have needed – and of course food at times when crops were scarce. The deer would not have had to be culled for the antlers because these are shed by the stags each year after rutting has taken place.

The reason the Neolithic and Bronze Age miners at Grimes Graves went to so much trouble and put themselves in undoubted danger to get at this particular layer of flint was that it was stronger, more resilient and, most importantly of all, easier to knap. Knapping of flint is striking pieces of it in very specific ways in order to achieve a good working edge. Visitors can actually climb down a ladder to experience a little of the conditions under which the miners toiled and for those who mix an interest in things prehistoric with a love of the natural world, Grimes Graves is also a site of special scientific interest and is the home of a great variety of plants and animal species.

Flag Fen

Flag Fen Causeway and Reconstructed Bronze Age Village, near Peterborough, Cambridgeshire

LATITUDE: 52° 34' 25.23" N   LONGITUDE: 0° 11' 31.74" W

Flag Fen is near to Peterborough, England and it is the site where over 1,000,000 ancient timbers, which made up an ancient causeway, were found. These were arranged in five long rows and have been dated to a period between 1365 BC and 967 BC. Such a strange find is not common in the British Isles because climatically speaking it is rare for wood to survive the ravages of time. As a result, the discoveries at Flag Fen both surprised and delighted archaeologists. As its scale became more and more apparent, people began to wonder what the structures at Flag Fen had once been.

What made the whole situation even more mysterious was the great number of apparently 'ritual' finds that were associated with the site. The place had originally been a fen and experts already knew that watercourses and some bodies of standing water had, at certain times in our history, been considered ritually or religiously important. Broken swords or other votive offerings had been found in streams and rivers and it appeared that the same reverence had been shown to Flag Fen, but in this case on a much greater scale. Not only broken weapons were found but, for example, a number of polished white pebbles of a type of stone not readily available around Flag Fen or indeed anywhere near to it. Someone had brought the pebbles from a long way off and deliberately thrown or placed them in the fen, presumably as an offering to the gods.

A Flooded Landscape

As long ago as 1000 BC the level of the water in the fen was much lower than it is today, but over a long period of time it increased as the climate in the British Isles became wetter. This meant that year on year the many posts and other timbers at Flag Fen were gradually covered by water and by rotting vegetation, which preserved it and made many of the timbers found there as good as the day the water closed over them. The discovery of such well-preserved wood was a godsend to archaeologists because in such a situation it isn't only carbon dating that offers a good knowledge of when a site was in use but the study of tree rings (dendrochronology). Tree rings are a reliable source of information about climatic conditions in the past, year on year. It is possible to match the ring sizes of a given tree to known and dated samples from elsewhere and in this way extremely accurate dating of any particular site can take place. In Flag Fen there were so many timbers that working out when any particular part of the site was built has been relatively easy.

Interestingly enough, not all the timbers used at Flag Fen were from trees one might have expected to grow in the area. Significant examples of oak have been found there, which must have been brought from a fair distance away. This has led experts to speculate that certain species of tree were considered especially sacred and that to bring them to the site and use them there may have added to the religious significance of the site or bring the favour of the gods.

The story of Flag Fen is told in the visitor centre there, together with an explanation of how the timbers are being preserved. After all, it was only their immersion in water that has saved them for so long. The moment they are exposed to air they begin to deteriorate rapidly. Techniques such as freeze drying have been tried, together with replacing the water in the sodden wood with silicone.

Also at Flag Fen there is part of a Bronze Age village on display, with roundhouses of the type our ancestors lived in. All in all, Flag Fen offers a great snapshot into our remote past, as well as raising more than a few questions about the religious preferences and general behaviour of the Bronze Age people of Britain.

Old Bewick

Old Bewick Rock Carvings, near Alnwick, Northumberland

LATITUDE: 55° 29' 16.8" N   LONGITUDE: 1° 52' 35.58" W

In the wonderful county of Northumberland, in the very north of England, close to the village of Old Bewick, there is a wonderful collection of prehistoric rock carvings that give as good an example of cup and ring, and circular, markings as can be found anywhere in the British Isles. The carvings can be found in a field boundary 0.6 miles (1km) east of Old Bewick and many are carved into a large block of stone. It was at Old Bewick, in the 19th century, that people began to realize for the first time that the cup and ring markings commonly found across the British Isles were of genuine historical significance. Around Old Bewick there are a number of prehistoric structures, for example the Blawearie Cairn and Cist, as well as a double Iron Age fort, making this a landscape rich in prehistoric significance.

On the rocks at Old Bewick can be found extremely elaborate cup and ring markings, many joined together by deliberately carved grooves. In particular there are two cups with multiple rings, offering a figure-of-eight structure that is not commonly found, but of a sort that does exist elsewhere and which is very reminiscent of the carvings at Newgrange in Ireland.

Not far from the main rock there are others, which have also been heavily decorated, so do have a good wander around the locality. Maybe our ancestors chose these rocks because of their secluded position, or perhaps partly because they were already naturally weathered into cup marks that were easy to enhance. However, 'easy' is a relative word in association with these carvings. Many of the cup and ring markings were made before the advent of any sort of metal, so they could only be done in either relatively soft rock, or with a great deal of patience and over a protracted period of time. The crispness of some cup and ring markings is such that it is obvious that when first created they were well defined and deep, so clearly these were not idle graffiti but objects of reverence.

Professor Alexander Thom showed (*see* Thom, Alexander) that some of the cup and ring marks, and especially some spirals, were extremely carefully created, using geometry techniques that we normally associate with the ancient Greek period, which was considerably later.

Set in this wild and lonely place the many carvings near Old Bewick are a slightly unnerving sight. It is odd to think that we can connect in this spot with people who lived such an unbelievably long time ago and that they could have created something that would be almost as enduring as these old rocks themselves.

Despite decades of conjecture, it is fair to suggest that nobody has an answer for cup and ring markings. It used to be suggested that the 'cups' were designed to hold some sort of votive substance, such as milk, crude beer or maybe blood, but this explanation doesn't make any sense because the cups are just as likely to be carved into vertical surfaces as horizontal ones. The truth is that we just don't know. Perhaps the answer lies in astronomy, and our ancient ancestors were telling us something about the knowledge they had of the Sun and Moon. Most likely of all is the possibility that cup and ring markings had a peculiar religious significance and were considered as votive offerings to the deities in their own right. Or maybe you have a better explanation.

Lambourn Seven Barrows

Lambourn Seven Barrows, Lambourn, Berkshire

LATITUDE: 51° 32′ 33.41″ N   LONGITUDE: 1° 31′ 37.12″ W

As I have intimated elsewhere in this book, many of our richest and most important prehistoric sites in the British Isles would not cause the average person to raise an eyebrow as they drove past in a car. Of course the impressive stones of Callanish or the vast bulk of Silbury Hill would cause a sharp intake of breath, but the vast majority of burial mounds of one sort or another, strewn across our landscapes, have become so weathered and now look so natural that one has to know specifically where they are in order to pay any real attention.

Such is not the case at Lambourn, in Berkshire, England. This site represents one of the most important and long-lasting landscapes of the dead to be found anywhere in Britain. It may not be as impressive as Newgrange, or as beautifully crafted as Meashowe, but in terms of scale it is still extremely impressive.

The area in question is known as Lambourn Seven Barrows, though why it should have gained this specific name is a mystery. There are at least 26 and maybe as many as 30 barrows in what must have represented a deeply revered ritual landscape, which endured for a very long period of time. The reason I mention it is not just because it is quite easy to see the barrows here, set out amidst the landscape, but that they represent a fair cross section of many of the *types* of barrows to be found within the British Isles. So, if you are the sort of person who wants to cross barrow types off on a list (a little like a trainspotter) at Lambourn you will be able to tick off bowl barrows, bell barrows, saucer barrows, disc barrows and even at least one long barrow.

A Wealth of Bodies

Just one of the barrows at Lambourn was found to contain parts of at least 100 different people, dating from a time long before individual burials were taking place in barrows. In these early days it seems likely that the dead were left in the open to decompose naturally before parts of their skeletons were interred on a communal platform that may eventually have been covered over to make the barrow. Different cultures over differing times built the barrows in their own peculiar ways – or maybe it was sometimes the same culture that was subject to its own form of 'fashion'. There is great debate these days about how many invasions into Britain really did take place in prehistory. Of course there are clues, such as long skulls and round skulls, that could define different genetic types, but many of the invasions that used to be taught in school are now thought to have been immigrations and not to have represented violent interludes. Amongst unearthed finds in the barrows were a number of grave goods of high status, so perhaps places were reserved for the elite; these included a ceremonial battle axe and a mace head made of deer antler.

If you are driving through Berkshire, or if you really do want to see what a prehistoric barrow cemetery looks like, Lambourn Seven Barrows is as good a place as any. The nearby villages are very beautiful and you may see quite a few horses around because this is racing country, with many stables and studs.

Hambledon Hill

Hambledon Hill Prehistoric Hill Fort, near Blandford Forum, Dorset

LATITUDE: 50° 53' 42.04" N   LONGITUDE: 2° 12' 12.07" W

Dorset is on the south coast of England, a lovely county and one that is especially wonderful in the spring and the autumn. There are many prehistoric sites in Dorset but the one that really stands out for me is Hambledon Hill. Although often designated as an Iron Age hill fort, which indeed it was, the site has an ancestry that goes back significantly longer. Hambledon Hill was dug first in the 1970s and was extensively examined. At this time it was discovered that the site had first been of significance as long ago as 2850 BC – a very long time before the Iron Age.

Actually this wasn't really in doubt because within the confines of the later henge there are the remnants of two sizeable long barrows of a type that were not being created in the Iron Age. The area seems to have been some sort of causewayed camp because the top of the hill once had two separate causewayed enclosures. As to the use of the site in these early days it seems likely that this was originally a place of the dead. The bottoms of ditches are always useful places for archaeologists to find evidence because so much washes down into them across a long period of time. At Hambledon the ditches revealed a number of skulls, which may have been there as a warning to would-be invaders or which could have been associated with ancestor worship. Deer antlers were found – which is not remotely unusual since they represented the Stone Age and even Iron Age pick axe and would have been used to excavate the ditches.

The Remnants of Feasts

A significant haul of animal bones was also found by the archaeologists. These were of various types but it was established that most of the animals eaten on the site were slaughtered in late summer or early autumn. Some commentators have taken this as evidence that the site was occupied only at certain parts of the year, though this is far from clear-cut. On the contrary, even in relatively recent times the killing of animals in the autumn especially was quite common. With little in the way of available fodder it was not possible to keep any but the most important breed-stock animals healthy throughout the winter months, so the autumn was a good time for a feast.

If the site was only used at this time of the year there may be an indication that celebrations were taking place, which may have been associated with the long barrows and some form of ancestor worship that seems to have been endemic to the Neolithic and the Bronze Age.

Although the Bronze Age appears to have been relatively peaceful, at least in comparison with the later Iron Age when inter-tribe fighting seems to have been a regular event and fortified areas were common, there is an indication that the area might have been under attack at some stage. The skeleton of a young man was found and he had clearly been killed by an arrow wound. Associated with this find was a great deal of charcoal, which tended to indicate that the wooden ramparts had been burned as part of an attack on the enclosure.

Hambledon is clearly an Iron Age hill fort that gradually increased in size until it eventually reached the dimensions we see today. Parts of the hill are less protected because they are so steep but where the lie of the land dictated, there is a multiplicity of ditches and banks, making this one of the most impressive of the Iron Age hill forts to be seen in southern England.

Stanton Drew

Stanton Drew Stone Circle, Stanton Drew, Somerset

LATITUDE: 51° 22' 0.5" N   LONGITUDE: 2° 34' 28.73" W

The stones at Stanton Drew are not the largest to be found in the British Isles but the site is large and complex and certainly worth a second look. I have been there on numerous occasions and am always fascinated, trying to work out what the builders were attempting to achieve.

Set amidst what seems to have been a deeply revered landscape, there is more than one circle at Stanton Drew. The site is not far from Bath (one of the most beautiful cities in England) and it was of particular interest to those who created Bath in the 18th century. John Wood, chief architect of structures such as the King's Circus, is said to have taken inspiration from both Stanton Drew and Stonehenge, and we have certainly found measurements in Bath that bear this theory out.

In addition to the three circles at Stanton Drew, one large and two much smaller, there are also two avenues lined with stones and a very strange arrangement of stones that is known as 'the Cove'.

The smaller stone circles are not really circles at all because they are elliptical in shape. Once again we have to ask ourselves what our ancestors were trying to achieve with these elliptical, egg-shaped and flattened circles. These ellipses are around 102ft (31 metres) in diameter and 136ft (42 metres) in diameter respectively. The smaller one has eight stones, four of which are now recumbent, whilst the other small circle has 11 stones, though none of these are standing and may have been deliberately tipped over by devout Christians back in the 17th or 18th centuries.

A Significant Circle

As far as the larger circle is concerned (and this one really is a circle) it is a sizeable 370ft (113 metres) in diameter. This means it is the second-largest stone circle in Britain and is only dwarfed by Avebury. It has, in total,

27 stones, even if only two of them are presently standing as they once did. Sockets in the turf show that there were originally 30 stones in what is known as the 'Great Circle', which represents a splendid monument that must have taken some time to plan and erect.

The strange group of stones known as the Cove are to be found about 550ft (168 metres) west of the southeastern circle. They are close to a modern (well, relatively modern) public house which is intriguingly (but quite wrongly) named 'The Druids Arms Inn'. The Cove comprises three stones. It has not been excavated in recent times and at present it offers no substantial clue as to what its purpose might have been. Together with the Great Circle the Cove creates a northeast–southwest alignment. To the north-northeast is a large standing stone, some 1,180ft (360 metres) away. It is likely that these outlying stones had some astronomical significance but the site would have to be accurately dated for this to become obvious and at the moment there is no absolutely reliable date for its construction.

It is likely that a timber structure once occupied this site, either at the time of the circles or perhaps before. A geophysical survey has shown concentric rings of post holes. The area is also surrounded by what must once have been a fairly impressive henge. The Great Circle and one of its smaller companions once had short avenues associated with them.

As is attested by the number of 18th-century 'Druids' that flocked to this site, and others around Britain when Druidism was very fancifully recreated, Stanton Drew has been a source of wonder for a very long period. In the main its stones, though knocked over, have not been smashed or buried.

As with other circles elsewhere, there is a local legend that the stones of Stanton Drew were once revellers. It is said that they sinned by dancing on a Sunday and for this most terrible of crimes they were summarily turned to stone.

Elegance and Complexity

This site is well worth a visit and it deserves more attention from those who study the prehistoric sky (astroarchaeologists) than it has enjoyed so far. It is very complex in design and without reliable dating it is difficult to know which sections of the site were developed first or what some of them might even have been for. Archaeologists are now less willing to excavate sites than they once were, believing that once a site has been disturbed, the secrets it contains will be lost for all time, whilst being willing to wait for technological innovation that might allow evidence to be collected without destroying what they would most wish to preserve.

Eighteenth-century antiquarians were as keen to look at Stanton Drew as they were at Stonehenge or Avebury. In particular, as I have mentioned, John Wood, one of the prime movers in the creation of the wonderful Georgian city of Bath, was virtually obsessed with Stanton Drew. Wood visited the site on many occasions where he took extensive measurements. His ideas regarding who built stone circles such as Stanton Drew, and the perceived truth today are far different but his meticulous approach to surveying both Stanton Drew and Stonehenge is a mark of respect from a man who was trying hard to get at the truth, even if he lacked the methods that are available to modern archaeologists.

It has been suggested, actually quite incorrectly, that the dimensions of Stanton Drew were used by John Wood in his wonderful circle of houses in Bath, which he named King's Circus. In reality Wood used the dimensions of the henge at Stonehenge. But he did write a book on Stanton Drew and clearly considered it to have been of great historical significance.

Arthur's Stone

Arthur's Stone Chambered Cairn, Dorstone, near Hay-on-Wye, Herefordshire

LATITUDE: 52° 4' 53.66" N   LONGITUDE: 2° 59' 43.28" W

If any one of us had a five-pound note for each time the legendary King Arthur's name was attached to prehistoric sites and structures up and down the British Isles, we would be quite wealthy. Yet another example is to be found at Dorstone in the county of Herefordshire, though it has nothing whatsoever to do with King Arthur. What you can see there today is the very impressive remnants of what was once a sizeable chambered cairn tomb. What makes this site so interesting is the sheer size and weight of the capstone, which stands on a number of surrounding stones and once formed the ceiling of the tomb. This capstone is shaped like a kite, is 19ft (6 metres) by 10ft (3 metres) and weighs an estimated 25 tonnes. True, it is not far up in the air as, for example, are the sarsen stones of Stonehenge, but it is still a colossal weight to be dragged to the site and then erected in its present position. How many willing or unwilling volunteers it took to place the capstone we will never know – nor can we do any more than guess at the technology they applied in order to get it into place.

False Entrance

It is thought that the cairn, which has now been dug away or weathered away, was probably oval and was in the region of 85ft (26 metres) in length; though not making this cairn a giant by any means, it was a fair size. One of the uprights in what was once the front of the tomb chamber carries cup and ring markings and it is thought that this stone probably formed part of the 'false entrance' which tombs of this sort in this area of England often possessed. Why these false entrances should have been present isn't known but in front of them was usually a courtyard, presumably where ceremonies of one sort or another took place. In some ways this tomb is more like examples that are found in South Wales, so it may well be a member of the same group and therefore created by the same people.

Although the reader may not choose to spend too much time at this particular site, it is a great example of how people, who only a few years ago were referred to as 'primitive', set their minds on a particular course of action and saw a task through that would totally intimidate most of us today. They were, in their own way, skilled engineers and planners. Most of the techniques they used have been shown to be allied to woodworking, though on a much grander scale. This is not at all surprising. There is no evidence, except in extremely rare cases such as Skara Bray in Scotland, that the builders of the tombs and the stone circles lived in stone houses themselves. Rather they occupied roundhouses, created in the main from timber, wattle and daub. They were farmers, used to corralling domestic animals and skilled at erecting shelters for their livestock, as well as houses for themselves. We know from places like Flag Fen that they were experts at creating wooden causeways and they probably also built bridges. Stonework was not common, it was definitely the exception and in most cases it was clearly allied to something 'above and beyond' everyday life and experience.

If you do go to Arthur's Stone, stand for a moment and take in the enormity of that capstone and ask yourself by what technique you could have brought it to this site and raised it onto its companion stones. Now imagine what the site must have looked like when it was covered in stones and earth. These are truly impressive structures and the realization of how sophisticated they were elevates our ancient grandmothers and grandfathers almost to the rank of giants, which is what our not-so-old ancestors thought they must have been.

Sutton Hoo

Sutton Hoo, Melton, near Woodbridge, Norfolk

LATITUDE: 52° 5′ 24″ N   LONGITUDE: 1° 20′ 18″ E

I freely admit that I have cheated by placing Sutton Hoo amongst the locations included in the Impressive Sites section of this book. Since the title of the book includes the word 'prehistoric', I suppose no site should be included if it was created after recorded history began. This is certainly not the case with Sutton Hoo, which only dates to around the 6th or 7th century AD – which is well within recorded history. However, the site is still shrouded in mystery and in any case it was the place at which the most fabulous treasure ever to be uncovered on British soil was found. And it is for these reasons that I have decided to give Sutton Hoo a special, if slightly undeserved mention.

Post-Roman Britain

When the Roman legions finally left the shores of Britain, in AD 410, the locals were left to their own devices and their own defence. In an effort to keep out invaders they did not want, the petty kings of England often resorted to introducing mercenaries into their lands, to bolster their defences. In the south of England especially, many of the mercenaries came from Saxony, or from the region in the very north of what is now the Netherlands. These people became known as the Saxons and the Angles, and it is from the latter that the name of England is derived.

The plan might have been a good one, if only the mercenaries had done what they were paid to do and left it at that. Unfortunately for the petty kings of the British Isles, the Saxons and Angles loved it so much here they decided to stay, and what is more they invited a large number of their relatives and friends to join them. Eventually the incursions became so great that open warfare started to break out between what were now clearly invaders, and the indigenous population. Without the legions to protect them the Britons put up a sterling fight but it was a losing battle from the start. They were forced back into Wales, Cornwall and Scotland, whilst the bulk of what is now England eventually fell to the Saxons and Angles.

Right from the start that area of England known as East Anglia proved to be very popular with the Germanic immigrants. They established themselves in Norfolk and Suffolk, where Anglo-Saxon kingdoms developed.

Sailors and Warriors

The Anglo-Saxons were great sailors and great warriors. In addition, they stood at the point in history at which paganism, which had always existed here, began to meet Christianity, which arrived from the west and Ireland, and from the east and the Continent. It took a while, but eventually the Anglo-Saxon kings of England became Christian. In that period before full conversion took place, we find a definite 'Dark Age' during which very few records were kept. Later, monastic chroniclers would have a great deal to tell us about the Anglo-Saxon period, but prior to around AD 700, historians and archaeologists know little of what was taking place in England.

What we do now know is that at least some of the early Anglo-Saxon kings, especially in the east and south of England, grew extremely powerful and prosperous. We also know much about the sort of objects with which they liked to surround themselves, as well as understanding from just how far away some of these objects came. We have become aware of some of the Anglo-Saxon burial practices and of the local craftsmanship, especially in precious metals, which was clearly far in advance of anything that used to be considered possible for this era.

We know all of this because of what was discovered near Woodbridge in Norfolk in 1939. It was known that a number of burial mounds existed in the area – in fact some of them had already been dug and looted. A few finds remained but in the main there was little except scars in the landscape to show what had once been there. Sutton Hoo overlooks a tidal estuary and is about 7 miles (11km) from the coast. The land there is mostly sand and it seems to have been of special significance for burials for a very long time. Some 20 mounds were known to exist and the ones that had not been disturbed were of special interest to Edith May Pretty, who owned Sutton Hoo House and the land upon which the mounds were located. By 1937 Mrs Pretty, who had been listening to local legends that 'untold gold' was buried beneath the mounds, enlisted the support of Ipswich Museum, in the form of Basil Brown, a talented amateur archaeologist. Brown began working on one particular site, known as Mound 1. It had clearly been at least partly excavated but Mrs Pretty was adamant it should be looked at in more detail. Basil Brown set to, with very little help, and patiently began removing the earth.

An Undisturbed Treasure House

When the burial chamber in the mound was reached, it became clear that it lay undisturbed. At this point the British Museum became involved because what Basil Brown had begun to uncover was the greatest ship burial ever to be discovered from the Saxon period.

Unfortunately the discovery came at exactly the same time as Britain was facing war with Germany. All the objects were removed, in great secrecy, from the site, and were shipped off to London, but were brought back again for a treasure trove inquest, which decided the treasure rightfully belonged to Mrs Pretty. With true generosity Mrs Pretty gave the whole Sutton Hoo treasure to the nation and it now resides, in splendour, in the British Museum.

The Sutton Hoo treasure is simply stunning, and breathtaking in its scope and amount. In addition to a fabulous war helmet there is a fine collection of silver plate, some of which had come from Byzantium. Many of the items were clearly favourites of the buried king, such as parts of a harp and personal adornments of the finest enamel-worked gold. There were shield fittings, silver bowls, spoons, swords, horse harnesses and the most fabulous solid gold belt buckle imaginable. And all of this is just a part of the Sutton Hoo treasure, which showed itself to have belonged to someone of immense wealth and power.

A Powerful King

It is now generally accepted that the burial was that of the Anglo-Saxon King Raedwald, King of the East Angles, who reigned between AD 599 and 624 approximately. Raedwald himself seems to have been a pagan, but his daughter married Edwin, the first Christian Anglo-Saxon ruler of Northumbria and so the ship burial came at that all-important pivotal point in the Dark Ages, just before written records were kept.

Of Raedwald's ship – a genuine ocean-going vessel, in which he had been laid to rest, little remained except the amazing pattern it had left in the earth. Nor were there any real remains of the king himself. But the treasure buried with him represents arguably the most important historical discovery ever made on English soil, not simply because of the artefacts themselves, but more because of the light they throw on such a dimly lit period of our history.

The site at Sutton Hoo is now administered by the National Trust. It is possible to walk around the entire site of the discovery and to learn a great deal about the burial itself and the story of its unearthing just prior to the Second World War. There is nearly always something significant taking place and Sutton Hoo is a great place to take the family. An award-winning exhibition is in place for interested visitors and there you can also see a full-sized replica of the burial chamber, together with facsimiles of many of the items that were discovered.

But if you want to see the real Sutton Hoo treasure, which I am pleased to say I have done on numerous occasions, you will need to visit the British Museum. There, you can stand in front of the glass cases and stare in open-mouthed wonder at some of the most beautiful works of art that our Anglo-Saxon ancestors were capable of producing. In the gleam of all that gold you, like me, might be left wondering whether the Dark Ages were really all that dark after all.

SCOTLAND

CONTENTS

Skara Brae

Skara Brae, Orkney

LATITUDE: 59° 2′ 54.78″ N   LONGITUDE: 3° 20′ 38.63″ W

For me, Skara Brae has to rank as one of the most surprising and the most magnificent of all prehistoric structures. True, most people will have to travel a fair distance to see it because Skara Brae is to be found on the island of Orkney, off the north coast of Scotland. It is, at one and the same time, impressive and somehow disquieting because it has a modernity about it that causes most people to change their attitude towards our Neolithic ancestors.

Lost to the Sand

Skara Brae is an entire village and it is built totally out of stone. The reason it survived is because not long after it was abandoned it became covered by sand, which protected it for many centuries until, in 1850, a great storm removed the sand and exposed some of the remains of the village for the surprised locals and experts alike to see. A few of the houses were excavated but by the late 1860s work on the site ceased. After all, it was difficult to get to Orkney in those days and modern archaeology, with its dating techniques, was still a long way off. Doubtless, at the time, historians considered the site to be medieval because the architecture was so advanced it could surely not be truly ancient. Further storms not long after the start of the 20th century revealed more of the dwellings of Skara Brae and caused a flurry of activity. Digging began again and by the start of the 1930s the whole of the site was available for study.

There are, in all, eight houses at Skara Brae. Each is self-contained but all are joined together by low passages, which were protected from the elements by being covered over, allowing free passage from one house to another in the very worst of the Orkney weather, at any time of year.

So, what is so strange about a lost village that is suddenly found again? After all, people since time out of mind have built villages. True, but this one is definitely different. Even the most die-hard sceptics regarding the potential age of Skara Brae were forced, by the 1970s, to admit that people had lived in these strange little houses as much as 5,000 years ago because organic matter from the site, of which there was an abundance, showed radio carbon dates between 3200 BC and 2200 BC.

A Village for Normal People

Perhaps what shocks those who see Skara Brae for the first time is the ultimate realization that it wasn't giants or mythical races of lost supermen that erected structures such as Callanish or Avebury, but normal people, just like us. We can see for ourselves a great deal about the domestic circumstances of the people. Each of the houses is built out of flat stones that were probably easy to find in the locality. The stones were fitted together skilfully, in a fashion that today would be called 'dry-stone walling' (in other words no form of mortar was used to tie them together). Their strength lies in their weight and in the way they are formed into an interlocking whole.

Each house has a large, central, square room. Each possesses a central fireplace and, surprisingly, a stone bed on each side of the room. Perhaps even more surprising is the fact that every house at Skara Brae has an almost identical stone-built dresser. It is this particular aspect of Skara Brae that has always fascinated me the most. It is the thought that people came in at the end of the day and looked at their prized possessions, standing on the dresser, as we might place ours these days. There might have been a particularly impressive animal tooth, an amber ornament from the far-off Baltic, or a polished stone axe left by some distant ancestor – the minutia of life, kept, not because any of it was intrinsically useful, but because it carried memories and emotions. And in this realization alone the people of Skara Brae, divorced from us by so much time, become as close as our next-door neighbours.

Living amidst the Rubbish

When the houses were first excavated, the stone slabs that covered the passageways between the houses were still largely in place. Between the houses, and perhaps acting as further insulation, was the rubbish that the people of the

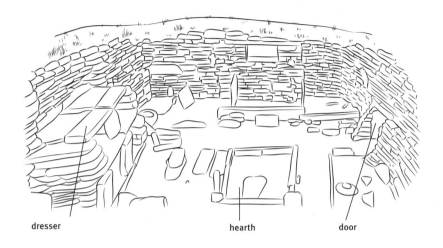

dresser   hearth   door

Figure 42: The inside of one of the houses at Skara Brae

village had discarded. As a result, a mass of animal bones have been found and it is these that have offered such good carbon dating analysis that the age of the settlement could be tied down so accurately.

Some experts suggest that this massive accumulation of garbage made the place unhealthy, but is this likely? It would have been simple to abandon the remains of their meals into the sea which, although not as close as it is to the settlement now, was no great distance away, or to have created a midden (rubbish tip) some way from the village. Skara Brae poses many questions. It has been suggested that the weather during the period the village was occupied was significantly better than it is today but the presence of the covered passages and such substantial dwellings tells a slightly different story. On the other hand, if life in this remote spot was so harsh, what were the people doing there at all? Certainly the site was not occupied for more than about 100 years.

When we look deep into the rubbish tips of Skara Brae we start to understand the components of a life that was at one and the same time very similar to ours and yet quite different. The people of Skara Brae were farmers.

They kept cattle and sheep and sowed barley and wheat, and were adept at using whatever bounty nature offered them for free, which in their case was a great deal. They had a diet that was heavy on shellfish, together with whatever fish they could catch from the shore. This included cod and other species. In addition, as has been the case even recently in this part of Scotland, they doubtless raided seabirds' nests for eggs when they were available and probably caught the birds themselves when they could. In short, by the standards of the time they had a varied and generally healthy diet, though their living conditions may not have been quite as comfortable as these snug dwellings might imply.

Not a Healthy Environment

We know that the houses at Skara Brae had no windows. Any fuel they burned would have been of a very inferior quality – probably low-grade peat and perhaps dried animal dung, since wood has always been at a premium in this part of Orkney. The central fires in the houses would have been very smoky and ventilation limited to one hole in the centre of the room. This would have let in a little light during the day, but in winter the Sun does not rise too high in the sky in these northern climes and so the houses would have been generally dark and fairly unhealthy. With so much rubbish accumulating so close by, it is possible that people became sick, though it also has to be remembered that they would have spent a great majority of each day out of doors, even in the winter. Another point that should be borne in mind is that they had experience on their side. Surely people who were as clever and resourceful as they clearly were at Skara Brae would not have provided themselves with conditions that ensured they would be perpetually picking up infections, parasites and diseases of one sort or another?

What we do know is that the village at Skara Brae was not occupied for a long period of time. After about only a century it was abandoned. It is possible that the area went through a series of extremely harsh winters, with the sea threatening to encroach on the village – we simply don't know. But, for some reason, people took their prized possessions from the dressers and moved away from this lovely, remote spot, disappearing into the mists of time from which they had emerged. What they left us was a time capsule, and incidentally one that is in constant danger from the sea and from the ravages brought about by so many visitors each year.

People who have a good imagination, which I think would be everyone who takes the trouble to read a book such as this, are sure to treasure memories of a visit to Skara Brae for the rest of their lives. Skara Brae is a Neolithic jewel of indescribable importance and a site that is a must for anyone who has an interest in the way ancient people lived in our islands.

The ancient Orcadians must have been excellent farmers and it is certain they raised cattle because amongst the rubbish that had accumulated between the houses in Skara Brae there were large collections of beef bones.

It is entirely thanks to changing weather patterns and the encroaching sea that Skara Brae was sealed by sand as a time capsule from the past. The people who lived in the settlement seem to have struggled against the all-pervasive wind-borne sand for decades before they finally gave up the struggle and abandoned the site.

Maeshowe

Maeshowe Chambered Cairn, Mainland, Orkney

LATITUDE: 58° 59' 46.28" N   LONGITUDE: 3° 11' 13.55" W

There would be absolutely no point in travelling all the way to Orkney in order to see Skara Brae without also taking in the other undoubted treasures from prehistory that adorn this most wonderful island. Chief amongst these has to be Maeshowe, indisputably the finest chambered cairn to be found in the British Isles (unless we count Newgrange in Ireland (*see* Newgrange) which rivals Meashowe in many ways). Here, on Mainland, Orkney, is a work of great artistry and intelligence.

The same sort of people who constructed the little stone houses in Skara Brae were also responsible for building Maeshowe and they certainly knew their business when it came to using stone. Whilst other peoples across the British Isles adapted their knowledge of woodworking to the art of building in stone, which they did fairly rarely, the Orcadians had little or no wood but must have become adept at working with what they had at a very early date. In their case it was stone, and plenty of it.

Figure 43: Maeshowe chambered cairn

The mound that covers the tomb at Meashowe is 115ft (35 metres) in diameter and at its highest point it is 24ft (7 metres) tall. This makes it an impressive structure, even when seen from a relative distance, and there is no doubting that this is an artificial construct, though anyone without knowledge of its contents might be astonished at its composition or what its interior looks like. Maeshowe probably isn't too different from any of the chambered cairns of its type. Its fame lies in the fact that it has remained generally intact and that we can actually enter it and gaze with wonder at what the prehistoric Orcadians were capable of achieving.

Within the centre of the mound is a veritable maze of passages. These were built out of sizeable flat stones before the mound was eventually raised over them. The work must have taken an age and it has to be remembered that some of the stones weigh as much as 30 tonnes!

The entrance of Maeshowe was carefully placed so that at the time of the winter solstice (around 21 December) the light of the Sun rising at dawn would pass down the passage and illuminate the wall at the far end. Why should this be the case? The most likely explanation has something to do with death and rebirth. Those who built Meashowe and the other monuments of the period clearly understood the year very well. They knew that the Sun travels south on the horizon after the autumn equinox and that it achieves its most southerly position at dawn by the winter solstice. After that it begins to move north again, through the spring equinox and onto midsummer. It could be reasonably suggested that the winter solstice represents the 'death' of the year. The weather in the northern hemisphere is at its coldest, days are at their shortest (especially in northern Scotland) and nature is caught in the iron fist of winter.

This is probably why the midwinter period was of the greatest importance to the prehistoric people of the British Isles. If the right ceremonies were carried out, the gods would relent once more and the world would gradually be freed from the icy hand of winter; if the world could reawaken, then why not the dead ancestors? Whether it was considered that they would be reincarnated into this world, or into some alternative existence, we cannot know, but there is surely no doubt that some idea of the sort prompted the builders of Meashowe (and Newgrange in Ireland) to create tombs with this specific orientation.

The Central Chamber

The passage at Meashowe is long and leads ultimately to a central chamber that is about 15ft (4.6 metres) square. The roof is corbelled, which means that slightly overlapping stones rise gradually upwards and inwards until they eventually meet in a beehive-shaped structure. The expert way the tomb was built shows just how conversant the Orcadians were with corbelled structures, of which there were once many in Orkney and the north of Scotland.

Unfortunately, when Maeshowe was first excavated in relatively modern times, in 1861, there was very little to find there. Even if there had been we might not have known about it because the man who conducted the 'dig' was

Figure 44: Drawing of the interior of Maeshowe in section

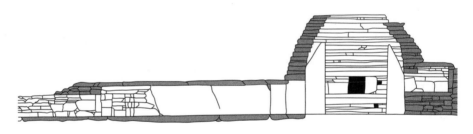

Southeast section

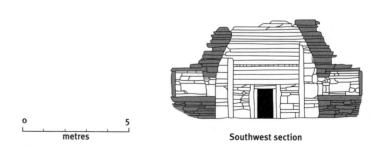

0   5
metres

Southwest section

a treasure seeker rather than a scientist. But in any case the tomb had been robbed many centuries earlier by the Vikings. They left runic inscriptions within the tomb that can still be seen by visitors today.

Estimates vary as to how long it actually took to create a tomb as large as Meashowe. The archaeologist Colin Renfrew has estimated 100,000 man-hours, though an edition of TV's *Time Team* a few years ago showed a reconstruction of a fairly small corbelled tomb that was actually completed in a staggeringly short period of time. In the case of the television programme, stone was brought to the site for the team to use, whereas with Maeshowe it had to be sought and dug out from the surrounding ground. This would certainly have increased the timescale considerably but I, for one, think that these prehistoric engineers were not in any particular rush to get their structures finished. I am sure the job was done mainly in winter when there was little else to do; it kept people warm and built social cohesion, and any particular project such as this one might have taken years to complete.

A Place for the Dead

When we consider tombs these days we tend to think of structures that are sealed after an interment and which stay that way more or less forever. It is likely that these large tombs from remote antiquity were slightly different in that they were probably re-entered on a fairly regular basis. Unlike the later round barrows that contained high-status burials with many grave goods, the earlier tombs started out as repositories for parts of many skeletons. These had often been de-fleshed in some way prior to placing them in the tomb within central chambers or side chambers. They may have been visited on many occasions and were certainly added to across time. This might make such tombs in a way more akin to temples, or places of ceremonies and celebrations, associated with a death cult about which we know little or nothing. It is very unlikely that the Vikings who raided the tomb six centuries ago, despite their thirst for treasure, found nothing much more than bones for all their efforts, though they were probably left with a sense of wonder that anyone would go to such trouble to protect anything that was so valueless, at least as far as they were concerned.

Maeshowe might be quite late in construction, and certainly later than many tombs of its class. It is thought that it was completed around 2800 BC, which still makes it very nearly 5,000 years old. It is a stunning achievement of planning and execution and sure proof that whatever religion these people did possess, it captivated them every bit as much as did the Christianity of the medieval church and cathedral builders. It must have represented a central and deeply important part of their lives. And just as surely as the men who threw up the massive bastions of Canterbury and York went home at the end of the day to their small hovels, so the people of the Neolithic period in Orkney would have lived generally in small and fairly squalid dwellings, in no way comparing with the artistry and solidity of Maeshowe. Despite this the existence of Skara Brae bears testimony to the fact that building domestic structures in stone was not unknown to the Orcadians, who after all had little or no wood to use for any purpose. That they became so good at constructing in stone is therefore not too surprising. Nevertheless, the determination, planning and persistence that went into any one of the tombs of the Maeshowe sort was colossal. It shows without doubt that although we may have advanced in terms of technology, our overall intelligence has not altered much across what seems to us to be a vast period of time.

The Legacy of Orkney

There was clearly something very special about the island of Orkney. In terms of the monuments it possesses from our prehistoric past it is rivalled only by the structures of Salisbury Plain in England, the ritual landscape around Thornborough in North Yorkshire, England and the Boyne Valley in Ireland. There are so many tombs, ruined and still standing, in Orkney that it is entirely possible that people, or their bones, came from far off to be interred there. Maybe the island had the same sort of importance in Neolithic Britain as Anglesey did to the later Celtic people of the British Isles. Slowly but surely our knowledge of these lost cultures grows, and with refined techniques and ever greater scientific skills, we may yet learn more about a remarkable people whose only real legacy to us so far has been the fantastic structures they created. Maeshowe is amongst the best of these.

The Ring of Brodgar

The Ring of Brodgar, Orkney

LATITUDE: 59° 0′ 7.5″ N　　　　　LONGITUDE: 3° 13′ 44.7″ W

The third of the prehistoric structures in Orkney I want to mention is the standing stone circle at Brodgar, which is not very far away from the tomb at Maeshowe. Brodgar is extremely impressive, probably partly because it is so remote it has not suffered much at the hands of man, even though it has been buffeted by the elements for so long.

Brodgar stands in an impressive location on an isthmus between the lochs of Stennes and Harray. All around it are the most stunning views imaginable and the site may have been chosen because of these, or on the grounds that there are good views of the sky on all sides, which would have increased its potential as an observatory and marker of astronomical events. Brodgar is within a natural bowl, with mountains on virtually every side, offering a multiplicity of backsights for would-be naked-eye astronomers to use.

A Very Large and Impressive Circle

Brodgar is the third-largest stone circle in Britain. The only bigger ones are at Avebury and Stanton Drew in England. Brodgar has a diameter of 341ft (104 metres) and though it originally contained 60 stones only 27 are to be seen on the site these days. However, the stones that do remain are extremely impressive and significant sentinels when seen at any time of year, but somehow especially so in the gloom and dark of the short Orcadian winter days.

Around the stones at Brodgar is a circular ditch that is about 9ft deep (3 metres) and which is 397ft (121 metres) in diameter. We might refer to this as a henge, except for the fact that there is no attendant bank, as is always the case with henges further south. The effort required to create this ditch was enormous. Whereas in the south, henges were often dug into gravels or relatively soft chalk, at Brodgar the surrounding ground is solid sandstone under a very narrow band of earth. Since the ditch is around 30ft (9 metres) wide, a great deal of rock had to be smashed and shifted to create such an impressive ditch. Despite the absence of a mound – which surely means that all the material excavated had to be taken away – the ditch has two entrances and has therefore been referred to as a Class II henge.

Within the circle at Brodgar there appear to be no other stones, though we cannot be certain that this is the case because the site has never been excavated to any great extent. This also means that dating is difficult. Most estimates place the Ring of Brodgar at around 2500 BC, though I for one would not be remotely surprised if it was subsequently discovered to be a good deal older.

A Lunar Observatory?

It is likely that Brodgar, like many of the northern Scottish circles, was used for lunar observations. Investigations of these circles by Alexander Thom (*see* Thom, Alexander), showed that this was clearly the case. The Neolithic and Bronze Age inhabitants of this part of Britain seem to have had a particular fascination for the tortuously difficult movements of the Moon, which they may have used as part of an assessment of the frequency of eclipses, or for maritime purposes since a good knowledge of the interactions of the Moon and the Sun allow a better understanding of spring tides.

As we have seen already, Brodgar is set within a landscape rich in prehistoric structures and it somehow seems appropriate that such a fine standing stone circle was erected on the island. The stones at Brodgar are quite peculiar in comparison with their more southerly counterparts. Builders of stone circles generally used what was available to them and in the case of this part of Orkney it was very flat stones, which vary in height between 7ft (2.1 metres) and 15ft (4.7 metres).

This is a wild, lonely and evocative place. Anyone viewing it after a visit to Skara Brae and a nosey around Maeshowe is sure to be suitably impressed. Maybe it's the colour of the stone but the large, flat megaliths of Brodgar always feel warm to me, no matter what time of year one touches them. I stand for ages, looking out across the lonely hills and I imagine the care that was taken in choosing the right stones for the site and then the physical exertion necessary in moving them to their places within the ditch. Where did all the stone and earth from this fairly massive ditch go? Was it cast into the loch? This seems like the most likely explanation but if so, why did the builders of Brodgar depart from the usual method of henge building, which kept the bank on site, at the far side of the ditch. Were there practical reasons, maybe to do with backsights, that meant the mound was not to be considered here? So many questions and so few positive answers. But then that is part of the appeal of the prehistoric structures across the British Isles. You can dream up your own answers, and if you think hard they are likely to be just as reasonable and likely as those put forward by any expert.

It is often suggested that the reason northern Scotland, and Orkney in particular, has so many Megalithic monuments is because the population of the area was quite high in prehistoric times. Climatologists sometimes suggest that the general climate of the British Isles was much warmer around the time the stone circles and burial mounds were being created and that the Scottish growing season was therefore longer and subsistence farming easier than it proved to be in more modern times.

Who am I to argue? I am definitely not a climatologist but, on the other hand, we are now beginning to realize that our species managed to survive in Britain way back at a time when the climate was extremely harsh, either just before or just after ice ages. True, the picture may have been different once farming became the norm but until very recently extremely isolated communities on the Scottish Isles managed quite well with crop growing and raising sheep and cattle. It should also be remembered that the Highlands of Scotland were not abandoned because it was impossible to farm them, but rather because greedy, mostly English, landlords wanted the land for sheep. Maybe our ancient ancestors were able to cope with Orkney's climate and also recognized that they were living in one of the most beautiful places on our planet?

Kilmartin

Kilmartin, Argyll

LATITUDE: 56° 8' 0.84" N   LONGITUDE: 5° 28' 58.47" W

If Orkney is rich in prehistoric sites, another area of Scotland, this time slightly more accessible, that is of equal interest is the region around Kilmartin in Argyll. The prehistory enthusiast could spend a considerable time wandering round this area and there is much to wonder at in a region that must always have been a special place of reverence for its inhabitants.

Part of the area is clearly a city of the dead because there are a number of burial cairns in Kilmartin Glen. Some of these have been excavated and all are attributable to the Bronze Age. However, probably the most fascinating structure in this most extraordinary area is the standing stone circle of Temple Wood. We don't know what our ancient ancestors called these stones and the name Temple Wood is extremely recent. Late in the 19th century a circle of trees was planted outside the circuits of the stones and that is when the name Temple Wood came into use.

The Circles of Temple Wood

There are actually two circles at Temple Wood. The southernmost example is around 40ft in diameter (12 metres) and presently has 13 standing stones, though there were undoubtedly more at one time, probably 22. Within the circle the ground is covered in polished river stones. This is not something I have personally seen at any other site and it seems to be a peculiarity of this location, since the northern circle also has them.

The northern circle is smaller, has far fewer stones and is generally of less interest than its large neighbour. Carved onto some of the stones of the southern circle are quite precise markings. One of the stones contains two spirals, which were used by Alexander Thom in order to demonstrate the geometric knowledge of the people who built these sites. There are also concentric rings and the ubiquitous cup marks.

Many burials have been associated with the circles of Temple Wood but the majority of them are much later than the stones (though most of them are, by definition, prehistoric). There is a cist burial at the centre of the large ring and many associated burials in the vicinity, making this just about the most used and reused site I have ever seen. This is a really strange place and well worth a look, especially since there is so much else to see in the district. Within striking distance of Kilmartin there are literally dozens of cairns, masses of carvings of one sort or another, hill forts, sacred places, standing stones and little fairy rings of stones nearly up to their necks in peat. It would be quite possible to spend a week or more simply wandering round with a good guidebook of the area. The whole area has an ambience that is unique, the locals are more than accommodating and the whiskey is especially good.

It is worth noting that the 'mystical' nature of the Kilmartin area does not restrict itself to the prehistoric period. Historians with a particular interest in a mysterious order of fighting monks that appeared in the 12th century have looked at Kilmartin with interest. Some suggest that the Knights Templar, who rose to become one of the most important religious orders ever created, retreated to Scotland when their order was betrayed and made illegal by the Roman Catholic Church in 1307.

Why the fleeing knights might have chosen this area could be partly due to its isolation in the early 14th century, and could also have something to do with the fact that the king, Robert the Bruce, was no fan of either the Catholic Church or its popes. The story goes that the escaped Templars began to live non-religious and fairly normal lives once they came to Scotland, and many of them, and their sons, were buried within the Kilmartin area in graves that are easily recognizable as being Templar graves.

Hardly prehistoric, but it does add to the fascination of the place. It is even suggested that some of these escaped Templar knights fought for Robert the Bruce and helped to win a great battle against the English at Bannockburn in 1314.

Mousa Broch

Mousa Broch, Shetland

LATITUDE: 59° 59' 45.37" N   LONGITUDE: 1° 10' 50.46" W

If the journey to Orkney or indeed the more remote Highlands is long, getting to Shetland is even harder. I mention Mousa Broch because it is by far and away the most well preserved of this species of fortified roundhouse, of which there are or probably were around 500 throughout Scotland. When seen from a distance a broch might look something like a ruined stone windmill and the gaunt and weathered stumps of these truly remarkable buildings can be seen all over the far northeast, as well as in the west and many of the islands.

There are brochs and parts of brochs numerous enough to comprise a lifetime's study for someone – and in fact that is precisely what they have done. However, the most complete and impressive broch is almost certainly that of Mousa, on the Island of Shetland.

Mousa Broch is of hollow-wall construction and created, as are all brochs, without any mortar. Perhaps fortunately for this particular tower, it is somewhat smaller in diameter than many of the brochs of Scotland. This makes it a good deal more solid and so it has stood the test of time, earth tremors, high winds and rain that are typical of these remote areas, much better than some of its fellow structures.

Climb to the Top

It is possible to climb right to the top of Mousa Broch and the view from the summit certainly makes the effort worthwhile. Mousa is only one of over a hundred brochs that were built in Shetland alone and is probably about the same age as most of them. It dates back to a period not so long before the Roman invasion of Britain but of course remote Shetlanders may never have even heard of the Romans, and certainly did not fear them as their southern neighbours must have done. Mousa is one of two brochs that seem to have guarded Mousa Sound.

The walls of the broch are incredibly thick, which visitors can appreciate when they walk down the passage that leads through them. Once inside there isn't all that much to see, except the construction of the inner walls and the staircases that lead upwards. Having said that, there is always a sharp intake of breath from visitors as they first gaze up at the stonework, which is still in remarkably good condition and which has stood the test of time incredibly well.

There never seems to have been a sizeable community of people living close to the broch, so it has probably always stood more or less alone. Exactly why it was built, and even absolutely *when*, is not known since no detailed excavation of the site has ever taken place.

Mousa is just one of 500 examples of brochs and it seems incredible that they still retain their basic secrets, despite the fact that there were so many of them. Somewhere in the mists of myth and legend the answer to the massive effort that went into broch building lies waiting to be rediscovered.

Many of the brochs occupy fantastic locations. One cannot help thinking that if they had been built in more accessible locations, for example in southern England, they would either have not survived the intervening period, or else more effort would have gone into uncovering the secrets of their construction and why they were built.

It isn't out of the question that if we were able to go back in time and ask the man who planned and built Mousa Broch why he had undertaken the project in such an isolated spot, we may have received the answer 'Because I could.' In other words, anyone who had designs on invading a particular area, and who scouted around first, would have seen the brochs and been impressed at the tenacity and also the obvious wealth of anyone who could create such a structure. In their original state all the brochs said the same thing – 'I am very powerful; I have many people at my disposal and my defences are virtually impregnable. Occupy my land at your own peril!'

In this respect the brochs were similar to Iron Age hill forts, many of which were so large there simply could not have been enough warriors to defend their banks. In other words, both hill forts and brochs dealt partly in bluff, but it was probably good enough to do the trick.

Ballymeanoch

Ballymeanoch Stone Row, Argyll

LATITUDE: 56° 6' 39.8" N   LONGITUDE: 5° 29' 2.73" W

Just about a mile southeast of Slockavullin is an impressive row of four large standing stones. The tallest stones in the row are 12ft (3.6 metres) and 13ft (4 metres) respectively. They are aligned northwest–southeast across 49ft (15 metres). This is one of the best stone rows in Scotland and as with most pre-historic sites in this spectacular country they stand in the most breathtaking landscape imaginable. Look carefully on the western side of the stones and you will see a wealth of cup markings. Despite their frequency all over the British Isles these never cease to amaze me. Why did people take so much time and trouble to make them and what are they trying to tell us? After over three decades of looking and thinking I am really no wiser than I ever was.

The stone row at Ballymeanoch was aligned to the midwinter sunrise but as my own investigations (together with my friend and colleague Christopher Knight) show, that means they are also aligned to the rising point of the star Sirius, which seems to have been particularly fascinating to the Neolithic people of our islands. This alignment to Sirius may have been coincidental in the case of Ballymeanoch but was certainly not the case at other sites, and especially not at Thornborough Henges in Yorkshire, England.

Alexander Thom was fascinated by this row and he also pointed out that the alignment in the opposite direction was to the most northern setting of the Moon at the time the stones were erected. Thom's original fascination with the Scottish standing stones and stone circles revolved around his absolute belief that 'Moon-tracking' was a major pursuit of our ancient ancestors and especially so in these most northerly sites.

About 140ft (42 metres) to the southwest of the stone row there are another two sizeable stones. Alexander Thom thought that these were aligned with the most southerly rising position of the Moon.

Stone rows still represent a significant mystery because if they were not created for astronomical purposes, what was their true function? Could they have been way-markers, telling travellers that they were on a particular route (practical or ritual) or were they built to commemorate specific individuals, perhaps priests or tribal chiefs? This has certainly been a popular explanation for the extremely long stone rows to be found in Brittany. The truth is that we don't know, but isn't it the mysteries of all prehistoric sites that make them so appealing?

Hauling huge stones around the landscape was certainly not easy, and we tend to forget about the logistics necessary to achieve the objective. For example, nobody could have moved stones such as these any distance without the aid of ropes and significant amounts of timber. Even if, as I have suggested, many of the largest stones in the British Isles were moved in winter, utilizing snow to make them easier to shift, a great deal of timber and many, many metres of rope would also have been necessary.

A commodity such as rope does not make itself, and there are no native vines in the British Isles, such as the ones employed by Tarzan to swing from tree to tree. From the most remote times in the British Isles rope had to be made by extracting and spinning fibres from various plant species. Presumably this would have been work undertaken by women and children, though it is likely that men took part too, probably around the fire in the evenings, when there was little else to do. Communities may have worked for months or years, simply to put together enough strings to make the massive ropes necessary to shift stones weighing so many tons.

Meanwhile many trees and saplings would have had to be cut to make the sledges and other timbers necessary for such a procedure. This undertaking too would have been no mean feat at a time when there was no metal and when axes were made of flint or other hard stones. Such timber then had to be trimmed and prepared.

All of this goes to prove that the people concerned were not only dedicated, but extremely hardworking. Surely they would never have gone to such trouble unless they considered the objective to be important?

Arthur's Seat

Arthur's Seat, Prehistoric Edinburgh

LATITUDE: 55° 56′ 37.09″ N   LONGITUDE: 3° 9′ 16.22″ W

It might surprise readers to learn that regal Edinburgh, Scotland's wonderful capital city, is about as prehistoric a location as one can find anywhere in Britain. This is because it was first inhabited by hunter-gatherers as long ago as 8500 BC. These hunters stayed for some time in and around Cramond, close to modern Edinburgh, and they seem to have set a trend that has shown the area to be inhabited by humans ever since.

Part of the reason people were drawn to this location was its defensible nature. Right in the centre of modern Edinburgh is a hill known today as Arthur's Seat (there's that semi-mythical king again).

Now part of Holyrood Park, Arthur's Seat is the largest of a group of hills in the vicinity, being 823ft (251 metres) in height and extremely defensible. The view from the top of Arthur's Seat is stunning, and there is no better way to experience Edinburgh, old and new, than from this location. But people were looking down from here long before any sort of city, town, or even village existed where Edinburgh stands today. This was the site of a significant and no doubt impressive hill fort. Remnants of the once strong defences can still be seen on Dunsapie Hill and above the area known as Samson's Ribs (so called because of the ditches and banks).

An Iron Age Defensive Structure

These ruined fortifications date back to the Iron Age, a period of history in the British Isles when it seems that everyone was taking up arms and sealing themselves into more or less impregnable fortresses of one sort or another. The idea amongst historians, and particularly teachers of history, used to be that when trouble threatened in the form of invading forces from elsewhere, everyone in the vicinity, including the livestock, would be corralled into the hill fort, which could be defended more easily than remote farms and tiny hamlets.

The combined effort of all the locals, now turned warriors, would see off the threat, or else sit out a siege that could not have been maintained for too long at such a remote period.

Whether this really represents what hill forts were for during the Iron Age is now in some doubt. It is possible that, like other structures such as brochs, hill forts were really more of a 'statement' than a practical way of dealing with an invading army. It has to be remembered that many of the Iron Age hill forts, including that around Arthur's Seat, were extremely large. It would have taken a substantial number of defenders to guard their perimeters, and if this was not possible the attackers could always find an undefended area where the banks and ditches could be stormed. It is known that the legions of Rome attacked and overran a number of even the most fiercely defended hill forts in England, Wales and throughout Gaul.

Even if Arthur's Seat is not as impressive as some of the hill forts further south, Cadbury or Old Oswestry for example, it is amazing to think that people have lived in this area for so long. One can also reflect on the fact that whilst at the top of Arthur's Seat, as is the case at Edinburgh Castle, one is literally on the top of a volcano. True, these ceased to be active a very long time ago, but how different the landscape must have looked when they were spewing forth steam and magma.

Most people who love prehistory are also fascinated with more recent periods and there surely could not be a better or more historic location than Edinburgh, whose very cobblestones reek of an often difficult but always fascinating past.

NORTHERN IRELAND AND EIRE

CONTENTS

Newgrange

Newgrange, Boyne Valley, Co. Meath

LATITUDE: 53° 41' 40.69" N   LONGITUDE: 6° 28' 31.67" W

Quite justifiably people come from all over the world to see Newgrange and doubtless some of them fail to realize that it is just one of a number of very similar tombs in the Boyne Valley of Ireland. Not so far away are Knowth and Dowth, which all together form part of what is known as the Brú na Bóinne, clearly one of the most important prehistoric landscapes in Europe or beyond. The Brú na Bóinne contains many tombs, standing stones, stone circles, remnants of timber circles and many other little-understood features from the very remote past. Taken all together the Brú na Bóinne is classified as a UNESCO world heritage site.

Newgrange itself is both spectacular and of the utmost importance when it comes to understanding the people who were living in the British Isles a good 500 years before a single stone was moved on the Giza Plateau in Egypt. Other Neolithic sites might suggest that, despite their abilities to move great stones around the landscape, these long-lost people were short on artistry and therefore probably lacking in culture, but one look at Newgrange will quickly dispel any such idea and shows just how refined its builders were. It must surely be certain that their subtlety, religious imperatives, and sophistication matched both their artistic skills and their engineering competency.

An Irish Passage Tomb

What we see at Newgrange today is a passage tomb. It has largely been reconstructed in terms of the way it looks from the outside, but every effort was made in the 1970s to merely put it back to what it was when first created, around 5,000 years ago. The visitor's first appreciation of the site is a very large mound, surrounded by a wall of white quartz stone that scintillates in even the feeblest sunlight. The tomb has a single entrance in its southeastern side and this leads along a passage for 60ft (18.95 metres) into the heart of the mound,

Figure 45: Newgrange in Ireland is one of the most impressive prehistoric tombs in the British Isles

where it takes on a cruciform shape. Once in this cross-shaped section the visitor can observe the corbelled roof above and also appreciate the size of many of the large stones that were used to line the chamber and the passage. Here, within what must surely have been a deeply revered and sacred spot, was where the bones or cremated remains of those long-lost people were laid – though for how long, why or with what ultimate intention in mind, we still do not know.

There are many observers of these truly ancient tombs who doubt that they were really intended to be tombs at all, at least not initially. True, most orthodox archaeologists still accept that this is what they must have been but other people point out that a church or cathedral, for example, contains the bones of the dead but that neither is ever considered to be, first and foremost, a tomb. However, if the chamber at locations such as Newgrange was not primarily a place of the dead, then what was it? Certainly it cannot have been a location where a congregation could have gathered because, as impressive as it is, it would not have been possible to assemble even a cross section of the community within its space. We are left with few clues, except the bones, but it is likely that it served a number of different functions. One possible explana-

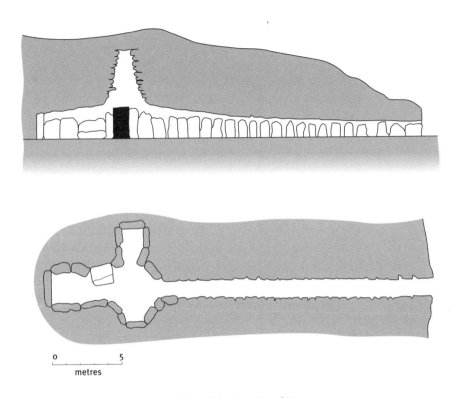

Figure 46: Plan of the interior of Newgrange

tion is that individual bodies, or even parts of them, were deposited within the chamber for only a specified period, maybe a year or less, until they could be somehow 'recreated' by the light of the rising Sun at midwinter.

The Magic of the Shortest Day

As is the case with Maeshowe in Scotland, the passage at Newgrange was cunningly and carefully created in such a way that the light of the rising Sun on the shortest day of the year would pass immediately down the passage and into the chamber beyond. Indeed, at Newgrange, a special 'box' was created above the tomb's entrance so that this phenomenon could take place, whether or not the tomb was sealed. So we might envisage a scenario in which individuals from the community who may have died during a particular year had their bodies prepared in a very specific way, perhaps being exposed until the flesh disappeared from them. They might then be placed in the chamber, which would be resealed until after the next winter solstice. It is even conceivable that after this had taken place the bodies of the dead, or parts of them, were not considered to have any merit or relevance, which is why they were not treated with any undue reverence subsequently.

I stress that this is just one idea that occurs to me. It seems to fit most of the facts but it is distinctly lacking in substance or detail, and that is because we simply do not have sufficient evidence to be certain. In this scenario the tomb would then effectively be a 'resurrection chamber', an initial idea which I credit primarily to my fellow writer and researcher Christopher Knight. If this was the case perhaps everyone in the community ultimately took their turn to be the focus of the winter solstice celebrations and to be recharged, or reborn, under the light of the pale midwinter Sun, either to be considered reborn into the normal world or to pass to some existence beyond it.

Whether or not this is merely fanciful nonsense we may never know for certain. What we do know is that the Neolithic farmers that created Newgrange, and its companion passage tombs, left us a snapshot of their lives and capabilities in many other ways. A significant number of objects were found in the passage and chamber of Newgrange over the years. Although most of these disappeared into private collections, or were eventually discarded, there were enough of them to show that people had come and gone within the tomb for a considerable period of time. These finds included pendants, stone marbles, flakes of flint, bone pins and other oddments of everyday life within this ancient community. Some of these were doubtless deliberate votive offerings, whilst others may simply have been lost or discarded.

Enigmatic Carvings

One of the things that Newgrange does show us is just how good the Neolithic people were when it came to stone carving. There is an assortment of large stones in and around the monument that were deliberately and painstakingly carved into all manner of (apparently) abstract patterns. In fact they are probably not abstract at all. Let's face it, the letters of our own alphabet only make sense because we are taught to understand their meaning. In the absence of this knowledge they could appear to be random shapes. The many swirls, spirals, lozenges and other designs still to be seen at Newgrange doubtless had quite specific meanings to the people who created them, although they defy interpretation as far as we are concerned.

Ireland is quite rightfully extremely proud of its flagship monument at Newgrange. The mound rises to a height of 40ft (12 metres) and covers an area of over an acre (0.4 hectares). The stones comprising the structure were not cut from the living rock to complete the project because it is clear that they were

Figure 47: One of the magnificent carved stones flanking Newgrange

extensively weathered before they were put into place. Nevertheless, the job of finding such a large amount of stone in the locality must have been daunting and it has been estimated that the task of creating Newgrange as we see it today probably took in excess of 30 years. It has also been shown that many of the smaller passage tombs in the same area are slightly older than Newgrange and so it has to be a possibility that the builders gradually refined their skills and techniques across a significant period of time.

Even when the primary purpose of Newgrange may have been forgotten, or had changed over centuries, the site did not lose either its significance or presumably its mystique. It is known from post holes that a significant number of wooden circles or other structures were erected on or near the site in the centuries following completion of the tomb. And much later, by the time of the Bronze Age, the site was still a place of reverence because a circle of stones was erected around the tomb, something that probably took place a good 1,000 years after building began on the site. This may have been a later culture subsuming the 'magic' of a site that was already ancient to them, or there may indeed have been a type of continuity – though it is hard to see how memories could have been passed intact by a non-literate culture for so many centuries. We can imagine that the passage tomb was already a deeply revered site for the stone-erectors of the Bronze Age and they might even have thought it was an entry into the 'other world' or was related in some way to the mysterious 'people of the hollow hills' who still represent a tangible component of Irish folklore.

Use and Disuse

The latest research tends to indicate that although the Bronze Age people of the area clearly did think the site was significant, their immediate forebears probably did not. There is evidence that the passage grave fell into disrepair before the Bronze Age began and that people were living around its broken edges – probably without paying it too much religious attention. Migrations took place regularly in the late Stone Age and Bronze Age British Isles. People probably arrived whose religious imperatives were different, and to them the passage grave may have had no particular significance. Only later, when the locals became detached from true memories of the original nature of the site, was it once again revered and the stones erected around it.

Newgrange is a truly remarkable place. I sometimes wonder if we, living here in these islands, have the slightest comprehension of what we have within our midst. At the time these structures were erected there was no civilization worth the name existent anywhere in Europe. Only the embryonic states of the Near and Middle East were starting to climb out of the obscurity of prehistory and great Egypt was also in a fairly infantile state. The British Isles at the time must have seemed a very advanced place in comparison with what surrounded it and a culture that existed in a relatively narrow swathe from parts of Scandinavia in the north, in an arc, down through Great Britain and Ireland and into Brittany, probably shone like a star amidst the surrounding darkness of primitive subsistence farming. No wonder the most ancient tales of other civilizations talk about those 'magical islands to the north', where the weather was always good, where people were learned and educated and where the technology was breathtaking. It is entirely possible, though they didn't realize it, that they were speaking about places such as Newgrange.

Freed from the wealth of immigrants and invaders that came and went across the water in England, Scotland and Wales, it is likely that the indigenous populations of Ireland endured for longer with their old beliefs and practices intact. There may also have been more continuity of belief, especially in the magical nature of certain locations such as Newgrange.

Newgrange stands within a deeply significant ritual landscape that retained its potency and significance into relatively recent times. The Irish themselves remembered those who had laboured to build such structures and they assumed the proportion of giants, or else people who had magical powers. It is likely that Irish oral history goes back many thousands of years and it may have much to tell us.

Carrowmore

Carrowmore Passage Tomb Cemetery, Co. Sligo

LATITUDE: 54° 14′ 53.68″ N   LONGITUDE: 8° 31′ 6.88″ W

It's a fair bet that a good cross section of those reading this book will never have heard of Carrowmore, and yet it should rank as one of the finest collections of truly ancient tombs to be found anywhere in the British Isles. It is located in Co. Sligo, on the Cúil Irra Peninsula, and it is one of the most significant mortuary sites ever to be created. What is more, it is the centre of great controversy and if some of its evidence is to be truly believed, it may tell us something quite remarkable about when at least some of these incredible structures were planned and executed.

There are presently a known 30 or so tombs to be found in the Carrowmore passage tomb cemetery, though there are probably more that are lost or still not discovered.

Most of the tombs represent 'dolmen circles' in which not particularly large dolmens (*see* Dolmen) were surrounded at a distance of around 13 to 16 yards (12 to 15 metres) by a ring of large stones. It used to be argued, and by some people still is, that the dolmens had originally been covered with a mound, though there are many knowledgeable experts these days who will state categorically that, in the case of the Carrowmore tombs, no mound ever existed. Some of the tombs have a pentagonal burial chamber, whilst others were roughly circular. Each monument was built on a platform, doubtless to level it in the undulating landscape, and many of the dolmens represent satellite tombs around larger and grander central tombs, towards which they face. In this case the site takes on a situation akin to some of the larger pyramids of Egypt, in which relatives of a particular pharaoh would have small pyramids built in close association with the much larger pyramid of the pharaoh himself, as if to gain their own immortality by showing themselves to be allied to him in death as much as they were in life. Maybe, therefore, the highest class of society occupied the central tombs at Carrowmore, with less elevated individuals dealt with in the satellite dolmen tombs.

Preparing the Bodies

Bodies or parts of bodies interred in the tombs at Carrowmore can be shown to have undergone a lengthy and complicated process of preparation before being laid to rest. Part inhumation, part cremation, seems to have been the norm, though subsequent advances in examination may throw more light upon what was really taking place in terms of burials at this extensive site.

And now we come to a situation of great controversy regarding the site at Carrowmore – namely, how old is it? Usually, radio carbon dating can be relied upon to offer a sensible age range for a site, but at Carrowmore this has not proved to be possible. Excavations meticulously carried out between the 1970s and the 1990s returned radio carbon dates from reliable sources as being around 5400 BC. This creates a great puzzle because it has been universally accepted that all the Neolithic structures were created by settled farming communities, whereas farming had not commenced in Ireland by this very early period. True, there were people living in Ireland at the time, but they would have been hunter-gatherers, who have never been associated with building of any sort that has survived the test of time.

Is the dating suspect? Are we wrong about the period when farming did reach our islands? Were the hunter-gatherers more capable than we have henceforth realized? At the moment the jury is still out regarding these issues, though the contentious carbon dates won't go away. People have tried to explain them away in terms of those who built the monuments having utilized wood that was already ancient when they found it, but this seems slightly implausible. Having said that, there is a great tradition in Ireland and in other parts of the British Isles for using what is known as 'bog oak'; trees that were flooded and which have survived as usable wood for many centuries. Whether this could be the case or not cannot be ascertained for certain though most bog oak is truly ancient, predating even a remote 5400 BC.

An Ancient Legacy

More and more people on the fringes of prehistory research are now suggesting that the period of building in our islands commenced very much earlier than we have hitherto realized and no doubt the arguments will rage for a long time to come. What is known is that other parts of the same site have revealed a dating broadly in accord with other tombs built in the Neolithic period – so the whole thing is deeply confusing.

Sligo, as a county, contains a number of different types of tomb of great age. These include classifications I mentioned in the A–Z section of the book, such as passage tombs, wedge tombs and of course the portal dolmen tombs. Whether these were all built, maybe at slightly different times, by the same culture, or if they represent new influxes of people is, at the moment, difficult to say. Doubtless as scientific skills increase, more and more evidence will come to light and many of these questions may be answered.

In the meantime Carrowmore is one of the most fascinating places imaginable, even though anyone without the slightest knowledge of matters prehistoric might drive past it without a second glance. The area is not hard-going on foot (though as with other such places the ground undulates and could not be considered to provide reliable disabled access). There is a visitor centre nearby, which is open from the late spring until the autumn, and as usual almost anywhere in the British Isles it would be advisable to have stout footwear and good waterproofs. One of the reasons that Ireland in particular in so green is because it rains on so many days of the average year!

Beaghmore

Beaghmore Complex, Co. Tyrone

LATITUDE: 54° 42′ 3.97″ N   LONGITUDE: 6° 56′ 14.46″ W

For anyone who relishes a real puzzle from prehistory, Beaghmore in Northern Ireland represents an interesting day out. Many of the monuments at Beaghmore defy description within the general classifications, though archaeologist Aubrey Burl commented that some of them have a commonality with vaguely similar structures in Cumbria, England.

Nothing was even known of Beaghmore until the 1940s, when peat cutting in the area began to reveal some intriguing features that had been covered for many centuries. Eventually a whole sequence of stone circles, cists, piles of stones and other associated structures became evident and the whole area began to take on such an importance that moves were made to preserve and safeguard the site.

It is thought that the structures at Beaghmore were created in the early Bronze Age, though since not all the site has been adequately excavated or dated it is entirely possible that parts of it are much older. In and around Beaghmore, and within a relatively small area, there are no less than seven stone circles. None of these have very high stones and some of them are definitely not circles at all. It is likely that in at least some of the cases they originally surrounded burials of one sort or another.

In addition to the circles, some of which seem to have quite definite astronomical alignments, there are also 12 cairns and 10 rows of stones. To find so many stone rows in such a small area is virtually unique and since it has been shown that stone rows quite often have an astronomical significance, we can assume that the same was the case here, even in the case of rows where no pattern relating to the sky has been discerned yet. It is known, for example, that three of the stone rows point to the winter solstice, which, as we have seen, had a tremendous importance to these early builders in stone. Astronomical alignments for the other rows may not have been found yet, but the sky is a complex subject for study and doubtless sense will eventually be made of all the rows.

At Beaghmore there are many small cairns in and around the site, some of which have been found to contain the remains of human cremation and since there are also burials at the centre of at least some of the circles, there does seem to have been a direct connection between Beaghmore and whatever funeral rites and beliefs were prevalent when it was built.

A Range of Purposes

Strangely enough, we find at Beaghmore a whole site that has been reused after originally having been put to a different purpose. Archaeologists have been able to show that the land upon which all the present structures stand was once farmed in the Neolithic period. It is possible that the land lost its fertility because the earliest farmers used a slash-and-burn technique of farming that easily exhausted nutrients in the soil. Once it could no longer be reliably farmed, it would probably have made sense to put the land to some other use and so an extensive ritual site began to develop there.

Eventually the natural vegetation grew up around all the structures and the bog overtook it. For century upon century the stones stood below the turf, getting deeper and deeper, until someone came along to cut the peat for fertilizer or fuel, and happened upon the stones. In truth, this already extensive site could turn out to be much larger than it looks right now, since other components could still be hiding beneath the adjacent peat. What went on here is unknown, but it can be fairly conjectured that it had a religious aspect and that ancestor worship may well have been part of the site's function. In addition, astronomical observation almost certainly took place at Beaghmore.

This is a particularly intriguing and fascinating area and although its stones are generally fairly small and therefore don't appear all that impressive, the many mysteries of a site which only showed itself again so recently are going to keep local experts interested for a very long time.

The Giant's Ring

The Giant's Ring, Shaw's Bridge, Belfast

LATITUDE: 54° 32′ 24.52″ N   LONGITUDE: 5° 56′ 57.87″ W

The north of England is not alone in possessing a super-henge in relatively good condition. There is also one to be found in Northern Ireland and it really is a giant. The henge that has come to be known as the Giant's Ring is almost exactly the same size as those to be found at Thornborough in North Yorkshire, England. In many ways it is very similar and probably served a similar purpose, though in the case of the Giant's Ring there is the added bonus in that the remains of a passage tomb lie at the centre of the henge. The tomb is almost certainly later than the henge and, in my estimation at least, the primary astronomical function of the henge had either been forgotten or abandoned by the time the passage grave was created. In other words, a deeply revered site that was already hundreds of years old, the function of which was no longer relevant, must have seemed like an ideal place to put a passage grave.

We know little or nothing of the people who created either the henge or the tomb, and if prehistoric research is sometimes significantly lacking in England and Scotland, it is worse in parts of Northern Ireland. This is probably because the landscape is still essentially rural in nature. Sites don't tend to encroach on habitation (though the Giant's Ring is not far from Belfast) and even the curious antiquarians of the 18th and 19th centuries were not so active here.

The Giant's Ring is slightly different from its English cousins in that there is no appreciable ditch to be seen around the henge. What is more, the centre of the henge is dished, as if material for the banks had been scraped from the surface of the interior. There are at least three entrances into the henge that seem to be original, though in a way it is hard to tell since this particular super-henge is now a major public amenity. At one time horse racing used to take place here and locals from Belfast come daily to fly kites, walk dogs, to jog or simply to take some fresh air in a wonderful location. Do be careful what time you visit though because the gates are allegedly closed at 4pm, though this is Ireland and so that might be something of an approximation.

WALES

CONTENTS

Bryn Celli Ddu

Bryn Celli Ddu, near Llanddaniel Fab, Anglesey

LATITUDE: 53° 12' 27" N   LONGITUDE: 4° 14' 8.89" W

Wales is alive with prehistoric structures of one sort or another and they are to be found almost everywhere within the principality. However, there is no doubt that one of the finest repositories of our ancient history to be found anywhere in the British Isles is Anglesey, a large island just off the northwest mainland of Wales. Cross the bridge and you are in a prehistoric heaven but to my way of thinking the most evocative and best preserved prehistoric structure in the whole of Wales is the passage tomb of Bryn Celli Ddu, near Llanddaniel Fab.

To get the best out of the site you will need to have a torch with you but humanity's interest in this site is likely to have started before the dark depths of the tomb itself was created. At first there was a henge and a stone circle on the site. It appears that the stones from the circle were taken down during the Bronze Age and that at least some of them were incorporated into the tomb itself. Bryn Celli Ddu might not be as large or impressive as Newgrange, but it is just as important, and it shares something in common with both Newgrange and Maeshowe in that it was deliberately aligned to allow the light of the midwinter sunrise to enter the chamber – indeed there may once have been a light box present as shown to be the case at Newgrange.

The Cylindrical Pillar

Inside the tomb at Bryn Celli Ddu is a curious pillar that is almost cylindrical. It is hard to believe that anyone in the Bronze Age 'found' a rock this shape. It carries ancient incised marks and stands in front of what could easily be a 'stone lens' (see p. 81). It is the combination of this pillar and the stone lens that convinced my co-writer Christopher Knight and his associate Robert Lomas to reach the conclusion that not only the Sun was tracked from Bryn Celli Ddu but also the planet Venus when it was setting as an evening star. This theory is contentious but in the light of what we were to eventually discover

233

Figure 48: The entrance to Bryn Celli Ddu tomb

about the Megalithic Yard (*see* Thom, Alexander) it makes great sense.

At the entrance to the tomb is a carved stone with a typical serpentine design. This is a modern replica because the original stone, which stood within the tomb, has been taken for safekeeping to the National Museum of Wales. Accounts differ but some reports suggest that this stone was never in the tomb and that it had been deliberately buried under the entrance at the time the tomb was created. Also outside the entrance those who created the tomb buried a whole ox. Why this happened is a mystery, though ox bones have been found associated with other Bronze Age tombs.

The mound to be seen over Bryn Celli Ddu these days is not original but rather a partial reconstruction of what is thought to have been the case when the project was completed in the Bronze Age. There are people who doubt that such a mound ever existed on this site and who maintain that it was solely a device for astronomical observations. Such people are in the minority, at least as far as orthodox archaeology is concerned and of course we know that most structures of this sort did have a cairn or mound over the top of them.

Not much in the way of burials has been found within the tomb, merely a few partially cremated bones and (strangely) an intact human ear bone.

This is a deeply mysterious and extremely atmospheric site – in fact much of Anglesey is atmospheric. Bryn Celli Ddu is best seen when there are few people around and when you can take your time looking closely at all it has to offer. I am sure that there are more carvings on the rocks within its interior than have been reported – see what you think.

I have completely lost track of the number of hours personally spent measuring carefully at this site or squatting in the interior, waiting for some astronomical happening, whilst measuring and even filming the results. On several different evenings, in different years, I have waited with my friends, drinking hot coffee from flasks, until the Sun set on moonless nights and Venus, resplendent as an evening star, started to dip low towards the western horizon.

Venus is the brightest object in our skies apart from the Sun and Moon and is quite bright enough on a moonless night to cast a shadow. And this is exactly what it does at Bryn Celli Ddu. What is more, the reflection of its light is cast upon the stone lens, travelling between marks etched into the stone, presumably just for this purpose. What were the Venus watchers trying to do? Were they anxious to work out that most precise relationship between the cycles of Venus and those of the Earth year? It is true that the two planets share a very precise relationship – such that some astronomers think they are gravitationally locked into a tight mathematical dance.

It is hard to know, but I don't doubt that whatever was taking place would have been seen within the broad conception of 'religion' – things of the gods and goddesses – because in these remote times there would have been no disparity between the scientific and mathematical workings of the starry skies and the forces that were presumed to have put them in place and regulated them.

Druids Circle

Druids Circle, Penmaenmawr, Conwy

LATITUDE: 53° 15' 9.58" N   LONGITUDE: 3° 54' 51.53" W

Not only is Druids Circle one of the finest standing stone circles to be found in Wales, it is set amongst a landscape that was well utilized by our prehistoric ancestors, and for more than one reason. On the slopes of nearby Cwm Graiglwyd there was an axe factory, where pieces of the hard local stone were turned into axes during the Neolithic period. These were not simply for local use but for trade, and together with axes made in England's Lake District they are found widely distributed. The stone for the axes was found or quarried; it was then pounded into shape before being laboriously polished. It is quite likely that the best of them were never intended to be used in a daily sense but were for ritual purposes and to be used as grave goods. Axes from this area have been found as far away as the south of Cornwall – which at this remote time was a significant distance to trade such heavy objects.

The Druids Circle itself comprises about 30 stones, set in a stunning landscape. It has a portal entrance and is one of several standing stone circles in the district. What is more, it stands close to an extremely ancient prehistoric track that was probably the one used for setting out to trade stone axes from the district.

A Sacrificial Altar?

One of the stones in the circle has a 'chamfered' top, which led archaeologist Aubrey Burl to dig out some still extant legends that this particular stone was once used to sacrifice infants – though of course there is no proof whatsoever that such a practice ever took place. Ritual human sacrifice has been suggested a great deal for our truly ancient ancestors and the remnants of bog burials show that in some places, and in some circumstances, it does seem to have taken place, though the examples we have are from very much later than the Neolithic or Bronze Age periods. Strangely, it used to be a practice in the locality to place babies under a month old on the 'sacrifice stone' for good luck!

Maybe bearing some sort of testimony to these strange local tales is the fact that several infant burials have been found within the circle. These were cremations, though one of the cremations was of a girl around 11 years of age. If this was a place of infant sacrifice, it seems that either babies were in short supply or else any child would do. Once again it has to be stated that we really don't know and that these could be perfectly normal burials of much-loved children who suffered a perfectly natural, if tragically early, death.

Such is the position of Druids Circle, surrounded as it is by mountains, that this site was almost certainly used for astronomical purposes. To the best of my knowledge no in-depth research regarding its observational potential has been carried out but it is quite remarkable that we find mountain plateau circles such as this one in so many parts of the British Isles.

Incidentally, the name of the circle has nothing to do with its ancient past. As I explained in the A–Z section (*see* Druids), the Druids existed at the time of the Roman conquest, whereas the stones of this particular circle were probably erected around 3000 BC. That means there was a bigger gap in time between the circle's creation and the Druids than there was between the Druids and us.

Look out for the other circles in the vicinity.

Dyffryn Ardudwy

Dyffryn Ardudwy Burial Chambers, Gwynedd

LATITUDE: 52° 47' 5.27" N   LONGITUDE: 4° 5' 32.8" W

If you happen to be touring around Snowdonia in North Wales, which let's face it is one of the most spectacular and rewarding regions within our islands, you might want to stop off at the small village of Dyffryn Ardudwy, which is not far from the charming seaside resort of Barmouth and also quite close to spectacular Harlech.

Close to the village you will find what turns out to be quite a strange rectangular-shaped cairn – strange because within the same structure there are actually two separate burial chambers. This is not at all common – in fact the way it is laid out here seems to be unique to this site.

The western chamber stands on a platform of large stones and is the earlier of the two. Its dolmen is shaped like an 'H'; the chamber is rectangular and is topped by a large, sloping capstone.

Further to the east is the other chamber. It is around 30ft (9 metres) away and although later in date it was, at one time, more spectacular. It may have had a forecourt and a portal guarded by two large stones. Both chamber entrances face towards the east – perhaps in the direction of the rising midwinter Sun.

Excavations at the site revealed a cremation burial, but this was of a date later than the tomb itself, which was probably first constructed around 3500 BC, in the heyday of monumental tomb building in the British Isles. Two plaques of stone from Mynydd Rhiw on the Llyn Peninsula were also found buried at the site. What they were for is unknown, but Mynydd Rhiw was the site of an important prehistoric axe factory of the sort mentioned above in the description of Bryn Celli Ddu.

Beddgelert

Beddgelert Marker Stone, Gwynedd

LATITUDE: 53° 00′ 29.93″ N   LONGITUDE: 4° 05′ 41.64″ W

I suppose that bearing in mind just how many prehistoric structures there are in Wales, and especially in Gwynedd, I might be taken to task for mentioning one specifically that may not be prehistoric at all. Personally I think it almost certainly is, and that below the ground here is something of true prehistoric worth. As it stands at the moment all you will see in the field at Beddgelert are a couple of ancient, weathered stones, which are reputed to be the grave of nothing more or less than a dog!

That's what Beddgelert means, 'the grave of Gelert', which was supposedly a wolfhound belonging to Prince Llewelyn ap Iorwerth. He came home one day to find his house ransacked and his favourite dog with blood all around its mouth. Not finding the infant that was supposed to be in the house the prince assumed it had been attacked and eaten by Gelert. Drawing his sword he slew the dog, only to find later his unharmed son under an upturned cradle and the body of a huge wolf, which Gelert had fought and killed. In remorse, Prince Llewelyn ap Iorwerth had a special grave dug for his brave and faithful dog, and it is said that he never smiled again.

It's a great story, though the stones in the field close to the village have probably been there for far longer than the period of Prince Llewelyn ap Iorwerth. It may be that Gelert was actually a 6th-century saint and it is just possible that this is his grave, though we have no real way of knowing.

If you go to Gelert's Grave just stand there and look around. There is no more beautiful or haunting place in the length and breadth of the British Isles and if I was going to place a monument to the gods anywhere in our islands, I would surely choose this wonderful spot in Snowdonia.

It may not be prehistoric, it may not even be provably ancient, but it is most certainly worth a detour and every instinct in my body (none of which have any scientific validity in this case) tells me that our truly ancient ancestors revered this spot as much as I do.

Gors Fawr

Gors Fawr, near Narberth, Pembrokeshire, Wales

LATITUDE: 51° 55' 52.76" N   LONGITUDE: 4° 42' 46.85" W

The name of this area literally means 'great wasteland', which it has probably been since time out of mind. It is the site of a sizeable circle but comprised in the main of small stones, none of which are more than about 3ft (just under 1 metre) in height. The circle has a diameter of around 24 yards (22 metres) and, despite being overshadowed by some of our other stone circles, is impressive enough. Like many stone circles in Wales it stands in spectacular countryside.

About 142 yards (130 metres) to the northeast of the circle are two larger stones. These are twice the height of those in the circle and one of them is charmingly known as 'the Dreaming Stone'. There may be a midsummer sunrise association with this site, which like many others in the area may be attributed to the late Stone Age or the early Bronze Age.

What sets this area apart is not just the circle of Gors Fawr but the fact that it is very close to the Preseli Mountains, and is extremely close to the site where it is suggested the bluestones came from that are found at Stonehenge. One of the greatest mysteries of all lies in trying to work out why the people who built the first stage of Stonehenge chose to bring their stones such a vast distance; after all, England has plenty of stones of its own (and the later sarsen stones which were local are much larger and more impressive). All sorts of theories have been put forward. Maybe the people who built Stonehenge had originally come from further west, but it is just as likely that this whole area of what is now Wales was held as being sacred from an extremely early period.

Roman Britain

S trictly speaking, Roman remains in Britain lie beyond the scope of what would truly be referred to as 'prehistoric'. We do have a good deal of written evidence for the Roman invasion and occupation of Britain, though there is very little known about the minutia of life in these islands under the Romans except for what is recovered from archaeological sites. Authors like Julius Caesar and Tacitus were so busy trying to make political ground and singing the praises of either themselves or other famous figures from Latin history that they singularly failed to tell us anything of interest about the way ordinary people lived or the composition of Roman Britain, except in the broadest terms. As a result the sudden finding, in a remote field or under some factory, of Roman mosaics, hypocausts or marching camps generally comes as a great surprise.

A Wealth of Villas

As an example, with land being given by the Romans, especially in the south of England, to retired veterans of the legions, as well as to natives who knew how to toe the line, there were once a great many Roman villas in our islands. The National Trust presently produces an excellent map of Roman Britain, which lists all the known villas, as well as Roman towns, forts and other structures from the period. But as wonderful as these maps are, many of the Roman roads, some of the towns, dozens of the villas and forts, together with marching camps and maybe even the odd city, are not present – simply because we don't know where they were located or even that they existed.

In terms of the surprises that come along every year for historians and archaeologists alike, these Roman remains are every bit as exciting and unexpected as a newly excavated Stone Age mound or the socket holes of a long-forgotten stone row. In addition, there are now many recreated or partly recreated Roman sites to be seen in our islands and these make excellent days out. Some have museums and visitor centres where artefacts discovered in these locations can be viewed at first hand. Finally, there are many re-enactment groups that go to great trouble to recreate aspects of life in Roman Britain and who are often to be found at Roman sites on high days and holidays.

Roman Sites are often Accessible

For all these reasons I decided to include a limited amount of Roman sites in Britain at the end of this book and these should at least whet the appetite of readers who may by this stage discover that they have a real fondness for tramping across marsh and mountain to explore our past at first hand. Not that this is always necessary in the case of Roman sites because our Latin forebears often thoughtfully placed their structures in areas that are not so hard to get to (though some of them are also notoriously remote).

Romans in Britain

The Romans first came to Britain as an army in 55 BC under the leader Julius Caesar, though in reality Romans had been coming here a lot earlier than that in order to trade. Caesar's expedition was never intended to conquer Britain, and in any case, during this invasion the Romans came under great pressure from the combined forces of the British tribes that inhabited these islands in the Iron Age. These would have represented diverse groups that would probably fight each other at the drop of a hat but there were many that would and did come together to counter a common threat such as that presented by Rome.

Caesar soon withdrew and Britain was left alone again until AD 43, when a much more concerted campaign started, during the reign of the Emperor Claudius. This time the Romans had come to stay and although the British warriors fought back ferociously on occasion, they didn't really stand a chance against the might of the Roman army.

Part of the Empire

England was conquered in total, as was Wales. In the case of Scotland some punitive expeditions took place, especially early in the invasion, but for one reason or another the legions soon withdrew behind a great defensive work (Hadrian's Wall) in the far north of England.

Although the Britons revolted again and again, especially in the north, the Romans could not be dislodged until, in the year AD 410, what remained of the

Figure 49: Housesteads (Vercovicium) on Hadrian's Wall

Roman garrisons in Britain were withdrawn to defend the heart of the Roman Empire, which was under attack and crumbling fast. Once the legions left, England was fair game to both local warlords and those that came from over the sea and this in turn led to the arrival of the Anglo-Saxons (*see* Sutton Hoo in Impressive Sites section).

Changed beyond Recognition

During this period of just under four centuries the islands of Britain had changed beyond all recognition, though of course much of Scotland and all of Ireland remained essentially untouched by the Roman Empire. But even these extremities were influenced greatly by the proximity of Rome. In Scotland especially there is still vague evidence of the fact that Rome did at least try to subdue the whole country.

I have picked what I consider to be the very best Roman sites in England, Wales and southern Scotland and in a couple of cases places where people who are not so good on their feet and who can't stride over the high places with impunity might choose to go. Of course Roman sites are dramatically different from anything that went before and the comparison itself is fascinating. Most rewarding of all is that even when it came to everyday life the Romans built 'to last', so that although we know little about the way pre-Roman British tribes-people lived, we are beginning to amass a great deal of information about life in Roman villas, towns and forts.

Hadrian's Wall

When it was built Hadrian's Wall was quite definitely one of the most impressive structures, if not the most impressive, to be seen anywhere in Western Europe. It ran from Wallsend (Newcastle) in the east of northern Britain, 80 Roman miles across country to a point close to the village of Bowness-on-Solway, on the Solway Firth. The structure was made mainly of stone but there were some timber sections. Much of the wall would have been around 20ft (6 metres) in height and there were mile-castles at roughly one-mile (1.6km) intervals. The wall was also accompanied by a sizeable ditch but where the topography allowed for it, the legions used rocky crags and natural fault lines to improve the defensive nature of the wall.

Hadrian's Wall was commenced in AD 122 and, as the name implies, it was built on the direct orders of the Emperor Hadrian who ruled from 117–138. Its purpose was thought for centuries to have been to keep the warlike Scots tribes at bay, though this is a misnomer for a number of reasons. First of all the people living north of the wall were not Scots at this time but rather Picts, and in any case the wall was more a 'statement' of intent than a direct obstacle to the fearsome little people from north of the border. There would never have been enough troops to look after every part of the 80-mile (129km) wall adequately but their mere presence in large numbers in bigger forts close to the wall would have acted as a significant deterrent. Also it is unlikely that the Picts ever had a cohesive enough society to consider an actual 'invasion' of Roman Britain, so the wall probably did serve its purpose of keeping small raiding parties at bay. It also controlled people coming and going and supervised trade between the two areas.

Contrary to popular belief, it was not British slave labour that created Hadrian's Wall; the quality of work and speed necessary made it essential that the work was carried out by the legions themselves. Just about anyone would have lent a hand in one way or another and the massive task was finished in only six short years.

Auxiliary Troops

At any one time during the period Hadrian's Wall was garrisoned it is likely that upwards of 9,000 soldiers were present along its length. These were not Roman legions but rather auxiliary troops, drawn from areas already under Roman rule elsewhere in the Empire but not from Britain itself.

Where large numbers of soldiers live there are always bound to be forts and these often attracted trade in such a way that the locations soon turned into

Figure 50: Steel Rigg, Hadrian's Wall

towns. In the streets of these settlements outside Roman forts there would have been bath houses, bars, brothels, shops and many houses for the women the Roman soldiers may have taken as common-law wives. In many cases such settlements still exist and although they may now be perfectly normal British villages or towns, they often have a story to tell when new excavations are made for shops, offices or homes. With so many soldiers garrisoning Hadrian's Wall there would have been a large number of such settlements and it is certain that some of them, which did not survive to the modern era, are still to be identified and excavated.

John Clayton and Hadrian's Wall Path

It is possible to walk along significant stretches of what remains of Hadrian's Wall and though much of it has now crumbled to dust, or else the stone has been stolen over the years to build other structures, at least the footprint of this massive undertaking is still visible in most areas.

Much of what remains of Hadrian's Wall does so because of the tireless efforts of a man named John Clayton. He lived at a time when large sections of the wall were being used for road building, but around 1830 the fairly wealthy John Clayton, who at that time was the town clerk of Newcastle upon Tyne, began to buy up stretches of the wall and to protect them from further attack by those wanting cheap, readily available stone. Clayton also bought farms along the wall and by running these judiciously and profitably, he was able to raise revenue that could be ploughed back into reconstructing parts of the wall and also into his archaeological exploits. He discovered or already knew about a number of the military settlements along the wall, including the most famous, Vindolanda, Carrawburgh and Housesteads.

There is now a path that follows the wall all the way from Wallsend to Bowness-on-Solway. Of course to walk the full length is a major undertaking, though some people do it in stages. Walkers are advised to follow the path during the summer months because much of the land is fragile and easily eroded by the treading of boots on the wet ground and in any case this can be a wild part of Britain in the winter.

Housesteads

Housesteads (Vercovicium) near Hexham, Northumberland

LATITUDE: 55° 00' 36" N   LONGITUDE: 2° 19' 26" W

Vercovicium was the Latin name for the modern Housesteads, which was once one of the most impressive of the Roman garrison forts that guarded Hadrian's Wall. Unlike other forts of its type it stood solely on the south side of Hadrian's Wall, with the wall representing its northernmost defence. (Other forts protruded into enemy territory.)

Vercovicium was large and occupied by parts of several different auxiliary legions during its four-century history. It was often altered and extended and a number of archaeological digs on the site, both back in the 19th century and much more recently, have unearthed much of the ground plan and also a great many artefacts that have helped to illuminate a dark part of history by showing the sort of lives lived by the auxiliary soldiers, their families and retainers.

It is now possible to walk around much of the site and although Vercovicium is situated in a very impressive location it is approachable by car. In addition it is administered for the National Trust by English Heritage. At the site you will find car parks, a tea room, toilets, even bus stops and a small but extremely interesting museum.

Vindolanda

Vindolanda, Greenhead, Northumberland

LATITUDE: 54° 59′ 30″ N   LONGITUDE: 2° 21′ 47″ W

There is no better place in Britain to see the way military life was lived in Roman times than at Vindolanda. Like Vercovicium, Vindolanda was a military fort on Hadrian's Wall, this one guarding an important trade route known as 'Stanegate'. Vindolanda is an almost unique time capsule, and for an important reason: the first of the forts on Hadrian's Wall were built almost entirely of wood and as a consequence they soon needed replacing. When this happened the Romans placed clay and earth over the demolished material, which they rammed down hard in order to create a suitable base for the next structure. By so doing they eliminated oxygen, allowing many of the artefacts buried in the soil to remain in almost perfect condition.

Modern archaeological techniques have allowed the most fragile of finds to be both located and preserved, offering a snapshot of the minutia of life in a Roman fort that would normally rot away to nothing. So, leather goods, writing committed to wooden tablets, pieces of clothing and all manner of objects have survived and many of these are placed in the museum that is to be found close to the extensive site.

The digs have been very extensive and in places it was necessary for the archaeologists to dig down as much as 13ft (4 metres), because not merely one or two but at least ten forts existed at Vindolanda during its 400-year history. At the site you can see reconstructions of buildings, exhibitions, Roman hypocausts, officers' residences, barrack blocks and so much more. For anyone with the slightest interest in our common history Vindolanda can make the past come to life. The work of the Vindolanda Trust to fully excavate this truly amazing site goes on. Who knows, you might be so captivated that you will want to become involved in archaeology yourself.

With a shop and café on site and with ample car parking available, even those who are not up to tramping across moorland and heather can have a great day out at Vindolanda.

Fishbourne

Fishbourne Roman Palace, Fishbourne, Chichester, West Sussex

LATITUDE: 50° 50′ 12″ N   LONGITUDE: 0° 48′ 37″ W

Worlds away form the northernmost outpost of the Roman Empire on Hadrian's Wall and in the very south of England lies Fishbourne Roman Palace. This site represents one of the largest and best Roman villas ever to be found on English soil. Its full importance did not come to light until a major excavation took place starting in 1960 and over a protracted period of time the true significance of this massive villa began to be understood.

The final villa (because there were several stages to the construction) was over 179 square ft (150 square metres). It had several wings and formal gardens, as well as accommodation for what was obviously a very wealthy family and all the necessary retainers to keep such a significant house running.

The site of Fishbourne also had a military significance and excavations are still taking place in the vicinity, exposing even more buildings that were placed adjacent to the villa itself. It is thought that the villa belonged to a local petty king and his family. The Roman invaders fought their enemies ferociously, but they were very generous to local British leaders who accepted their presence and who helped them to subdue the less welcoming tribes. One of these, a man by the name of Togidubness, was rewarded with the villa where he, his family and their descendants, began to live a totally Roman style of life.

The true glories of Fishbourne Palace are its mosaics, each created by the use of thousands of pieces of stone. Originally these were monochrome, but later examples are in many colours and their artistry and complexity rival examples found much nearer to the heart of the Roman Empire.

Even in its excavated form, Fishbourne is well worth seeing and remains the largest Roman villa ever to be found north of the Alps. It is worth visiting whatever the weather because much of the excavated site is under cover. The going is easy and the atmosphere serene. With a museum attached and lots for children to do, Fishbourne Palace makes a wonderful day out. It is a great introduction not only to Roman Britain but also to archaeology and associated studies.

Bath

The Roman Baths, Bath, Somerset

LATITUDE: 51° 22′ 57″ N   LONGITUDE: 2° 21′ 38″ W

If there was one thing the Romans loved to do it was to bathe. On just about any significant Roman site archaeologists find the remnants of bath houses, where soldiers and civilians alike would spend as much of their spare time as proved to be possible. Bathing was much more than a chore to Romans, and to Romanized Britons. It was a social exercise, and even business was transacted on the tour around the different sorts of bath that existed in even the remotest bath houses. Even in the most far-flung parts of the Empire (on Hadrian's Wall for example) extensive and comfortable bath houses have been located.

After the passing of so many centuries it would be a miracle if something as complex and amazing as a truly magnificent Roman bath could possibly have survived, but the miracle happened and it can be seen at first hand in the centre of the stunning southern English city of Bath in Somerset.

The Romans called this place Aqua Sulis, probably after a British deity that was already being worshipped there when they arrived. There are natural hot springs in the vicinity and these were used to supply the baths. Housed within a custom-built building and allowing access from above and alongside, the Roman baths in the centre of Bath are extensive and utterly fascinating.

You won't need your hiking boots or your trusty stick and when you have finished looking at the baths, you can either take the water at the spa, which tastes foul, or better still retire for a leisurely lunch or a cup of coffee in one of the many cafés and restaurants that are to be found in the centre of this most beautiful city. There is plenty to captivate the history buff in Bath that is not Roman, and of course the stone circles at Stanton Drew are not far away.

Brading

Brading Roman Villa, Brading, Isle of Wight

LATITUDE: 50° 40' 21" N   LONGITUDE: 1° 08' 40" W

Brading is another of my favourite Roman villas. It is much less extensive than Fishbourne but to me it is just as fascinating. It comprises what remains of 12 rooms, some of which have wonderful mosaic floors. The first of the rooms was discovered in 1879 when the local farmer accidentally broke through with an iron bar into a void that contained the magnificent Bacchus mosaic. Although the excavation that followed was not as scientific and careful as it would be these days, at least the majority of the villa was preserved. The villa originally dates from a period shortly after the Roman invasion of Britain in AD 44 but the site was developed over a century or more.

Like most villas, Brading was also the centre of an extensive farm and there are the remains of agricultural outbuildings, and replanted Roman gardens give an indication of the surroundings that the Romans and their British counterparts enjoyed.

On site there is an exhibition centre, offering a wonderful view of life in Roman Britain and this is another location for a wonderful family day out.

Wales

The Romans were represented in great numbers in Wales, all the way from the south to Anglesey in the north. In the main, Roman sites in Wales are the remnants of forts – built to keep the residents in check. However, there are some larger and more complex sites, the best of which is at Caerleon.

Roman Headquarters at Caerleon, Newport, Gwent

LATITUDE: 51° 36′ 33″ N   LONGITUDE: 2° 57′ 21″ W

The principality of Wales represented a fairly tough nut for the Roman legions to crack. In the early days of occupation a great deal of opposition to Roman rule was organized in the area and so it isn't surprising that a section of the most formidable of the Roman army's might was located in Wales. To the Romans Caerleon was known as Isca.

The headquarters of the second Augustinian legion was created at Caerleon from as early as AD 75 and because an entire legion was garrisoned in the area the site is extensive, and contains the remains of some of the most impressive Roman garrison buildings to be found anywhere. It's true that a great deal of what once existed at Caerleon was robbed by locals as a cheap and easy way to get their hands on quarried stone, but the extensive foundations are interesting enough.

Nearby is a Roman amphitheatre, with seats for as many as 6,000 spectators, making it one of the largest in Britain.

What really sets the seal on this site is the nearby National Roman Legion Museum, which has artefacts, exhibitions and activities at any time of year. Entry is free and Caerleon represents an economic and interesting way to keep the family amused, whilst at the same time indulging one's interest in ancient structures and archaeology.

Scotland

The Antonine Wall

It is known that on a couple of occasions the Roman army marched well into Scotland and it may have been the intention of Rome at one time to absorb the whole area into the Roman Empire. A few factors worked against this wish. The terrain is formidable, the weather can be atrocious and what Rome would get out of its subjugation of Scotland would never be paid back by what the area could supply in terms of Rome's needs.

Nevertheless, and most probably because of pressure placed upon northern England by the Caledonian tribes, several punitive expeditions into Scotland did take place. One of these led to a defensive structure being created well north of Hadrian's Wall. Because it was built on the orders of the Emperor Antoninus Pius (commenced in AD 142) it came to be known as the Antonine Wall.

The Antonine Wall took far longer than Hadrian's Wall to create, partly because of the topography but also on account of the weather and probably the unfriendly locals. It ran from the Firth of Forth to the Firth of Clyde, across the central belt of Scotland and was built from stone and turf. The Antonine Wall was 39 miles (63km) in length and about 10ft (3 metres) in height, with a formidable ditch on the northern side. It took the legions 12 years to complete but not long after AD 208 it was finally abandoned and the Romans contented themselves with an empire that extended only to Hadrian's Wall.

There are several features on the Antonine Wall that are still evident, though few remain in such a good state of repair as parts of Hadrian's Wall or have been reconstructed in a similar way. In most places the ditch is still discernible but fortifications are not much in evidence. There are a number of forts and fortlets along the wall and most of these are administered by Historic Scotland. The Antonine Wall does not presently offer the ease of access that is to be found on parts of Hadrian's Wall and the going across this part of Scotland is often tough. Perhaps the best way to explore the Antonine Wall is by recourse to the Ordnance Survey maps of Roman Britain.

Sites of Interest by County

Some prehistoric sites of interest mentioned in the book are listed below in the counties where they are to be found, with page references to the relevant sections in the book.

England